Don't Wait For Someone Else To Fix It

Don't Wait For Someone Else To Fix It

8 Essentials to Enhance your Leadership Impact at Work, Home, and Anywhere Else that Needs You

Doug Lennick
Chuck Wachendorfer
with Kathy Jordan, PhD

WILEY

Published by John Wiley & Sons, Inc., Hoboken, New Jersey.
Published simultaneously in Canada.

For general information on our other products and services or for technical support, please contact our Customer Care Department within the United States at (800) 762-2974, outside the United States at (317) 572-3993 or fax (317) 572-4002.

Wiley also publishes its books in a variety of electronic formats. Some content that appears in print may not be available in electronic formats. For more information about Wiley products, visit our web site at www.wiley.com.

Library of Congress Cataloging-in-Publication Data is Available:

ISBN 9781394175796 (Hardback)
ISBN 9781394175819 (ePDF)
ISBN 9781394175802 (ePub)

Cover Design: Wiley
Cover Image: © Steppeua/Getty Images
Author photos: © Doug Lennick; © Chuck Wachendorfer
SKY10042781_021423

Contents

Foreword

Today's workplace is in continual flux. The workplace is less and less predictable. Increasingly it's up to each of us to define our own purpose and fulfillment in this ever-moving landscape. We all want our days infused with meaning and impact. Most of us spend most of our days at work. So, it's no surprise that the workplace is the number-one place we go to find meaning and impact. It's also up to smart, people-wise leaders to meet their workers halfway and offer resources (like this book) that can help create a purpose-driven culture.

Mostly though, people need essential tools to create their own success—over and over—as they grow as humans. This is a book that will meet you where you are now and provide the stories, ideas, and essentials that will help you thrive at work.

Everyone loves a good story, and this book has a lot of good stories to tell. Storytelling is a natural element of human evolution. It's how we make meaning of our experiences and our lives. Throughout this book, Doug and Chuck share their own stories and the stories of leaders, workshop attendees, and others who embody the book's purpose mindset. People just like you who have made it work at work and in life.

You have your story. I have mine. Our stories are us. Each of us is unique—a story of ONE.

To be absolutely clear: I'm not talking about the version of life story either of us might write. I'm talking about the story you know like the back of your hand, the complete, unabridged account of how you and I came to be here at this very moment, me writing this, you sitting there with this book or e-reader. Only you know exactly how your story begins and whether it's gone uphill or downhill.

But do you know *why*? Why do you get up each morning? And *why* lead? That's what this book is about. It offers seasoned guidance on how our stories influence both the *why* and the how we lead.

Because *why* we lead determines how well we lead.

One of the most insightful questions you can ask someone in any leadership role is, "*Why* do you want to become a better leader?" The answer to that question, as it turns out, will make a significant difference in how well you lead.

I began wrestling with the *why* question some 50 years ago. Across years of study and practice, I've tried to share what I've learned about those questions with my readers, especially about how we can express our highest calling in the work we do. After all, the way we spend our days will end up being the way we spend our lives.

I've learned how imperative it is to heed our calling—to discern the difference between a job, a career, and a calling. And I've observed that Doug and Chuck have worked hard at heeding their own callings. In this book they write from their insights to clarify eight essential truths with elegant simplicity and grounded experience.

When the authors first asked me to write this Foreword, I was honored but uncertain. I asked, "Why not a famous leader?" They replied that this was not an ordinary leadership book but one that shares the stories of ordinary people doing extraordinary things—everyday people in all walks of life. The ultimate leadership challenge is "self-leadership."

Why are some leaders so amazingly good at self-leadership? When we are inspired by an extraordinary leader, we naturally tend to conclude that that person is different from me—perhaps they were born with something a little extra. "She is so gifted," we say. "He has a natural gift for that."

But is it really so?

For many years, I have coached leaders of all persuasions. I have dug into their self-awareness (or lack of). And over time, I've come to the same conclusion that Doug and Chuck have come to in this book: the best leaders are "people-wise."

First, people-wise leaders see the big picture beyond themselves—they sense their part in the larger scheme of things beyond their own career success and self-absorption.

Second, people-wise leaders see that no problem ever comes to them that does not have a teaching in it. They are true learners sensing that the future belongs to the learners, not the knowers. They see problems as teachers in disguise.

Third, they see the path to trust as a path of service. Serving others is what they make their role about. They connect their role with their soul. They are aware that what will ultimately determine their meaning and impact will be the worthiness of their aim—the aim to serve with compassion.

Embracing the *why* lead question is a crucible test for self-leadership in all areas of our lives. The workplace is not just a realm of key performance indicators and profit-and-loss statements. It can be rather a supremely humanized place where we are energized to go to work every day. Rarely is a book as timely and timeless as this one. If you want to wake up on purpose every day and thrive at work, you won't want to put this book down.

Let's get started. . . .

Richard J. Leider
Founder, INVENTURE—The Purpose Company
International author of many bestselling books,
including *The Power of Purpose, Repacking Your Bags,
Life Reimagined, and Who Do You Want
to Be When You Grow Old?*

PART ONE

THE BIG PICTURE

CHAPTER ONE

Everyone Is a Leader

Tuesday, September 11, 2001, dawned as a surprisingly cool and cloudless late summer morning in the northeastern United States. It would soon become memorable for all the wrong reasons. Between 8:46 and 9:03 a.m. Eastern time, hijackers flew two large commercial airliners into the North and South Towers of the World Trade Center in lower Manhattan, New York City. The towers quickly caught fire. By 10:28 a.m., both towers, each more than 100 stories high, had collapsed. Meanwhile, at 9:37 a.m., a third hijacked plane crashed into the Pentagon in Washington, DC, igniting an explosive fire. Within an hour, five stories of the Pentagon had collapsed. A fourth hijacked airline, United Flight 93, was rerouted toward Washington, DC. It never reached its target, likely the White House or the United States Capitol, thanks to heroic resistance by passengers who had learned through cell phone communication with loved ones of the previous attacks. Flight 93's hijackers decided to down the aircraft before passengers could breach the cockpit, and at 10:03 a.m., the plane crashed in rural western Pennsylvania.

All told, nearly 3,000 people died that day, and more than 6,000 others were injured. These coordinated attacks remain the deadliest terrorist operation in world history.

Osama bin Laden, who founded the radical Islamic organization al-Qaeda in 1988, was the mastermind of the September 11, 2001 attacks. Bin Laden was an unusually charismatic figure, obviously capable of influencing his followers to sacrifice their own lives to destabilize Western civilization. Under bin Laden's leadership, the 9/11 terrorist attacks were brilliantly conceived and diabolically successful.

Fortunately, bin Laden had competitors in the global leadership space, leaders committed to positive change based on universal principles and positive values. These leaders answered an urgent call to arms in the aftermath of the 9/11 attacks. One such leader, Ken Chenault, was well known to coauthors Doug and Chuck, then senior leaders at American Express Financial Advisors (AEFA). Ken Chenault, a 20-year veteran of American Express, had become CEO and chairman only 10 months earlier. Suddenly, Ken faced a leadership crisis of monumental proportions. At the time of the attack, American Express was headquartered at the World Financial Center, just across the street from the twin towers of the World Trade Center. The World Financial Center building sustained massive collateral damage from the attack and had to be evacuated. Tragically, the company also lost 11 employees who had worked in the American Express Corporate Travel office on the 94th floor of the World Trade Center's North Tower.

Ken immediately understood the impact of the terrorist attack on the American Express workforce. Ken's gift for empathy meant that he knew personally and deeply how the American Express community would respond to the attack, no more so than when he met with the families of the employees who lost their lives on that dark September day.

On September 20, 2001, only nine days after the attacks, Ken held a town hall meeting at Madison Square Garden for all New York City metropolitan area employees. Coauthor Doug, at the time one of Ken's senior advisors, recalls his conversation with Ken on the day following the attacks:

> Ken and I were on the phone discussing the emotional impact the terrorist attack had and would have on the workforce. The American Express headquarters workforce would be displaced for at least several months across a three-state area: New York, New Jersey, and Connecticut. Ken knew it would be challenging to keep the American Express community together. So, he began by scheduling a meeting for all employees in the Northeast United States to be held at Madison Square Garden.

On the 20th anniversary of the September 11 attacks, Ken shared with us his thoughts at the time about preparing for the Madison Square Garden meeting:

The first thing that came to my mind was this quote from Napoleon, "The role of the leader is to define reality and give hope." I knew that's what I had to do, especially under those terrible circumstances. Second, I realized the need to demonstrate genuine compassion. Everyone's emotions were pretty raw, as were mine. Third, I felt it was important to be very authentic and personal, and to share my vulnerability without losing track of my strength. Finally, I wanted to speak from the heart.

According to the American Express employees who filled the seats of Madison Square Garden that day, Ken accomplished what he set out to communicate. He was authentic and compassionate. He supported the employees dealing with the trauma of their escape from the World Financial Center and the lower Manhattan area on September 11. He expressed his shared grief over the deaths of their colleagues. And he acknowledged the disorientation they would all face in the coming months. But Ken also voiced confidence in employees' ability to unite as a community to weather the difficult times ahead. As Ken recalls saying, "Our company is strong, but our hearts are stronger, and over time, our minds will get clearer. We will overcome."

In the weeks and months following the terrorist attack on the World Trade Center, Ken unfailingly aligned his leadership actions with the compelling messages he had conveyed at Madison Square Garden. Fortunately for the American Express team, Ken's leadership positively influenced the company's employees well beyond those who had been eyewitnesses to the New York City tragedy. For example, coauthor Chuck was at the time group vice president for the Southeast Michigan and Northern Ohio region of American Express Financial Advisors. Chuck recalls Ken's leadership in the days following 9/11 in this way:

During the 16 years I had worked for American Express, I had great pride in the brand. I was proud of our company's reputation for helping people when in trouble, especially while traveling. When September 11th struck, it was personal to us, not just in New York, where the trauma of the attacks was most acute, but also in Detroit, my region's headquarters, and everywhere American Express employees were stationed across the globe. Ken's response to the September 11 attacks was inspiring but not surprising. Ken embodied the kind of leadership I expected from our company. Ken carried the baton forward in the difficult months that followed September 11, 2001. Ken's reach extended well beyond the fabled Madison Square Garden meeting. He was a great leader who inspired my colleagues and me to be the best leaders we could be during a time of enormous crisis. Ken made us believe that, even in this unprecedented time, it was our opportunity to shine and not shrink from the situation. We paid attention to how Ken dealt with things and did our best to emulate his leadership in supporting our people.

Though Ken needed to make tough decisions to deal with the financial downturn post-9/11, ultimately including layoffs, he succeeded in his mission to accurately define reality and give hope to the expansive American Express community. He communicated often, holding frequent town hall meetings with employees across the globe so they always knew what to expect going forward. Ken encouraged employees to develop innovative products and services that would excite customers and help offset losses in struggling post-9/11 business lines. Because Ken demonstrated such compassion and respect for employees, even people laid off told him how much they appreciated how compassionately he had connected with them throughout the crisis.

What explains the remarkable leadership Ken Chenault demonstrated in the wake of 9/11? Ken had a high degree of *leadership intelligence—the capacity to positively influence and engage the best efforts of others.*

More than 20 years after 9/11, the entire global community suffers increasing threats to human happiness and security, including a European war, nuclear saber rattling, terrorism, a persistent pandemic, an endangered climate, anti-democratic movements, racial injustice, and economic disruption. Sadly, there is a worldwide shortage of leaders with the leadership intelligence to help us overcome these crises.

Consider, for example, the impact of inadequate leadership on the response to the coronavirus pandemic that exploded in early 2020. At that time, the World Health Organization (WHO) commissioned an independent panel of experts to analyze the causes of the pandemic and make recommendations for preventing and mitigating future pandemics. One media outlet reported on the panel's findings with this headline: *World leaders had the ability to avert the COVID-19 pandemic but failed to do it, a scathing WHO-commissioned report said.*[1] Years from now, history books will tell the story of global heads of state who ignored their duty to protect the health of their fellow citizens.

Fortunately, there are heartening examples of political leadership, such as New Zealand's Prime Minister, Jacinda Ardern, widely credited for taking swift action to help New Zealand avoid the mass infections and deaths that devastated the United States and Europe at the beginning of the coronavirus pandemic. As Vox reported:

> *Ardern responded swiftly, with an early lockdown that essentially eliminated the spread of the virus. She also spoke directly to New Zealanders with a warmth and empathy that's been lacking in other world leaders, helping to soothe New Zealanders' anxieties and getting them on board with coronavirus restrictions. To date [April 2021], New Zealand has reported fewer than 2,000 cases and 25 deaths due to COVID-19.*[2]

Arden's leadership during the pandemic also inspired in New Zealanders "a rare sentiment in the COVID-19 era: A deep sense of pride in the country's response,"[3] according to Dr. Robert Borotkanics, a senior research fellow at Auckland University of Technology in New Zealand. By January 2022, with the highly infectious coronavirus omicron variants raging, Arden continued her leadership with stringent measures designed to protect life. New Zealand, with just over 5 million population, was determined to combat a weekly average of just 33 daily cases. Since the beginning of the pandemic, New Zealand had suffered a minimal death rate of 10 cases per million. Compare this to the United States death rate of 2,600 per million. There's no doubt that leaders' decisions accounted for many of the differences in the impact of the pandemic on different countries.

[1] Marianne Guenot, "World leaders had the ability to avert the COVID-19 pandemic but failed to do it, a scathing WHO-commissioned report said," *Insider* (May 12, 2021), https://www.businessinsider.com/leaders-could-have-stopped-covid-19-pandemic-but-failed-who-says-2021-5.

[2] Anna North, "New Zealand Prime Minister Jacinda Ardern wins historic reelection," *Vox* (October 17, 2020), https://www.vox.com/2020/10/17/21520584/jacinda-ardern-new-zealand-prime-minister-reelection-covid-19.

[3] Annalies Winny, "In New Zealand, A Response to be Proud of," *Global Health Now* (April 15, 2021), https://globalhealthnow.org/2021-04/new-zealand-response-be-proud.

It's a no-brainer that the world is fortunate to have star leaders such as Jacinda Ardern or Ken Chenault. But we can't sit back and hope that the leaders we need to help us survive and thrive will magically appear. Fortunately, we don't have to rely on a relatively small set of enlightened traditional leaders to improve the world. Outstanding leadership comes from unexpected places. It comes from us. We are the leaders we have been looking for! Creating a safer, happier, and healthier world is in our hands. You may think you're "not the leadership type." You may have no interest in being a leader, but like it or not, you *are* a leader.

You don't get to choose whether or not to be a leader.

You only get to choose what kind of leader you'll be.

For instance, look at the choices made by a COVID tester in India, one of the countries hardest hit during the coronavirus pandemic:

Shilpashree A.S. (Like many people in India, she uses initials referring to her hometown and her father's name as her last name.) dons PPE, including a protective gown, goggles, latex gloves, and a mask. Then, she steps inside a tiny booth with two holes for her arms to reach through to perform nasal swab tests on long lines of patients.

. . . To prevent the spread of the coronavirus, she is not allowed to have contact with her family. For the last five months she's only been able to visit with them on video calls. "I haven't yet seen my children or hugged them," she said. "It is like seeing a fruit from up-close but not eating it." Still, there is no other job she would rather be doing right now. "Even though this involves risk, I love this job. It brings me happiness," she said.[4]

The sacrifices Shilpashree made embody the essence of good leadership. Shilpashree is anything but a marquee leader. She was an ordinary person down in the trenches of the coronavirus battle. Shilpashree took on the dangers of a COVID-19 tester in her community in service of the common good. She could have isolated herself at home and tried to stay safe in the company of her husband and children. Instead,

---

[4]Bill Gates, "7 Unsung Heroes of the Pandemic," GatesNotes (September 8, 2020), https://www.gatesnotes.com/Health/7-unsung-heroes-of-the-pandemic.

she chose the route of influencing others in service of doing good. How many of us would make the sacrifices Shilpashree endured to make a positive difference in her pandemic-ravaged community?

Reading Shilpashree's story, you might think, "I could never do that." Maybe not, but each of us can make a difference as leaders in our own way. Leadership is not about having a certain title or performing a particular role. Leadership is about the power to influence others. Everyone is a leader because everyone influences others, through what they do and what they don't do. Take these examples of nontraditional leaders who have influenced others to have a positive impact on our world:

Albert Einstein. Einstein's famous scientific theories, such as his general theory of relativity, were created primarily between 1895 and 1904. Perhaps because they were so revolutionary at the time, people in the scientific community were reluctant to adopt them. Many of them thought Einstein was essentially a crackpot. Faced with such skepticism, Einstein could have retreated into a corner and licked his wounds. Here's where leadership intelligence comes into play: Einstein spent the rest of his life trying to influence people to accept his scientific findings. Today most people think of Einstein as a scientist, not a leader. But had he not used his leadership intelligence to advocate for his theory of relativity, his scientific discoveries might easily have been lost.

Ruth Bader Ginsburg. Justice Ginsburg is most famous as a long-serving member of the U.S. Supreme Court. However, her most enduring legacy may be her trailblazing work in advancing gender equality and women's rights, including winning multiple anti-gender discrimination cases before the Supreme Court early in her legal career. As with Einstein, we don't think of Justice Ginsburg as a leader in the traditional sense, but she is undeniably a role model when it comes to influencing positive change. Acknowledgment of her leadership influence included the $1 million 2019 Berggruen Prize for Philosophy and Culture, which recognizes "thinkers whose ideas have profoundly shaped human self-understanding and advancement in a rapidly changing world." Late in 2020, Justice Ginsburg passed away after a life well-lived. In years to come, her leadership impact will only grow as she continues to influence others to pursue their passion for justice and equality of opportunity.

Bill Gates. Gates is the legendary cofounder of Microsoft Corporation, the world's largest software company. Gates is widely recognized for helping transform modern life through technology. Over the last 20 years, Gates has shifted his focus from business success to philanthropic leadership. Gates' reputation has been clouded by personal failures, prompting a divorce from his former wife, Melinda French Gates. Despite their marital challenges, Gates and his former wife Melinda continue co-chairing the Bill & Melinda Gates Foundation, the world's largest private charitable foundation. Gates sold $35.8 billion worth of Microsoft stock to fund the Gates Foundation. According to the *Economist,*

> *The Gates Foundation is central to the global alliance trying to eradicate polio by vaccinating everyone and to ease the burden of malaria and find a vaccine against it. It has been several years since he [Bill Gates] warned that a new disease causing a global pandemic was a matter of when, not if, and called for the world to hold "Germ Games" along the lines of the wargames carried out by armies.[5]*

Since 2020, the Gates Foundation has allocated more than US$2 billion to the global COVID-19 pandemic response.

These are famous examples of nontraditional leaders. But for every Albert Einstein, Ruth Bader Ginsburg, or Bill Gates, thousands of ordinary people are untapped resources for the kind of positive leadership that can change the world. The world needs you to be the best leader you can be. That's true whether you're a CEO or a soccer coach, a senator or a social worker. Leadership happens everywhere. And even small acts of leadership can make a positive difference.

> *You are a leader at work—even when you help a new teammate learn the ropes.*
> *You are a leader in your family—even when your teenage kids roll their eyes at your parental wisdom.*
> *You are a leader in your community—even when you send an email to officials about a dangerous traffic intersection.*

[5]"The Covid-19 Pandemic Will Be Over By the End of 2021, Says Bill Gates," *The Economist,* August 18, 2020, https://www.economist.com/international/2020/08/18/the-covid-19-pandemic-will-be-over-by-the-end-of-2021-says-bill-gates.

Right now, the world is calling you to "step it up"—to use your leadership intelligence to encourage others to join you in positively impacting your world, whether that world is your family, your community, your workplace, or the whole planet.

Take Denny Bavaria. Denny has stepped it up throughout his adult life, influencing others through his passion for basketball. Denny was born and raised in a tight-knit working-class community in northeastern Pennsylvania. His father was an expert slater and volunteer firefighter. His mother was a gifted tailor. Though Denny's family lacked material wealth, they enjoyed the riches of a loving and deeply religious family. Denny's mom and dad did everything they could to support their neighbors in times of trouble. His mom repaired clothes at no cost for neighbors during tough times. Each Friday night, his parents turned their garage into a social hall where neighbors stopped by for food, music, and laughter. Denny's mom and dad were community leaders long before the term existed, and Denny never forgot what he learned growing up in a family culture of compassion and leadership.

Denny's first formal leadership experience came when he served as captain of his high school basketball team for several years. After graduation and a brief stint at community college, Denny joined the United States Air Force, where he served worldwide before retiring as a highly decorated noncommissioned officer.

Denny, who had played and coached basketball wherever he served with the Air Force, parlayed his love of the sport into a series of rewarding coaching jobs in central Pennsylvania. Over the next decade, he coached high school basketball. He expanded opportunities for girls' basketball. Denny also established the first Harrisburg, Pennsylvania, area youth basketball program, which included travel teams, expanding opportunities for high-potential players. Before long, Denny developed the reputation as "Mr. Basketball" for central Pennsylvania. Denny's commitment to helping players grow was part of his life purpose. Denny always points out that he could never have accomplished all he did in making central Pennsylvania a basketball force to be reckoned with without his wife's consistent support, although she had imagined a more leisurely retirement.

Despite Denny's contributions to youth basketball, he knew he could do more. Denny was dissatisfied with the limited opportunities for girls to develop skills to play basketball at the college level.

With the support of community leaders, Denny established Capital AAU, central Pennsylvania's first AAU (Amateur Athletic Union) program for girls. At the time, the region had several AAU programs. However, none were exclusively girls' programs. What is more, most were primarily money-making ventures rather than programs designed to help kids with the potential to maximize their performance.

Denny already had too much on his plate and already was missing too many nights and weekends with Claire. Still, Denny agreed to stand up the new AAU girls' program under certain non-negotiable conditions. First, as leader and coach, he would refuse any compensation. Denny's insistence on working pro bono contrasted with other regional AAU programs that paid coaches' salaries. Second, Denny wanted to ensure that it would be affordable for kids to play. This contrasted with most area AAU programs that were expensive for players to join. Third, the program would only play tournaments that college coaches attended so that players could showcase their talents to the decision-makers who counted. That contrasted with other regional AAU programs that sent players to tournaments that would be easy wins for their players, thus giving players and their parents overly optimistic views of their potential to play at the college level. Finally, Denny vowed that Capital AAU would never mislead families about their kids' potential. He did not want players' parents to waste time and money participating in the AAU program if their girls had no realistic future as college players. This contrasted with other regional AAU programs that accepted any players with the financial resources to play, even if they lacked the talent to get to the next level.

Denny's leadership attracted many aspiring players to the program. During the 10 years that Denny led the Capital AAU, 50 girls achieved college basketball scholarships.

In 2013, the love of his life and chief cheerleader, Claire, died suddenly and unexpectedly from pancreatic cancer. In addition to staying involved in girls' basketball, Denny has taken on a new leadership challenge, organizing frequent fundraising events for the Lustgarten Foundation, the largest private funder of pancreatic cancer research worldwide.

Denny is only one of many inspiring leaders who answered the call to step it up to use their leadership intelligence to make a positive difference. For instance, coauthor Doug's older daughter, Mary Lennick, is someone who stepped it up by dedicating her career to helping others. Mary, who has a master's degree in social work, is the executive director of Family Alternatives, an innovative family-based foster care program intended to overcome the limitations of the Minnesota state foster care system. Mary is a mindful leader of 13 staff members who provide enhanced training and support to 150 foster parents. When it comes to foster care, crises are the norm. Mary takes her responsibility as a crisis leader seriously. She understands exactly how much her behavior influences those she leads. For example, a while ago, one of Family Alternatives' foster parents was arrested for soliciting a minor and killed himself. Mary's staff was understandably traumatized by this event. In responding to that challenge, she saw her job as helping her people stay emotionally in the here and now so they could continue to be effective and help the kids affected by such a disturbing situation. In circumstances like these, Mary says, "I need to stay level-headed because leaders set the tone. My energy matters if I want to help people move through the mess."

In addition to leaders like Mary Lennick and Denny Bavaria who achieve formal leadership roles, volunteer leaders like Kristin Pradko step it up in service to a meaningful cause—in Kristin's case, gun violence prevention. In December 2012, when the public mourned the horrific Sandy Hook elementary school massacre, Kristin was three months pregnant with her second child. Kristin was profoundly affected by the tragedy, though it took several years for her to decide how best to respond. In the aftermath of Sandy Hook, the gun control advocacy organization "Moms Demand Action" was formed. By that time, Kristin had already resigned from her job as a kindergarten teacher in northern Virginia to become a full-time mom, which is a significant leadership position in its own right. In leaving her teaching career, Kristin made a critical decision about how she wanted to influence the trajectory of her family life.

As each of her children started school, Kristin felt increasingly uneasy. "I never felt safe sending my kids off to school," she worried. Finally, Kristin saw an opportunity to do something about her concern. In June 2016, the Pulse nightclub massacre in Orlando got her attention, even though Kristin was a busy mom and only a month away from giving birth to her third child, an adorable sister for her two growing boys. Not long after, Kristin noticed a mention on social media about a meeting of the Alexandria, Virginia, chapter of *Moms Demand Action*. The invitation spoke to her fears about her kids' safety and her hopes for their future. *Moms Demand* was planning an annual event to bring attention to the cause of sensible gun control. Kristin signed up to help and before long was asked to join *Moms Demand's* local leadership team. As Kristin recalls, "Gun violence prevention has always called to me. Even with a full plate at home, I decided to get involved. *Moms Demand Action* was an easy organization to be involved in, and over time I've made so many friends, so I look forward to meetings."

Kristin relishes her opportunities to advocate for gun control legislation with members of Congress, noting that "Friendly legislators are delighted to talk with us." Kristin's experience underscores that stepping it up has many benefits beyond the opportunity to serve a worthy cause. She is burnishing key leadership skills that will help her when her kids are older, and she is ready to re-enter the job market. Meanwhile, her involvement in *Moms Demand Action* offers the social benefits of meaningful friendships along with the satisfaction of working to make her community a safer place for all.

Doug Bavaria, Mary Lennick, and Kristin Pradko are powerful role models who show how we can make a difference in our communities, whether in paid or volunteer leadership roles. That said, other ways, seemingly more internal than externally focused, allow us to influence others. Dana Marie Ferrell, CEO of Bellevue, Washington-based Servitium Wealth Management, focuses on changing her world through self-leadership. Dana has an enviable track record as a successful leader and respected member of her local business community. Not long ago, Dana had an epiphany. In her interactions with people, she had to admit that she often wasn't very nice. That bothered her, so she found a coach to help her learn to be more kind. Dana's coach helped her see that she wasn't just hard on other people; she was tough on herself. If she wanted to be consistently compassionate toward others, she'd have to be more compassionate with herself. To help her develop the habit of kindness, her coach asked her to send a daily text about something she did to be kind to someone and something she did to be kind to herself. For example:

> *Christmas Eve—I picked up poop in the dog area so someone else wouldn't have to.*

I slept in and cuddled with my puppy.

Over time, the nature of her acts of kindness has become more profound and has stirred more self-reflection. For example,

I went to a conference. I smiled and was kind to people I previously had some resentment toward. I really feel like I let that go and just felt at peace.

I took a trip to Hawaii. I sat with a socially awkward gentleman who was alone on our tour. I engaged with him. He was slow to respond but then started talking. It was a good conversation and an essential human moment for me. I realized I shouldn't prejudge others. I can learn from all different kinds of people.

The more Dana practices acts of kindness toward others, the more she discovers that she is not just influencing others but improving her state of mind. She says, "Being kind is becoming a habit that makes me feel good. I get more by being kind and humble than in any other way. And that's the way I want to live." Dana's kindness practice also seems to have positively impacted her business. Her wealth management practice has been doing better than ever. Dana doesn't think that's a coincidence.

As Dana's experience demonstrates, the choices you make about what kind of leader you will be begins with the decisions you make about the type of person you want to be. Our friend and colleague Richard Leider, best-selling author and legendary personal and business coach, sees those choices as part of a process of discovering your purpose in life. Richard tells us that there are two aspects of purpose: The "Big P," your life purpose, that is, "what I'm meant to do and be while I'm here on earth," and the "little p," those countless things you do every day to fulfill your Big P. Big P and little p come together as a "cradle-to-grave, 24/7, moment-to-moment choice in our daily lives."

Though your Big P sets the overall direction of your life, it is all those little p's that define the direction of the influence you have as a leader. You can be an effective leader, that is, skilled in influencing others to act in certain ways. But unless your little p's support a worthwhile Big P, your effectiveness as a leader will be wasted, if not harmful.

So, take a few seconds right now to think about your Big P. Then ask yourself:

> *Is my purpose a self-centered one, or is the life I'm trying to live focused on having a positive impact on the world?*
> *Are my daily actions and decisions aligned with a worthwhile purpose?*

If you can answer yes to both questions, you are already doing an excellent job of stepping it up. And you are also demonstrating leadership intelligence. Like most of us, you know that you can always do better. Being a good person and someone with leadership intelligence is not a lifetime achievement award. It is something you need to work on actively every day. But many of us have an idealized view of our leadership impact. In numerous surveys, corporate employees rate their leaders as far less competent and engaging than leaders themselves do. For example, a 2022 survey by Deloitte found the following:

> *More than 8 out of 10 global executives believe their people feel "excellent" or "good" in their physical, mental, social and financial well-being, according to a February [2022] survey of 2,100 people from Deloitte and Workplace Intelligence. However, employees rate how well they're doing in each category much lower. In one big misalignment, though 81% of C-suite leaders think their employees are doing well with their finances, just 40% of employees actually feel that way.*[6]

In another survey by Gallup, in 2016, employees indicated that 82 percent of managers are not very good at leading people. Gallup estimated that this lack of leadership capability costs U.S. corporations up to US$550 *billion* annually.[7] Though these two surveys come from the world of corporate leadership, their results would likely be similar for leaders in any area of life.

What's the solution? How can you eliminate the gap between the leader you are today and the one you aspire to be? Practice. Every day. Just as daily physical exercise maintains physical fitness and strengthens

---

[6]Jennifer Liu, "88% of Executives Think They've Made Excellent Leadership Decisions During Covid—Only 53% of Workers Agree," *CNBC* (June 22, 2022), https://www.cnbc.com/2022/06/22/executives-are-overestimating-how-well-theyre-supporting-employees.html.
[7]Rasmus Hougaard, "The Real Crisis in Leadership," *Forbes* (September 9, 2018), https://www.forbes.com/sites/rasmushougaard/2018/09/09/the-real-crisis-in-leadership.

it, daily practice of certain leadership essentials will sustain and grow your leadership intelligence.

As authors, we have spent our lives in all sorts of leadership roles—in corporations, in education, as sports coaches, and in various community organizations. When we founded our company think2perform in 2002, we felt a strong sense of gratitude and responsibility to the many leaders who had influenced us over the years. We wanted to step it up by sharing what we had learned from them to help others. That is why the heart of think2perform is a team of people dedicated to helping leaders at all levels and in many different walks of life enhance their leadership intelligence. That's also why we wrote this book—to help you—no matter what kind of leader you are—step it up in a way that allows you to fulfill your purpose in life. To step it up with maximum impact, you will need to strengthen your leadership intelligence. Every day.

When we use phrases such as "step it up," "leadership intelligence," and "making a positive difference," we are not talking platitudes. We are talking about a purpose-driven, concrete approach to leadership that will allow you to be the best leader you can be in any area of your life and at any stage of your life. In the following pages, you will discover eight practices essential to stepping it up and cultivating your leadership intelligence. We call these practices "the eight leadership essentials." We developed the eight essentials model with the help of a variety of sources:

> *What we have learned from our own leadership successes and failures throughout our lives.*
>
> *What we have learned from numerous leaders and thought leaders around the globe about the skills needed to become the kind of leader you want to be.*
>
> *What we have learned from an extensive body of research on the keys to purpose-driven, high-impact leadership.*

We authors—Doug and Chuck—invite you to join us on a challenging, lifelong leadership learning adventure. Take advantage of the eight leadership essentials to turbocharge your positive impact on everyone in your life. As your leadership guides, we want you to know that *we* know we are by no means perfect. We have made our fair share of mistakes as leaders and have learned that mistakes can be some of our best teachers. We think of ourselves not just as guides but companions on our shared leadership journey. As leaders and followers, experts, and students, we are always learning more about outstanding leadership from everyone around us—our colleagues, clients, family members, and friends. If you were here with us in person right now, we would also be learning from you. And if you believe, as we do, that no matter your life circumstances, you *are* a leader, and want to have the most significant positive impact in your world, then step it up! Commit to mastering the eight leadership essentials! Now, let's dive in!

CHAPTER TWO

Follow the Leadership Logic Chain

It's a stunningly sunny day at the 2018 Winter Olympics in Pyeongchang, Korea. Rick Bower, head U.S. Olympic snowboard team coach, is standing at the top of the giant 22-foot halfpipe, surveying the international crowd of thousands below him. All his male and female athletes had just qualified in the top eight for the pressure cooker finals of the Olympic medal competition. An impressive feat, to be sure, but Rick is particularly grateful for this moment as he reflects on the despair he felt four short years earlier. The 2014 Olympics in Sochi, Russia, had been a vastly different experience for Rick. The U.S. men's halfpipe team, widely expected to win the gold and dominate the podium, returned home empty-handed. "It was one of the low points in my career as a coach," Rick shared. The weight Rick carried wasn't so much about his athletes' performance but his own disappointing performance as head coach. Rick knew he had let his team down. He had allowed his emotions to betray him and thus compromised his leadership of the team.

Arriving in Sochi in 2014 with sky-high expectations for his team's performance, Rick's heart sank as he and his team inspected the venue. Conditions were deteriorating rapidly. Usually, at top events like the Olympics, the walls of the 22 foot giant halfpipe would look like glass. Frozen solid and cut with an imposing, million-dollar machine called a Zaugg Pipe Monster, halfpipes can cost up to $3,000,000 to build. First introduced at the 1998 Winter Olympics in Nagano, Japan, the halfpipe competition had become one of the most popular events at the games, watched by billions of people around the globe. This pipe, however, was in the worst shape Rick and his team had ever seen.

Barely holding together under the Russian baking sun, with uneven, undulating walls, the Sochi halfpipe's dismal condition took people's breath away. Not only would the quality of the riding be affected, but the risk of injury would significantly increase. Snowboarders train for months and years to land five to six incredibly difficult tricks while running down the 600-foot-long pipe. Any variance in the wall of the pipe, even a few inches, could lead to a medal-ending fall or worse, a life-threatening crash. Rick and his team were in shock. The question that repeated in Rick's mind was, "What am I supposed to do now?"

As other teams arrived and training began, daily meetings with team coaches and Olympics officials about conditions deteriorated into heated, intense shouting matches. Rick found himself caught up in the madness. He felt helpless, as though he was letting people down and had failed to prepare his athletes properly. His dark mood was contagious, creating a downward spiral among his team. The athletes' practices suffered, and their frustration escalated.

Though everyone on the U.S. men's team qualified for finals, not one athlete landed their run on the day of the competition. The U.S. men's snowboard halfpipe team was shut out of the Olympic medal podium for the first time. Rick knew his athletes were not singularly responsible for their performance that day. He recognized his contribution to the team's meltdown. "I let the environment dictate how I responded," Rick shared dejectedly. "I should have done more to control my focus and attitude with the team."

Rick's willingness to analyze and improve his coaching performance perfectly illustrates the model of effective leadership we call "the Leadership Logic Chain."

EFFECTIVE LEADERSHIP AND THE LEADERSHIP LOGIC CHAIN

A *logic chain* is a model that defines a linked series of stages that contribute to the desired outcome. We applied the concept of a logic chain to leadership and coined the "leadership logic chain" to capture the sequential high-level steps that result in effective leadership. Being an effective leader is a necessary foundation for practicing leadership intelligence. If you're not effectively influencing others toward a particular purpose or goal, you can't deploy them to achieve a positive purpose. That is why the leadership logic chain is so important to leadership intelligence. The leadership logic chain guides you to implement three crucial stages of effective, intelligent leadership.

Effective leadership begins with *self-awareness*. You need to know yourself as fully as possible—what you think, how you feel, and what you do. As you'll see later, you develop self-awareness through examining your thoughts, feelings, and actions and with the help of those around you who are willing to be honest about how they see your strengths and challenges as a leader.

Armed with accurate self-knowledge, you have critical information that can strengthen your leadership effectiveness. But you need to take two intervening steps before you can capitalize on self-awareness to boost your leadership effectiveness. The second link in the leadership logic chain is *decision-making*. Many people believe that decision-making is the defining role of the leader. After all, most leaders spend much of their time each day making decisions. But according to a classic study by Chris Argyris, leaders tend to look exclusively to external data, such as typical business metrics, to help them understand the source of problems and make decisions to solve them. Few leaders look inside themselves for insights about the impact of their thoughts, emotions, and behaviors on the challenges they face and their ability to tackle them successfully. That's why self-awareness is a vital building block on the road to effective leadership. Without self-awareness, it's unlikely that a leader will make optimal decisions.

The third link in the leadership logic chain is *self-management*. Self-management is the ability to regulate your emotions and manage your thoughts and behaviors to achieve productive results. Self-management clearly requires self-awareness. But just being aware of a tendency to get upset easily, for instance, doesn't mean you can automatically control that behavior. That's where decision-making comes into play. Many people think of self-management as a function of good choices. And that's true. But it's also true that we'll be more successful at managing ourselves if we "automate" those positive choices by turning them into habits. James Clear, the famed self-improvement expert,

CHUCK: SELF-AWARENESS AND DECISION-MAKING

Several years ago, I got life-changing feedback from a friend who knew me well. One evening, I was talking with her about how worn out and exhausted I felt. She said, "Chuck, you say that a lot." Initially, I denied it was true, but I started paying more attention and discovered that she was right. I did say things like that a lot. With the self-awareness that my friend helped me cultivate, I could dig into why I was feeling so tapped out all the time. I was doing too much across the board, not enough of what I wanted to do, and I wasn't spending enough time with people who inspired and energized me. Once I understood the root causes of my fatigue, I could make better decisions about how I spent my time. With the help of Sarah, my executive assistant, I stopped saying yes to everything. I started saying no a lot more often. I figured out how many meetings each day would be optimal for my well-being and, therefore, that of my clients. And I shortened my meetings, so I had time for quick breaks to refuel between appointments.

points out that forming positive habits is the most reliable way he can produce positive results as a leader.[1] If you lack positive habits, self-management can become overwhelmingly difficult. That's because, without a base of good habits, self-management would require starting from scratch to figure out how best to manage yourself whenever you face a challenging situation. As James has demonstrated, establishing positive self-management habits makes it much more likely that you'll manage yourself in a way that results in effective and intelligent leadership. And the good news is that establishing positive self-management habits doesn't require dramatic changes in how you behave. As Chuck's story shows, he didn't need to change his personality to transform his work life from painful to positive. A few simple scheduling changes, with the assistance of a positive enabler, made all the difference.

Finally, having enhanced your self-awareness, leveraged that awareness to make good decisions, and demonstrated self-management through the decisions you make and the habits you establish, you have reached the top of the leadership logic chain, and its ultimate goal, effective leadership.

[1]As discussed in James Clear, "Continuous Improvement, How It Works and How to Master It," https://jamesclear.com/continuous-improvement.

The Leadership Logic Chain

Effective Leadership

⬆

Effective Self-Management

⬆

Effective Decision-Making

⬆

Self-Awareness

IMPLEMENTING THE LEADERSHIP LOGIC CHAIN

As you've seen, leadership effectiveness is fundamentally about influencing others. We've pointed out previously that effective leadership doesn't necessarily mean influencing for good. Throughout the book, we will focus on the leaders who want to make a positive difference. These leaders use their influencing skills to inspire others to pursue a worthy purpose and make a difference in the world.

If you expect to be an effective leader who creates positive results, you can't go it alone. You need a team of followers willing to be flexible in accomplishing the mission and goals you want to achieve with their help. In many cases, engaging your team in support of positive goals will mean helping your followers change their behavior. You may need to encourage them to do more of some things, less of other things, and in some cases, adopt completely new behaviors. The catch is that you can't *make* people do anything. The only person whose behavior you *can* control is your own. Therefore, any change in others' behavior needs to begin with you, the leader, changing your own. You need to manage yourself. If you are not getting the results you'd like from others, you must make different choices. Only when your behavior as a leader begins to change can you influence others to change their behavior. That's the essence of the leadership logic chain.

The best way to make the leadership logic chain come alive in your pursuit of leadership effectiveness is to follow this four-step process:

1. Develop awareness of your effectiveness as a leader.
2. Decide to adopt new behaviors.

3. Demonstrate new behaviors.
4. Give those you influence a chance to change their behavior in response.

Step 1: Develop Awareness of Your Effectiveness as a Leader

Being a successful leader begins with paying attention to what you're doing, that is, being consistently aware of what's working and not working in your thoughts and actions as a leader.

Self-awareness is not just a crucial component of the leadership logic chain. It is fundamental to leadership intelligence. And you'll discover in Chapter 4, "Get to Know Your Real Self," paying attention to your thoughts, feelings, and behavior is vital. For now, try to spot triggers for unproductive behavior, such as times of the day or certain kinds of people. One leader we know became irritable like clockwork every day around 3:00 p.m. If her team met around that time, they could count on her being sarcastic and unreceptive to their ideas. Her employees coped by making jokes about "the three o'clock monster." It wasn't until a brave colleague approached her about her mid-afternoon drop in civility that she learned to avoid scheduling meetings at that time and to take a 10-minute break for some deep breathing and a healthy snack.

Noticing patterns is another form of self-awareness and one of the most powerful ways to gather information about your leadership effectiveness. Patterns are thoughts, feelings, or actions that you repeat over and over, as if on "autopilot," in response to certain situations. Some patterns may work well for you as a leader; for example, when interviewing job candidates, you always make a point of sharing your values and asking about theirs. Including a discussion of mutual values during each selection process gives you essential information about whether a prospective employee is a good fit for you and your team. When your values and those of a promising candidate are aligned, you also get a jump start on emotional bonding with a likely new team member.

When you're aware of successful patterns, you can expand their use to other situations where they may have even more impact. For example, you could use awareness of the benefits of discussing values with job candidates to expand this practice to others, thus enhancing your influence with peers, clients, family members, and friends.

Other patterns don't work so well. None of us is perfect. We all get trapped in unproductive patterns at some point in our lives. Certain patterns may once have been positive, helping you accomplish important goals earlier in your life or leadership roles. But as you grew and developed, they became negative or limiting.

Negative patterns often persist precisely because they served as success strategies in the past. We were rewarded for following those patterns and, in the absence of self-awareness, continued them out of habit, even when they no longer produced successful results. That was the case with Randy, CEO of a large financial services business. Randy was a superstar who rose quickly in his career thanks to his smart and strong work ethic. But Randy was somewhat of a "Lone Ranger," conscientious to a fault, expecting far more of himself than others. Eventually, the very conscientiousness that had propelled him to the top took its toll on him. As Chuck coached Randy, he opened up about how overwhelmed he had felt with all that was going on in his firm. "I just feel like I have 15 balls in the air all the time, and I can't let any of them drop," he explained. "I don't know how much longer I can go at this pace. Maybe I'll hang in there for another five years, then retire because I'll be all out of gas by then."

Chuck sensed that Randy was about to burn out. So, Chuck suggested, "What if you shared some of those responsibilities with your executive team?"

"But these are *my* responsibilities," Randy countered. "I can't just offload my job on them."

Chuck was empathetic. "I can appreciate where you're coming from," he said. "You don't want to overwhelm your team. But have you ever thought about who might want your job someday? Empowering them to do some of what you do now could be a great development opportunity. Sharing your CEO responsibilities might also inspire them to create development opportunities for their own teams."

Randy sat quietly for a few moments. Then he took a deep breath, exhaled slowly, and replied, "It never occurred to me that I might be denying them growth opportunities, that they might want to step up and demonstrate that they could handle more." Randy saw that he didn't need to stay stuck in a negative pattern. He could improve his own life and, at the same time, create opportunities for others on his team. Randy immediately started talking about what projects he could share and with whom. Then Chuck asked, "Okay, let's say you've done that. What would you do with your new free time?"

"I've always wanted to learn how to fly," Randy said with a big grin. True to form, Randy didn't waste any time. He enrolled in flying lessons, and within a year earned his pilot's license, got his instrument rating, and bought his own plane. Empowering others allowed Randy to renew his energy for life outside of work while providing leadership development opportunities for his executive team. Win-win.

Randy's story is just one example of the need to recognize patterns that become less effective as you mature and your team or organization grows. When you're a leader, everything around you is constantly changing. That's why self-awareness is so central to your success. Some behavior patterns that helped you when you led a team of five people don't work when you're leading an organization of 500. Patterns you relied on when leading a group of experienced professionals may not cut it when leading a group of rookies. When what you've been doing no longer seems to be working, consider how and why your previously successful behaviors aren't working for you anymore.

Identifying negative patterns was also key to helping Anna, another of Chuck's clients, enhance her leadership intelligence at work and home. By all accounts, Anna was the picture of success: plenty of money, a beautiful home, and a thriving business with clients who loved her. But in her heart, Anna was miserable. Every day she felt stressed and overwhelmed. Anna was the sole breadwinner of her family—an unemployed husband and adult children living at home with her. Anna worked nonstop every day, never taking time for lunch or even a quick break. She stayed late at the office most nights, finishing work her employees should have done. When she finally got home around 8:00 p.m., exhausted and hungry, she gulped down whatever high-calorie convenience foods were on hand, then fell into bed. Before she knew it, Anna had packed on an extra 100 pounds.

With Chuck's help, Anna identified a crucial pattern: her failure to care for herself and her tendency to put everyone else's needs before hers. Most people will occasionally prioritize others' needs and think nothing of it. In fact, most overachievers have learned that to succeed, they need to help others periodically as a kind of "quid pro quo" to get their own needs met. Anna took that principle to the extreme and *never* got her needs met. She consistently put her own needs last.

During one of Chuck's coaching conversations with Anna discussing her lack of self-care, he asked her where she learned that her responsibility was to care for everyone else and not take care of herself. Without any hesitation, Anna shared that she was raised by a single mom. When Anna was seven years old, her mom was diagnosed with cancer. From then until her mom died when Anna was 11 years old, Anna was responsible for taking care of her mom. Most children at that age can count on parents who care for them and do their best to meet their kids' needs. Anna didn't have that luxury. With no other family to help, Anna had to attend to her mother's needs if they were both to survive. But now Anna was 55 years old and still caught in the same pattern. What had helped Anna and her mother when Anna was a child wasn't helping her now. Anna took care of her clients, her employees, and her family. Instead of working through others, she took on everything others didn't do. Sacrificing herself for everyone else was wrecking her health and happiness. When Anna expressed frustration that her kids were not functioning independently, Chuck's coaching helped her realize how she had contributed to their "failure to launch." Anna's well-intentioned but misguided pattern wasn't just detrimental to her family's growth and happiness. It also robbed her employees of the responsibilities and accountability that would allow them to develop professionally.

Knowing the origin of patterns that no longer serve you can help you begin to make new choices once circumstances have changed. To illustrate, Rick Bower had been the U.S. snowboarding team coach since 2006. His coaching approach had been stellar for the eight years that preceded the 2014 Winter Olympic Sochi games. But some of Rick's coaching patterns were not a match for the challenges of the disastrous Sochi games. Rick saw that there had been a fundamental breakdown in communication between the coaches and athletes. According to Rick, "People were siloed and isolated. Because we weren't talking, athletes didn't adjust their runs to the current conditions and were rigid in their approach to the competition." As the 2018 Olympic Games approached, Rick decided to change his approach. He chose to be less autocratic and more collaborative with his team. He made suggestions and sought input from the team and other coaches about what they thought would be most helpful, then incorporated their ideas into a new training routine. Rick encouraged his athletes to spend more time together as a team. In addition to their usual solo training runs, they now spent time watching their teammates perform. They did their conditioning workouts as a group. They also started attending video reviews together and often ate dinner as a team. Rick's new team-centered approach to coaching fostered better communication, camaraderie, and commitment. Working as a team also paid off in individuals' performance since the new regimen offered continuous opportunities to learn from other athletes.

REFLECTION QUESTIONS

What did I do in my past that seemed to be working well but isn't working well now?
In what areas could I be more effective as a leader?
What might be holding me back?

Step 2: Decide to Adopt New Behaviors

In step 2, we focus on decisions to adopt new ways of acting that counter unproductive patterns. That's because removing obstacles to effective leadership is much more challenging than continuing successful practices. Implementing the leadership logic chain includes making conscious choices to continue or expand behaviors that contribute to your leadership effectiveness.

Also, it's essential to think of the term "behavior" in a broad sense. Your behavior consists not only of actions others can see, such as speaking kindly to a follower, but of your private thoughts, such as "I'd like to spend more time coaching my new employee." Psychologists often refer to thinking as "cognitive behavior."

With that in mind, let's explore ways of changing patterned behavior to enhance your leadership effectiveness. These three practices can help you transform an unproductive pattern:

- Envision your ideal day or optimal situation.
- Define what you would do differently to have an ideal day or situation.

- Identify incremental steps you could take that would contribute to an ideal day or optimal situation.

In Anna's case, once she recognized not only her nonproductive caretaking pattern but where it originated, she was faced with a choice—continue that pattern or begin to take better care of herself. When Chuck asked Anna to envision her ideal day and the actions she could take to make that ideal day a reality, Anna decided to start very gradually by focusing on a day in which she would make time for strategies to achieve a healthier weight. For instance, part of her ideal day would include taking time for a nutritious lunch. Although there were many more elements to Anna's vision of her ideal day, her decision to focus on small steps made it more likely she could eventually achieve her goals for change. Anna's plan to make modest changes that would gradually move her in the direction of her ideal day is consistent with performance improvement expert James Clear's advice:

> So often we convince ourselves that change is only meaningful if there is some large, visible outcome associated with it. Whether it is losing weight, building a business, traveling the world or any other goal, we often put pressure on ourselves to make some earth-shattering improvement that everyone will talk about.[2]

Meanwhile, improving by just 1 percent isn't notable (and sometimes it isn't even *noticeable*). But it can be just as meaningful, especially in the long run.

In the beginning, there is basically no difference between making a choice that is 1 percent better or 1 percent worse. (In other words, it won't impact you very much today.) But as time goes on, these small improvements or declines compound, and you suddenly find a big gap between people who make slightly better decisions on a daily basis and those who don't.

[2]James Clear, "Continuous Improvement, How It Works and How to Master It," https://jamesclear.com/continuous-improvement.

REFLECTION QUESTIONS

Are there former behaviors you'd like to reintroduce that worked in the past?
Are there behaviors you'd like to adjust or modify?
Are there new behaviors that you'd like to try?
Are there behaviors you want to stop doing altogether?

Step 3: Demonstrating New Behaviors

Our colleague Ray Kelly tells this riddle: Five frogs are sitting on a log. One decides to jump off. How many frogs are left on the log? Five. That's because deciding to do something and actually doing it are not the same. Once you've figured out what new behaviors will contribute the most to becoming a more effective leader, it's time to put those decisions into practice.

Chuck's client Anna followed through on the behavioral changes she had decided would improve her life and work. She started bringing healthy snacks to work and made a point of drinking more water throughout the day. Over the following year, she took regular walks and started using the office stairs instead of the elevator. Gradually, Anna began to feel better, had more energy, and lost weight.

Now that Anna was on track with changes supporting her physical health, she recycled back to step 2 (Decide to adopt new behaviors) to envision elements of her ideal day related to work practices. For example, much of Anna's business success had resulted from long hours devoted to client work. One cause of Anna's overwork was allowing her assistant to overschedule her day. That meant Anna was burdened by far more daily appointments and meetings than was reasonable over the long term. For years, Anna had simply accepted the schedule that her assistant arranged, leading to extreme stress and fatigue. Fortunately, Anna managed to keep her clients happy, but it was only a matter of time before her work overload would result in mistakes that could affect clients and damage her brand. So, Anna took the next step of meeting with her assistant to clarify what Anna's schedule would ideally be like day to day. Anna needed to scale back her appointments to give her time to think more strategically about how to sustain and grow her business. She needed time to manage the practice—not just her firm's clients. That meant that Anna would have to hold her employees accountable for their respective client responsibilities rather than routinely picking up the slack for her employees when they dropped the ball.

Thinking back to Rick Bower's coaching challenges at the 2014 Winter Olympics, Rick realized that he needed to change his coaching patterns. By the time the next Winter Olympics in Pyeongchang, South Korea, arrived, Rick was a different coach. Not only was Rick more positive, but he had also prepared his team for all possible conditions and made sure his athletes hadn't over-trained. Rick was hyper-prepared mentally and physically for all possible scenarios. That included ensuring the team had extra batteries and clothing and insisting that he and his team showed up early for practice and competition events. This pattern shift enabled him to focus on his athletes and their performance. Rick's self-management allowed him to focus on what he could influence—his athletes. The result? The Pyeongchang Games were far different from Sochi. The U.S. Men's and Women's snowboard teams dominated easily, winning four gold medals, the only team to win multiple golds in snowboarding, and seven medals overall. Never before had a team taken home so much hardware at an Olympic game. Four years later, Rick demonstrated the same level of preparedness and open communication during the 2022 Winter Olympic Games in Beijing, where he was coaching Chloe Kim, a 2018 Olympic gold medal winner. Chloe had had a rough practice ahead of the final event. She and Rick knew they needed to make some adjustments to her final run. So, he sought input from fellow coach JJ Thomas. The spirit of collaboration and teamwork that Rick and JJ shared undoubtedly contributed to Chloe's second gold medal in women's snowboard halfpipe.

As you start to practice new behavior, keep these three ideas in mind:

Changing your behavior is not an easy task. That means accepting that you won't always have an ideal day or get the results you ideally want in certain situations. But you're more likely to be successful if you take an incremental approach. As author James Clear points out:

> *. . . breaking a bad habit is like uprooting a powerful oak within us. And the task of building a good habit is like cultivating a delicate flower one day at a time.*[3]

---

[3]Ibid.

Also, if you remain committed to acting in ways that support your current purpose, values, and goals, we're confident you'll have more good days than bad. And you'll achieve better results as a leader than ever.

Expect to make mistakes. If you aspire to be a more effective leader, you're likely a high performer who hates making mistakes. You may expect to consistently perform at your best. That's unrealistic. It may even lead you to stay in your comfort zone and avoid taking the risks needed to learn and grow. One of the most successful pattern changes you can make as a leader is experimenting with doing things differently and accepting that your initial attempts to change your routines won't always succeed. The good news is that when you don't succeed, you can use what you learned from a mistake to be more effective going forward. That's precisely the type of experience Don MacPherson had when he was president of the human capital measurement company Modern Survey. As Don recalls:

> *I had an employee who was not performing up to expectations, even though she had all the capabilities and tools to be a stellar sales representative for our company. I spent a lot of time coaching her and was frustrated when her performance didn't improve. When I reflected on my efforts to help her, I realized that all my coaching was focused on what she wasn't doing right. Since that wasn't working, I decided to change my approach. I started meeting with her at the end of each week to discuss what she was doing well. Right away, her attitude improved. I could almost see her floating out of my office, optimistic and feeling like she was capable of anything. She started crushing her sales goals, and within a year became our top sales rep.*

Communicate why you're engaging in new behavior. Whether you're engaging in new behavior as an individual leader or spearheading organizational changes, one of your most powerful tools is the ability to acknowledge any mistakes you may have made; to explain to followers why you are shifting direction, and to communicate how these changes will benefit them as individuals or as a team. For example, because of the coronavirus pandemic, think2perform, where Doug and Chuck are part of the leadership team, changed its business delivery system from one that primarily offered in-person consulting and training, supplemented by a few online products, to a heavily digital delivery system. At the time of this writing, the constraints against in-person delivery imposed by the pandemic were easing. But, like many firms, think2perform made a strategic decision never to revert to its pre-pandemic delivery system. Digital offerings would become a permanent and major component of the firm's delivery system. This might have made some team members worry that the company was trying to replace them with online product offerings. However, as CEO Doug pointed out at the time,

> *We want to avoid having our consultants think we don't care about them, and that we're shifting away from consulting to a product business, which is not our intent. We need to explain this quite artfully. We need our people to know that we care a lot about them and are prepared to invest in helping them succeed in a permanent digital environment. It's not going to be an easy thing. But if we communicate carefully and repeatedly, we can pull it off.*

REFLECTION QUESTIONS

What could I do that would make my unproductive behavior harder to continue?
What could I do that would make it easier to begin and sustain my new behavior?

Step 4: Give Those You Influence a Chance to Change Their Behavior in Response

Once you've established new ways of leading and communicated with followers your desire to make any needed changes, it's time to encourage them to follow your example. Share your journey with them. Encourage them to be self-reflective and determine how they can improve their own behavior. Your new behavior will affect how others act, but it will rarely result in an instant change on the part of your followers. This step is often the most challenging for leaders to adopt for several reasons. First, it may take some time for those you hope to influence to trust that you're committed to the behavioral changes you promise. Followers may understandably assume that your changes are only temporary, much like the New Year's resolutions to lose weight that fall by the wayside after just a few weeks. Followers may hesitate to get on board with your changes for fear that your "new and improved" leadership approach won't last.

Second, remember that you have had much more time to prepare for your change than your followers have. Be patient. Give your people time to accept and adapt to the changes you are making in your leadership behavior.

Finally, when you communicate about change, it's helpful to repeat your intentions often—announcing a change in your leadership approach once is far from enough. Many leaders over-rely on a single email announcing a change, only to be disappointed that followers did not respond to the message as they'd hoped. When communicating about your planned change, once is not enough. "I sent an email" to announce a change in a leader's behavior is far from influential. You will likely need to use multiple forms of communication for many months to reinforce your message of change. To further help followers understand and support any change, make sure you consistently communicate answers to these questions:

- Where are we going?
- What's in it for me to go there with you?
- What's expected of me?
- What can I expect from you?
- If I need support or help, where do I go, and whom do I talk with?

...

As leaders, we're influencing people constantly, whether we intend to or not. We need to ensure that our actions are consistent with our intentions. The American philosopher Ralph Waldo Emerson once famously stated, "What you do speaks so loudly, I cannot hear what you say." The examples in this chapter, including the experiences of Rick Bower and Anna, clearly demonstrate that managing our behavior—doing what we intend to do—begins with self-awareness. It's almost counterintuitive that to build a great relationship with or influence others, the person I must pay the most attention to is me. But what is the ultimate purpose of that focus on myself? And how will I know I'm managing myself well? To answer that question, I need a benchmark, and that benchmark is my *ideal self*. In the next chapter, "Aim to Be Your Ideal Self," you'll have a chance to discover who you want to be ideally and how living in alignment with that ideal will benefit you and those you hope to lead.

PART TWO

EIGHT LEADERSHIP ESSENTIALS

CHAPTER THREE

Aim to Be Your Ideal Self

oug Lennick was in the car with his son Al and daughter Mary
on the way to the airport for a flight to their vacation home
near Palm Springs. Doug was thinking about the meeting his family had with him only a few weeks earlier. Before the family meeting,
Doug thought he had been hiding his drinking from everyone, even
his wife, Beth Ann. But apparently, he had been fooling himself. Now
Doug recalled exactly where each person was seated that morning in
the family room of Doug and Beth Ann's suburban Minneapolis home.
Doug heard Al's voice telling him, "Dad, you're out of alignment."
That was really all Al had to say to cut through Doug's denial. Suddenly Doug remembered all the times that Beth Ann and his children
had expressed concern about his drinking, only to have Doug brush
them off. Finally, Doug had to admit his behavior threatened his family's happiness, which was very important to him. With the encouragement of his wife and family, in a few days, Doug would be entering an
outpatient alcohol rehabilitation program at the California Hazelden
Betty Ford Center not far from his desert home.

Returning to the present, Doug glanced out the car's front window.
To his surprise, they were headed north instead of east toward the airport. "You're going the wrong way!" Doug pointed out.

"No," Mary calmly replied, "We've got you a spot in the inpatient program at Hazelden here in Minnesota."

Doug had been a relatively light social drinker for most of his adult life. At business dinners, he would often forego a second drink to get home to spend time with his wife and kids. But in 2015, things started to change. As Doug recalls,

> When I turned 63, that was the age my mother was when she died in a car accident. I had always known that my mom was just 20 years older than me, but I didn't really think about that when she died. At the time I thought, 'Well at least she had a good life.' Now, 20 years later, it really hit me hard to realize how young my mother actually had been. I started drinking more tequila, and sometimes without the margarita mix. I would sit alone with my drink and keep thinking about how young my mom had been, how much of life she had missed, and how much time our family had missed with her.

But it was more than delayed grief that gripped Doug around that time and during the next few years. One of his children was going through a very painful divorce. His father-in-law suffered a serious fall. His daughter-in-law's father died just days after a stroke. Two close cousins died unexpectedly. As someone who cared deeply about his family, each of these blows hit hard. As Doug remembers his reaction to those events:

> I felt like I was still doing well. But I really wasn't. I had developed a number of troubling neurological symptoms that were affecting my balance and mobility. With everything going on emotionally and physically, I became that frog in the water which is heating up so gradually that the frog adapts until the water nears the boiling point and it's too late to save himself.

Doug's spirits rebounded for about a year when he served as a temporary senior executive in a big company. It was an energizing role, and Doug felt that he was really making a positive difference. But that assignment ended in early 2020, followed closely by the business disruptions of the coronavirus pandemic.

Suddenly, by mid-March of 2020, life shut down. There was this big void. That's when I really hit the skids. Beth Ann and I had come out to the desert for our usual March break. We were disappointed when the annual pro tennis tournament we always attended was canceled. Recognizing how dramatically the world was changing, Beth Ann had the good judgment to fly back to Minneapolis to be with friends and family right away. I wanted to stay in the desert for a few extra days, but then the airlines started canceling flights and I ended up stranded there by myself for six more weeks. I couldn't go to the gym to lift weights because it was closed. So was the tennis club. And the swimming pool. And the restaurants. But the liquor stores, along with grocery stores and gas stations, which also sold liquor, were all considered essential businesses, and they stayed open. I had less work to do because my temporary executive job was winding down and it was taking time for my clients and me to reorganize the way we worked during the early pandemic lockdown. Living alone, with a lighter schedule and almost none of my usual health practices to keep me in alignment with my values, I used alcohol to counter the disorientation and discontent I felt. I found myself making one or two margaritas in the afternoons. I did that every day until I started drinking in the morning too. Soon, drinking became an all-day affair.

When Doug finally got back to Minneapolis, he brought his new drinking habits home with him. Addiction was now firmly embedded in his daily life. Doug's neurological problems persisted. He didn't feel like himself. His work productivity suffered. And he lied to his family about his drinking. As Doug recalls, "I was far less happy with myself than I had ever been. And I certainly was not contributing to family happiness. Everybody was anxious, wondering what was wrong with dad. Does he have dementia? Does he have some serious brain disease?" Doug, who years before had created the groundbreaking alignment model and had long been a highly respected role model for living a life aligned with moral principles and personal values, was dangerously out of alignment.

Now Doug needed to absorb that he was being unexpectedly transported to an intensive inpatient rehabilitation program. Doug had been relatively comfortable with the ideas of outpatient rehab, which he considered "rehab lite." He thought that an outpatient program near his desert home could help him regain his ability to "drink responsibly" and would allow him the freedom to enjoy most of his usual vacation routines. But Doug rightly thought of inpatient treatment as hard core. The fact that Doug's family thought he needed an inpatient program made Doug realize that the stakes were high. His ability to have a good life and reestablish family stability and happiness meant he would have to adopt a sober lifestyle. Social drinking could never again be part of Doug's lifestyle. During that family meeting, Doug had never agreed to an inpatient program. Now he had a choice to make. Did he ask Al to turn the car around? Then he reflected on his situation: "My behavior lacked integrity. I was out of alignment with all of my personal values: family, happiness, wisdom, integrity, service, and health. My family was hurt and upset. My wife Beth Ann experienced the worst of me. I shattered our trust and in so doing hurt her deeply. I had to change." With all that in mind, Doug began his new sober life by spending four weeks at Hazelden.

Doug thought that he had made the most of his experience in the treatment program. Along with the tools he learned there, Doug discovered that the tools he had developed years before for living in alignment were powerful aids to his recovery. But just two days out of treatment, February 28 and leap day February 29, 2021, the disease came calling once again, and Doug relapsed. On March 1, Doug entered Hazelden Intensive Outpatient care. As Doug worked on his own recovery, he also renewed his commitment to support his fellow travelers on their recovery journey.

Today Doug is physically, emotionally, mentally, and spiritually much healthier. His neurological symptoms have resolved. He is regularly clocking 10,000 to 20,000 steps a day on his fitness tracker. He is working to strengthen his family relationships. He is refocused on helping his company make an even greater positive difference in the world. And he is again able to help others do their best to live in alignment, while working to stay in alignment himself.

However, despite all the positive momentum in Doug's life, especially the joy of improved relationships with his wife and family, the disease was not finished with him. On December 29, 2021, Doug drank again, not for long and not much. But for someone who had been sober for nearly a year, a little alcohol went a long way. He deeply hurt his family once again. Fortunately, recovery tools were still within reach, and Doug was able to quickly resume his recovery journey. December 30, 2021, became Doug's new first day without drinking. Doug renews his decision not to drink every day. That "one day at a time" decision is an essential part of Doug's commitment to live in alignment every day.

THE ALIGNMENT MODEL

As Doug's story illustrates, making a positive difference is only possible when you work every day to become the best person and leader you can be. Living in alignment is shorthand for the notion of aiming to live your real life as closely as possible to your ideal self. It means behaving every day in ways that support a meaningful purpose and goals that flow from universal principles and values. Since we're all fallible humans, it's safe to say that we are not always ideal people. But you can come much closer to living in alignment with your ideal self if you have a framework to guide you (see Figure 1).

Think of living in alignment as the interconnection of these three frames:

- Moral Compass: The principles and values that guide you
- Goals: What you want to accomplish as a person and leader
- Behavior: Decisions you make and actions you take to achieve your goals

FIGURE 1 THE ALIGNMENT MODEL

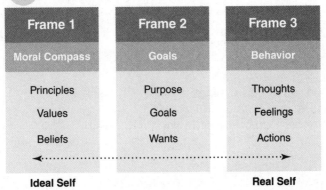

MORAL COMPASS

Frame 1, your moral compass, includes the core moral principles and personal values that are the foundation of who you would like to be ideally as a productive person and influential leader.

Principles. Principles are fundamental beliefs that have been embedded in human society for so long that they are now recognized as universal. Values, on the other hand, tend to be an expression of what's uniquely important to us as individuals.

In Doug's previous book, *Moral Intelligence*, he and coauthor Fred Kiel surveyed the research on universal principles and identified four held in common globally:

- Integrity
- Responsibility
- Compassion
- Forgiveness

What do these principles look like in practice?

- We show **integrity** when we act consistently with principles and values, tell the truth, stand up for what is right, and keep our promises.
- We demonstrate **responsibility** when we take responsibility for personal choices, admit our mistakes and failures, and commit to serving others.
- We exemplify **compassion** when we actively care about others.
- We express **forgiveness** when we let go of our own and others' mistakes.

OUTCOMES OF PRINCIPLES-BASED LEADERSHIP
- Integrity breeds trust
- Responsibility fosters inspiration
- Compassion reinforces retention
- Forgiveness enables innovation

Your ability to implement these principles defines your character as a leader. Coauthors Doug and Chuck have studied the dimensions of effective leadership and interviewed hundreds of leaders for more than 20 years. Our research validates the powerful impact that principles-based leadership has on followers' behavior. It's undeniable that the most influential leaders, independent of style or personality, all pay attention to these principles when forming relationships with followers and making leadership decisions.

Values. Values are the second element of Frame 1, our moral compass. Values represent personal beliefs about what is important to us as individuals. Our experience with successful leaders tells us that their values are closely linked to the principles. In helping thousands of leaders explore their values, we've found that influential leaders' top values are always aligned with principles. That doesn't mean there is always a one-to-one relationship between certain principles and particular values. Many different values can shape our choices about how we individually express a principle. For example, responsibility is a key principle, but our values shape how we express that principle. At think-2perform, one of our values is *growth*. By that, we mean we invest in continuous improvement of our firm, ourselves, and our clients. We integrated our commitment to the principle of responsibility and the value of growth when we founded the think2perform Research Institute. Through the Institute, we invest in research by top experts in performance, leadership, and organizational growth. We share results freely with the global leadership community; then, we use results to create state-of-the-art skill-building seminars for current and emerging leaders.

Living in alignment with principle-driven values is characteristic of the most influential leaders. The best leaders know their most treasured values and consistently make decisions aligned with those values.

Discovering your values. To act in alignment with our values, we must first deeply understand what they are. What is the set of values that anchors you? Can you name your five most important values? If you're like many of us, your values may not be top of mind. That doesn't mean you lack values. It does mean you will benefit from bringing those values into your conscious awareness, so you can take advantage of them to guide your life and leadership choices.

RESOURCES FOR CLARIFYING YOUR VALUES

- Values cards from think2perform. Each card in this pack names and explains a value. They come with instructions to help identify your most important values. Order at https://www.think2perform .com/product/the-original-values-card-deck
- Free virtual values cards and exercise from think2perform. Access at https://www.think2perform.com/values#start.

Aligning with values. Once you've figured out your short list of values, what do you do with that awareness? For starters, make sure you keep those values in mind day-to-day. Put a list of your top five values somewhere you can see it regularly. Make a habit of saying your values to yourself at particular times each day, say, while brushing your teeth. "Go public" with your values by sharing them with family, friends, and followers. Letting others know your values is a great way to help you be accountable for acting consistently with them. Use the exercise that follows, "Values and Behavior Alignment," to help you prioritize your top five values and determine to what extent what you *say* you value is aligned with the time and energy you invest in *living* those values.

EXERCISE: VALUES AND BEHAVIOR ALIGNMENT WORKSHEET

Step 1: In column A, rank order from 1 to 5 the values you most want your life to represent.

Step 2: In column B, rank order these values from 1 to 5 based on time and energy invested in each over the last year or so.

Step 3: In column C, quantify the alignment between importance of each value and the time and energy you invest in that value.

Step 4: Reflect on the alignment or gap between how I prioritize my values and the time/energy I devote to each value. Ask yourself, "How does what I say I value stack up against the way I demonstrate the importance of each value in my daily actions?"

Value	A: Importance	B: Investment	C: Alignment
List Top Five Values	What I Want My Life to Mean (Rate importance from 1–5)	Time and Energy I Spend (Rate from 1–5 1= little effort to 5 = significant effort)	Alignment Level (Subtract column B from column A)
1.			
2.			
3.			
4.			
5.			

Instructions: In the Values and Behavior Alignment exercise, the larger the positive number in column C, the more I invest in this value relative to its importance. The larger the negative number, the less I invest in that value relative to its importance. For instance, I may rank "Fame" as 5 in importance but 3 in my investment of time and energy. That leads to a gap of 2, which suggests that I may be spending too much time on a value that is not so important to me. As another example, I may rate "Family" as 1 in importance, but a 5 in my investment. The gap of –4 indicates that I'm probably not investing enough time and energy in my family relative to their importance. A score at or close to zero (–1 to +1) suggests close alignment between a value's importance to me and the time and energy I invest in that value. Such numbers are only rough estimates of alignment between values and behavior. However, it's a useful way to begin to think about how well you are using your time and energy relative to what you believe is most important to you. And it will give you a head start in thinking about how values can inform your goals when using the goal achievement process we'll be discussing in Chapter 9, "Achieve Purposeful Goals."

GOALS

Frame 2 of the alignment model includes two levels of goals:

Your *purpose*, the overarching reason for your existence. Residents of the Japanese island of Okinawa, perhaps not coincidentally known for its high number of centenarians, have a word for life purpose: Ikigai (eek-y-guy), which means "the reason for which you wake up in the morning."

Your *goals*, which are specific, often quantifiable, aspirations.

Purpose. Purpose is a high-level goal that represents what we want our life to mean. Zach Mercurio grew up the youngest of three high-achieving, highly competitive brothers who excelled both in sports and academics. As the kid at the bottom of the pack, he put a lot of energy into competing with his older brothers, alert to how his skills stacked up to theirs, even though it wasn't a fair comparison given his younger age. Zach was fortunate to attend school in an excellent educational system, which only intensified his tendency to value external measures of success. After Zach graduated from college, he landed a highly desirable job with a top advertising firm. It didn't take Zach long to realize he was miserable. He didn't have a clue about why he was working there. Zach's company only cared about whether he could make as much money as possible for them. But when he met with prospective clients, he realized they wanted more than a transactional discussion of their advertising requirements. Zach was struck by their need to connect with him on a human level, usually by telling their life stories. In the process, he discovered that in contrast to the architectural principle "form follows function," most people expected to form their lives without understanding their function. Devoid of the context of their life's purpose or function, most people's days lacked meaning. The most striking evidence of this was how many people on Mondays would ask, "What are you doing this weekend?" For a time, Zach used this question as a "go-to" conversation starter. But he could not ignore the sadness beneath this question. Finally, Zach had an epiphany: In his words, "No way I'm going to live for 2/7ths of my life. I need every day to be meaningful. I want a job that's like a book, so good that in the words of the poet Stephen Dunn I'd be finishing it for the rest of my life." Zach became obsessed with learning how to lead a meaningful life every day and teaching that skill to others. Today, Zach is a highly regarded consultant and coach to leaders and organizations. He specializes in helping others discover and live meaningful lives, whether as individuals, leaders, or organizations as a whole.

Zach's story is the embodiment of living in alignment with the second frame of the alignment model, which contains our purpose and goals. Goals range from the lofty (your life's purpose) to the ordinary (a larger house that can help you and your spouse telecommute). According to Zach, there is a difference between having a purpose and being purposeful. Having a purpose is a longer-term concept. It's about discovering the overall arc of your ideal life, the big picture meaning you want your life to have. What exactly is purpose? According to Richard Leider:

> *Our purpose is the essence of who we are and what makes us unique. Our purpose is an active expression of the deepest dimension within us— where we have a profound sense of who we are and why we're here. Purpose is the aim around which we structure our lives, a source of direction and energy. Through the lens of purpose, we are able to see ourselves— and our future—more clearly . . . . Purpose is what gives life a meaning.*[1]

Many of us may, in Richard Leider's words, ". . . believe we have a purpose but are challenged by what it may be or how to find out." If you're not already clear about your life's purpose, and have a longing to find out, be prepared to spend some time in reflection. To help you better understand your life purpose, use the exercise "What Is Your Life's Purpose?" based on Richard Leider's work, to help provide you more insight into your life's purpose.

EXERCISE: WHAT IS YOUR LIFE'S PURPOSE?

Take some time to reflect on the following questions. Answering these questions can help you clarify the high-level meaning and direction that you would like your life to take. You may also find it useful to discuss your responses with a close family member or friend.

1. What are my talents?
2. What am I passionate about?
3. What do I obsess about, daydream about?
4. What do I wish I had more time to put energy into?
5. What needs doing in the world that I'd like to put my talents to work on?
6. What are the main areas in which I'd like to invest my talents?
7. What environments or settings feel most natural to me?
8. In what work and life situations am I most comfortable expressing my talents?

*With permission from Richard J. Leider

---

[1] Richard J. Leider, *The Power of Purpose: Find Meaning, Live Longer, Better* (Oakland, CA: Berrett-Koehler Publishers, 2015).

Some of us have understood our purpose from an early age. Others of us are still searching for purpose in later life. Neither scenario is better or worse. What's important is that, wherever you are in life, it is vital to care about why you are here on this planet. Richard Leider suggests occasionally taking a day away from your regular routine to reflect on what matters to you. You may also discover that taking the time to explore your life purpose is not just an important process—it's also a lot of fun. Focusing on your life purpose can help you feel more joy as you release obstacles to happiness and move closer to making your ideal self your real self.

Once you're feeling confident about your life purpose, you're much more likely to fulfill your purpose if you can imagine what your life would be like when you are acting in alignment with your purpose. In Doug Lennick and Roy Geer's book, *How to Get What You Want and Remain True to Yourself*, they discuss a self-image theory, which says, "You will become what you believe yourself to be."[2] Doug and Roy advocate taking advantage of a powerful practice used by elite athletes—using their minds to visualize themselves performing perfectly. This practice has become commonplace in sports training, and it's just as effective when living a happy and fulfilled life. Visualizing life purpose may be even more critical than visualizing perfect performance in sports, where athletes typically only need to operate at peak performance for a short period. Life is a full-time sport, so the impact of visualizing ourselves successfully living our purpose 24/7 can be profound.

CHUCK: ENVISIONING A LIFE OF PURPOSE

I was 28 and sitting in the audience at a company conference listening to an expert on performance and creativity talk about thinking "outside the box." His central premise was that to discover what might be possible in life, it was helpful to project yourself to the end of your life and look backward. He challenged us to complete the following steps:

[2]Doug Lennick and Roy Geer, *How to Get What You Want and Remain True to Yourself*, (Minneapolis, MN: Lerner Publications Company, 1989).

1. Write about all you would like to have experienced and accomplished by the end of your life. Include what you'd like to be remembered for, almost as if it were a eulogy someone might read at your funeral.
2. Make a list with all your significant milestones and identify a date (month or year) by which you'd like to accomplish it.
3. Pick your top three milestones, and for each, list all the reasons accomplishing it would be important in your life.

One quiet afternoon after returning from the conference, I shut the door to my office and started writing. Imagining that I'd live into my 80s, I had a lot to write about over potentially 50 more years of life. When I finished, I was stunned at how many milestones, opportunities, and contributions I listed that I had never given any thought to in the past. From this backward-looking perspective, I was now thinking about the possibilities in my life.

I still keep that list in a file. Periodically, I'll pull it out just to reflect on what I wrote almost 30 years ago. When I do, it always amazes me how that list consciously or unconsciously has guided my life. Recently I realized that the list I made so long ago was entirely consistent with what my life would look like if I lived out my purpose.

I often recommend a version of that exercise to help clients clarify what a life of purpose and possibilities would look like for them. Envisioning their future as a series of concrete steps and milestones makes it much more likely that they'll be able to reach their goal of having a life that is personally meaningful and makes a difference in the lives of others.

Hopefully, by now you have clarified your life purpose and can share it with others you trust. For example, Zach Mercurio knows his life purpose, which he says is to help people realize their own significance. As important as it is to know our life purpose (what Richard Leider refers to as the "big P") it may be even more helpful on a practical level to understand how to be purposeful every day (Richard Leider calls this the "little p").

Being purposeful means rising to the daily challenge of figuring out the most meaningful actions you can take in any given day to fulfill your "Big P" by positively impacting those around you. As an example, Zach told us that during the 2020–2021 pandemic, many of his clients talked to him about the stress they felt and the threats to their purpose. Some of his clients would say, "I don't know how I'm going to get through this" (the coronavirus pandemic).

Zach would respond, "Who do you need to help to get through this?"

By reframing leaders' purpose-related questions, Zach helped leaders focus on those small but powerful moment-to-moment purpose-driven communications with followers that made all the difference in maintaining meaning and momentum. As Zach's perspective demonstrates, emphasizing being purposeful every day helps to ensure alignment of Frame 2 with each of our leadership decisions.

Goals. Goals is both the shorthand label for Frame 2 of the alignment model and the second of two elements of Frame 2, which includes both purpose and goals. Goals are a subset of our purpose. They are the more concrete objectives we set that tell us whether or not we are fulfilling our purpose. When Zach realized that his purpose was to help others recognize their meaning and significance, he had to achieve certain goals that would enable him to achieve his purpose. As in Zach's case, purposeful goals must be consistent with your purpose and aligned with your values. Achieving purposeful goals is an art that we will help you cultivate in Chapter 9, "Achieve Purposeful Goals."

BEHAVIOR

Frame 3 of the alignment model contains your behavior, including your internal thoughts and feelings, as well as your external actions. We often say that the Behavior Frame puts the "living" in "living in alignment." Frames 1 and 2 are aspirational in that principles, values, purpose, and goals aim toward the ideal self we aspire to be. Frame 3 is where the rubber meets the road. Frame 3 takes principles and values from Frame 1 and your purpose and goals from Frame 2 and ideally makes them real. We can only be successful leaders when we embrace principles and values, define our purpose and goals, and act accordingly. When we make choices that are not in alignment, we may give ourselves the benefit of the doubt, but those around us often don't. So, keeping our behavior in alignment is essential if we want to positively influence others.

Spenser Segal is a leader who exemplifies the power of living in alignment. Spenser is the CEO of ActiFi, a software company that provides a powerful suite of tools to financial services companies and their financial advisors. ActiFi's flagship platform, SuccessPro, helps financial services companies and their advisors identify and track goals and the activities that lead to those results. One of the unique features of SuccessPro is that it doesn't just follow traditional measures of business performance. It also helps advisors assess their values, identify values-based goals, and track the achievement of those goals. Spenser believes so strongly in the connection between values, behavior, and successful business performance that ActiFi has built those connections into its technology for advisor practice management and driving organic growth. As a leader with high integrity, Spenser also believes in "practicing what you preach." He reminds his team daily, "We have to do for ourselves and our clients what we recommend they do for themselves and their clients." In his mind, acting in alignment with values is as critical to ActiFi's success as it is to the success of the client organizations they serve.

· · ·

How can you tell if *you're* living in alignment? How can you know whether your real self is consistent with your ideal self? That's the job of self-awareness, a topic we'll explore in depth in the next chapter, "Know Your Real Self."

CHAPTER FOUR

Know Your Real Self

As the 30-year-old CEO and owner of Destination Services, a company that designed and managed corporate events for Fortune 500 companies, Kathy Fort Carty knew she still had plenty to learn. Having moved to Vail, Colorado, after college to live the ski bum lifestyle and help friends start their own company, Kathy decided to buy her own business from a local entrepreneur who wanted to move to a warmer locale. Only 23 years old at the time, Kathy borrowed $5,000 from her parents, then used $2,500 to buy the firm and kept $2,500 as a cash reserve. Fast forward seven years and thousands of exhausting hours later, Destination Services was now grossing over $2.5 million in annual revenue. As a college grad and former student athlete, Kathy was no stranger to hard work. But she had no formal business training. Kathy had learned everything she knew about growing her firm on the job.

Realizing she needed to bring a more formal structure to the business for it to grow, Kathy hired a human resources (HR) consultant to help evaluate her leadership. Kathy brought the entire company together for a full-day retreat with the HR consultant. The first thing the consultant did was pose a question to Kathy's employees: "What don't you like about Kathy's leadership style?" Kathy gulped. She had no idea the day would start this way. The consultant asked each employee to write their answers on the whiteboard at the front of the room. Kathy sat on pins and needles, watching her employees walk in single file up to the whiteboard to write their answers. Though most employees were her friends, they gave brutally honest answers. Their assessment of Kathy's leadership style was disturbingly negative. As each person set the marker down, a little more color drained from Kathy's face. "This is awful," Kathy thought. "They think I'm a terrible leader." As the last employee wrote their final thoughts, Kathy had an epiphany. "I'm not one of them." In a flash of self-awareness, Kathy realized, "I am the president of this company. I am the leader." That day taught her that she was no longer one of the gang. She was at the helm of a multi-million-dollar business and needed to step up her game.

Kathy's experience highlights the importance of accurate self-awareness to successful leadership. Before the retreat, Kathy still felt like that young novice entrepreneur who had cobbled together a group of ski-mates to run a business that would keep them on the mountain slopes of Vail, Colorado. But Kathy's self-concept, the collection of her conscious and unconscious beliefs about who she was, was years out of date. Our real self tends to change over time. Kathy's circumstances had evolved significantly in the previous decade, but her self-image had not caught up with who she now really was. Though Kathy wasn't fully aware of the magnitude of the change in who she was, she luckily had enough self-awareness to recognize that she needed help dealing with the challenges of a rapidly expanding business. Hiring an HR consultant turned out to be one of Kathy's smartest decisions as a leader. Her consultant gave Kathy's team permission to offer feedback about her leadership style that most employees had been reluctant to share. Though her team's feedback was painful in the short term, it opened Kathy's eyes to her current real self. Like Dorothy in *The Wizard of Oz*, who famously said to her dog, "Toto, I have a feeling we're not in Kansas anymore," Kathy now knew that she was in uncharted territory. She needed to embrace her role as leader of a multimillion-dollar enterprise. That meant she would have to change her behavior and make different leadership decisions than the ones that had been effective when she first took ownership of her business.

As Kathy recalls,

First, I had to accept that I was the leader. I was not their friend, peer, or sister at work. That was a difficult concept for me, as I viewed myself as equal in many ways. I was in my mid 20s and had no formal training in management or leadership and I certainly didn't think I had signed up for that role!

Once I accepted my responsibility as the leader, I considered the impact that I had on the team and gave serious thought to how I wanted them to feel and behave at work.

It was in my best interest (and the company's) to have staff that were happy, motivated, and willing to work hard.

I acknowledged that my behavior, demeanor, and mood mattered. That was tough to accept as well, but their perception was my reality.

But how would Kathy translate that self-awareness into better decisions and the most intelligent leadership plays possible? Kathy's first response was to make a conscious effort to be more friendly. Kathy decided that she should do her best to kick off each day in a positive way. Kathy now made a point to be warm and open when she arrived at the office. She stopped by everyone's desks to say hello and briefly check in with them. But Kathy was not satisfied with creating the optics of a caring leader.

Initially I didn't understand all that employees needed from me if they were going to be able to do their job well. I believed they should be self-starters, and self-motivated. And while all of them were both, they also needed to be reassured that I was happy with their work and performance. I had to undo many years of programming based on how I was raised in order to begin to give my employees what they needed and deserved, both emotionally and as their coach.

Kathy describes how she adapted her leadership practices to better address her employees' needs:

I tried to acknowledge good work more consistently. I realized that our staff wanted to get more praise and be told they were doing a good job. It seemed like a silly thing to me since I am intrinsically motivated. But positive feedback was important to so many who worked in our company. So, I monitored my compliments to ensure that people I thought needed my positive feedback would get it and did my best to boost individuals up regularly.

But that's not all Kathy did to align her real self with her ideal self. Kathy also worked to become an authentically accessible leader. As she puts it:

I tried to work with my office door open more regularly so staff didn't feel like I was "angry behind closed doors." I regularly talked to the staff and explained that sometimes my door needed to be closed so I could concentrate on difficult work or have private conversations. I also talked to the staff and told them that I had very little experience in being a boss and that I was trying my best. I showed them my vulnerability and asked them to be patient with me.

As with everyone who cares about being a positive influence, it was not easy for Kathy to evolve from the solo star she was into the leader she was determined to become. But from the day she held the team retreat, Kathy vowed to become the best leader and coach she could be for those who worked with her.

Wow. . . I think I worked on being a good leader from that day forward! I became much more aware of myself, my communication, my body language, etc. I worked for the next 30 years to be a positive influence on my staff. I learned how to set clear expectations with them, but I also focused on recognizing good work, achievement, mistakes made in good faith, and accomplishments by leaders and staff.

Kathy also recognizes those who helped her make the transition from independent performer to leader:

I invested heavily in coaching and Emotional IQ training as well. The 1:1 time with Chuck [Wachendorfer] and Rick [Aberman] made a huge difference in my career as I learned more about my strengths and weaknesses and those of my staff. This was often hard, painful, and personal work, but it was worth it. I also hired excellent HR managers and consultants the remainder of my career and made it clear to them that they needed to be direct and honest with me and help me be a better manager/leader. They had to really support me through difficult staff situations, legal battles, staff terminations, behavior incidents, coaching up my general managers, etc. I couldn't have done what I did without those supporters.

But, high achiever that she was, even those significant investments in her leadership development weren't enough for her. Kathy decided to do even more:

I outlined an aggressive schedule for myself to travel to each of my offices at a minimum of once a quarter. Typically, I visited more often. When I went to one of our offices, I always hosted a lunch, or happy hour. I talked to the team, listened to their concerns, and thanked them for their work. I attended their events, met the clients, and the vendors. I complimented them on work well done (and made sure to refrain from criticism in the midst of these events). I also made it a point to learn about their spouses, kids, pets, hobbies, etc. and engaged them in sharing more information about all of that.

This new high-touch approach to leadership paid off for Kathy. As she describes the impact of leveraging self-awareness to strengthen her self-management style:

I think the impact and my greatest accomplishment in business is that my staff still reach out to me to tell me I was the best boss they ever worked for! I have had staff confiding in me about the influence I had on their lives—taking a chance to hire them, training them, trusting them to grow, to learn and make mistakes, and giving them opportunities to take ownership in their work and our business. Several of my staff have started their own businesses and reach out to me to mentor them, give advice on how to grow, and how to be a good leader. That is pretty cool.

Beyond the culture of positive leadership that Kathy created within her company, self-awareness and good decision-making on Kathy's part turbo-charged her company's business results. Kathy is rightly proud of the accomplishments of her company as it expanded:

My business grew exponentially over the 25 years following the HR deba-cle when the staff reamed me. We racked up revenue from $1m to $25m over the course of those years.

My business scaled to 7 offices and 100+ staff, which could have never happened if my leadership style had not improved dramatically.

I was able to be one of the most productive and profitable businesses in my sector because our offices and staff had clearly outlined goals, boundaries in which to work, insisted on consistent communication and shared in the profits that they helped to generate. We had a bi-weekly company meeting to quickly review goals, we recognized individuals and teams that had done exceptional work, and we tracked their financial progress. But mostly we reinforced our culture of collaboration, risk taking, work ethic, celebration, and success.

Ultimately, I sold my business successfully for six times earnings, which was unheard of in a privately owned, service business, with no recurring revenue. I was told for years there would be nothing to sell because "I was the business." Thanks to coaching in effective and intelligent leadership, I made certain that was not the case.

ANSWERING THE QUESTION, "WHO AM I?"

For Kathy Fort Carty, the path to growing a $25 million business from scratch began with heightening her self-awareness. Getting to know your real self means finding ways to accurately answer the question "Who am I?" Kathy Fort Carty used feedback from her team to help her answer that question. Though people around us are not always entirely accurate in their perceptions of who we are, they can often provide valuable insights into our real selves.

When answering the question "Who am I?" it's easy to fall prey to two types of errors—a Type 1 (false negative) self-concept or a Type 2 (false positive) self-concept. When we make Type 1 errors in our self-concept, our estimation of our real self is more negative than our actual self. You, or some people you know, may be too quick to blame yourselves for the accidents or mistakes of others. When complimented for personal qualities or professional achievements, some may brush off positive feedback as though they don't believe they deserve praise. Such reactions are red flags that indicate someone has trouble accurately assessing the nature of their real self.

Another false negative error in self-concept happens when leaders take one of their skills for granted. They may assume everyone has that ability, so they don't fully take advantage of that strength. For instance, a leader may expect everyone on their team to see the strategic importance of a customer relationship intuitively, so when their team fails to engage with the customer in a way that the leader thinks is a "no-brainer," the leader may get frustrated and lash out.

In contrast is a false positive self-concept, one in which we tend to think of ourselves, our beliefs, and our actions in a more positive light than is accurate. This is the case for people—maybe even you—who tend to see themselves in the best possible light. Such individuals have an idealized self-concept. In their minds, who they really are is who they believe themselves to be ideally. When confronted with negative feedback, people who make Type 2 errors (false positives) in their assessment of their real selves may become defensive. They typically brush off criticism and may even lash back at you, questioning your motives for offering constructive feedback.

Thinking about ourselves in a favorable light can be a very useful quality. We all need self-esteem—a feeling of valuing and liking ourselves. Many research studies have demonstrated that self-esteem not only enhances our own well-being, but positively influences those around us. However, to maintain our self-esteem, we may sometimes ignore or try to explain away mistakes and failures. As Stephen M. R. Covey, author of *The Speed of Trust: The One Thing That Changes Everything*, says, "We judge ourselves by our intentions and others by their behavior."[1]

Those around us notice when we overestimate our strengths and ignore our weaknesses. They can tell we aren't being honest with ourselves, which keeps them from trusting us. If followers don't trust us, they won't let us lead them, no matter how good our intentions.

Whenever we minimize or exaggerate our capabilities, we limit our ability to influence others in a positive direction. So how do we keep ourselves grounded in a more accurate self-assessment? For Kathy Fort Carty, feedback from her employees was a game-changer in becoming aware of opportunities to improve her leadership influence. But others' input is only one way to enhance self-awareness.

---

[1]Stephen M. R. Covey, *The Speed of Trust: The One Thing that Changes Everything* (New York: Simon & Schuster, 2006).

THE EXPERIENTIAL TRIANGLE

Some of the most valuable information about our real self comes from our awareness of "the experiential triangle." The experiential triangle contains three elements—our thoughts, feelings, and actions. At any given moment, we are always thinking, feeling, and acting. Let's look at each of the three elements of our experiential triangle in turn (see Figure 1).

Thoughts. As human beings, we think one thought at a time. Even trying not to have a thought is a thought. Our thoughts and beliefs in many ways shape how we're feeling and how we act in response to people and situations in our lives. Those responses in turn make a critical difference in the feelings and behavior of those we seek to influence. Consider, for example, the impact of the varied thoughts and beliefs of corporate leaders in 2021 as the availability of COVID-19 vaccines lowered the coronavirus infection rate and made it possible for more people to return to pre-pandemic work life. For a year and a half, almost everyone who could work from home did so. When it became safer to congregate in indoor spaces, some companies began to require that employees come back to the office. Leaders of some companies focused on thoughts and beliefs that working onsite would provide employees with greater learning opportunities and that in-person collaboration would result in higher levels of productivity and innovation. For instance, CNBC reported that David Solomon, CEO of Goldman Sachs, described the remote-work culture as an "aberration." Solomon said the nature of business within the financial sector clashes with the

F I G U R E   1   THE EXPERIENTIAL TRIANGLE

work-from-home model.[2] "I do think for a business like ours, which is an innovative, collaborative apprenticeship culture, this is not ideal for us."[3]

Jamie Dimon, CEO of JPMorgan Chase, was similarly vocal about what he viewed as the downsides of remote working. "How do you build a culture and character? How are you going to learn properly?" he said, similarly referring to junior workers as Solomon did, per *Financial News London*. According to Dimon, "a lot of work takes place not at the meeting, but before or after the meeting, when people share ideas."[4]

Leaders of other companies thought differently. In May 2020, then Twitter CEO, Jack Dorsey, for instance, told his employees that they could work from home permanently if they wished, after he experienced an increase in his own productivity from working at home. In the spring of 2021, Spotify announced a permanent flexible work schedule:

> *The new occupational strategy lets its 6,550 global employees choose how they want to work at the company—in an office, remotely, or at a co-working space that the company will pay a subscription for, as* Insider *previously reported.*
>
> *Employees will be given more choice over the town, city, or country they want to work from.*[5]

In pointing out these different thought processes, we don't intend to judge company leaders' varying decisions about remote work. But

---

[2]Vicky McKeever, "Goldman Sachs CEO Solomon Calls Working from Home an 'Aberration,'" *CNBC* (February 25, 2021), https://www.cnbc.com/2021/02/25/goldman-sachs-ceo-solomon-calls-working-from-home-an-aberration-.html.

[3]Ibid.

[4]Paul Clarke, "'How Are You Going to Learn Properly?' JPMorgan CEO Jamie Dimon Warns of Increasing Negatives of Working from Home," *Financial News* (October 16, 2020), https://www.fnlondon.com/articles/how-are-you-going-to-learn-properly-jpmorgan-ceo-jamie-dimon-warns-over-increasing-negatives-of-working-from-home-20201016.

[5]Zahra Tayeb, "The Great Divide: Business Leaders Are Split on Long-Term Remote Working. This Is What Spotify, Twitter, Goldman Sachs, and Others Have Announced," *Insider* (March 7, 2021), https://www.businessinsider.com/what-spotify-twitter-goldman-sachs-said-about-long-term-remote-working-2021-3.

it's clear that different thought processes will lead to different decisions, which will influence followers differently. For example, imagine the impact of these different beliefs about remote versus in-office work. Even though concerns about COVID-19 are greatly reduced compared to the early days of the coronavirus pandemic, the majority of workers indicate a strong preference for working remotely, as reported in a 2022 Pew Research survey:

> 60% of workers with jobs that can be done from home say when the coronavirus outbreak is over, if they have the choice, they'd like to work from home all or most of the time. This is up from 54% who said the same in 2020. Among those who are currently working from home all or most of the time, 78% say they'd like to continue to do so after the pandemic, up from 64% in 2020.[6]

Interestingly, Jamie Dimon, who in 2021 insisted that all JPMorgan Chase employees return to corporate offices, found that his thoughts evolved as employees pushed back on a return to full-time onsite work. In an early 2022 report to shareholders, Dimon announced a more flexible work location policy: About half of its workforce would be required to work full-time in the office. Roughly 40 percent would be able to work part-time at home, while the remaining ten percent of employees would allowed to work remotely full-time.

When it comes to Jamie Dimon's thoughts regarding remote versus in-home work, his message to shareholders represents a major change in perspective. And it's a reminder of the importance of checking in frequently on your experiential triangle in order to be mindful of the thinking that underscores critical leadership decisions.

Now, consider your own thought processes: Each of us has about 12,000 to 60,000 thoughts per day. Of those tens of thousands of thoughts, 80 percent are negative, and 95 percent are the same thoughts we had the day before. What's more, scientists have found that 85 percent of what we worry about never happens. Massive and unfounded negative thoughts cause mental and physical stress, limiting our ability

[6]Kim Parker, Juliana Menasce Horowitz, and Rachel Minkin, "COVID-19 Pandemic Continues to Reshape Work in America," Pew Research Center (February 16, 2022) https://www.pewresearch.org/social-trends/2022/02/16/covid-19-pandemic-continues-to-reshape-work-in-america/.

to manage ourselves and positively influence others. Imagine, then, the positive impact of taking control of our thoughts. What positive influence might we accomplish if we decided to consciously manage what we think? Fortunately, we have the power to do just that. We can decide what to think.

Noted leadership consultant Dr. Marilee Adams agrees that since much of what we think about internally tends to manifest itself externally in our lives, it's important to be mindful about what we think. According to Adams, one helpful way to manage what we think about is to be purposeful about the questions we ask ourselves.[7] So, if you want to change a particular aspect of your life or business, begin by changing the questions you ask yourself. For example, instead of asking, "Why did this happen to me?" or "How could I be so foolish?" ask, "What can I learn from this? How can I do better next time?" or most importantly, "Where do I want to take my life? Does my career suit me?" Changing our questions shifts our focus and attention. Whether or not we can answer those questions immediately, our brain will continue to operate in the background until it comes up with productive answers to our questions. It's like losing your car keys. You don't always know where they are right away, but a few hours later, you usually remember where you left them.

The Power of Your Thoughts. Before reading further, try these two quick experiments that demonstrate the power of deliberate thinking:

Experiment 1: Take a minute to concentrate on something that made you angry. Close your eyes and imagine the situation in your mind's eye as vividly as possible.

Now focus on the experience you had when recalling that anger-provoking situation.

- *What thoughts did you have about that past situation?*
- *How were you feeling just thinking about it?*
- *How were you responding physically?*

[7]Marilee Adams, *Change Your Questions, Change Your Life: 12 Powerful Tools for Leadership, Coaching, and Life* (Oakland, CA: Berrett-Koehler Publishers, 2016).

If you're like most of us, thinking about that past experience made it come alive for you, almost as though it was actually happening. You likely recalled what you thought about at the time. There's a good chance you felt yourself getting angry all over again. You may even have noticed physical changes such as your heart beating faster or your jaw clenching. Isn't it remarkable that simply *thinking* about a previous disturbing experience actually changed you for the worse, both emotionally and physiologically?

Before moving on to the second experiment, take a deep breath and let go of any tension that you may still feel from that first recollection.

Experiment 2: Imagine that your brain is a radio receiver with a Love Channel, a Beauty Channel, and a Gratitude Channel. When you access these channels, they play all the "greatest hits" about whom you love, what you find beautiful, and what you're grateful for. As you've already discovered, you can visualize whatever you're thinking about. So, choose a channel you'd like to play in your mind, say, the Love Channel. Think about all the people (and pets), alive and deceased, for whom you have unconditional love.

> *Now focus on the experience of listening to your Love, Beauty, or Gratitude Channel.*

- *What thoughts came to mind?*
- *How were you feeling as you listened to the channel you chose?*
- *How were you responding physically?*

If you're like most, thinking about whom you love, what you find beautiful, or what you're grateful for, shifted you into a more positive state of being. As you focused on your channel, you probably felt more loving, more attuned to the beauty in your life, or more grateful. Tuning into your channel also may have led to positive physical changes such as feeling calmer and more relaxed.

Just as thinking about a past disturbing experience likely changed your emotions and physiology for the worse, thinking about positive experiences probably resulted in an improved emotional and physical state of being. These two experiments demonstrate that we can always decide what to think. Our ability to activate our cognitive mind in any situation, no matter how challenging, is one of our superpowers.

Emotions. As with thoughts, emotions provide valuable information about a situation, but only if you're paying attention to them. Unlike your thoughts, however, you can feel multiple emotions simultaneously. Our brains are hardwired to be emotionally reflexive. Being emotionally reflexive means that when we feel something, our brains have a rapid, automatic response, typically leading to some action. In many cases, this reflexive response may save us. Think about how quickly we stop moving when we step into a walkway and see a car speeding toward us. In other cases, being emotionally reflexive can work against us. When the stock market crashed in 2008 and 2020, many investors lost money because they reflexively acted on fear, selling tumbling stocks that recovered before long and even exceeded their pre-crash values.

Many emotionally reflexive responses become a pattern or typical way of responding because, at some point, that response seemed to protect us. Interestingly, emotionally reflexive responses, such as panic-selling stocks, become patterns because they are emotionally satisfying, even if they are not objectively in our best self-interest. That's why investors who panic-sell during market downturns don't learn from their experiences. The immediate emotional gratification they gain from reducing the anxiety caused by stock market volatility overwhelms any objective data about long-term market performance.

Our emotions tend to sacrifice accuracy for speed. Emotions want us to respond quickly but are often wrong. Emotional intelligence is "knowing" how we're feeling. Emotional competence, or becoming "emotionally reflective," is about managing those feelings and choosing the appropriate response.

Let's return to Anna, the successful executive you met in Chapter 2. As you'll recall, from a very early age, Anna had developed a pattern of reflexively responding to others by caring for them, usually at her own expense. When she was a child, she needed to care for others to survive. Taking care of others was emotionally rewarding. It helped her feel safer and more in control of an otherwise chaotic family situation. But as Anna became more self-aware, she recognized that this pattern was no longer working for her. Anna moved from being emotionally reflexive, in her case automatically caring for others no matter what, to becoming emotionally reflective. It's worth noting that being "emotionally reflective" is actually a cognitive process. When reflecting on emotions, we are engaged in thinking rather than entangled in raw emotion. It is that shift from pure emotion to reflection (i.e., thinking) about the impact of our emotions on our actions that allows us to choose steps that lead to the best outcomes for ourselves and those we lead.

Why is it so challenging to be emotionally reflective? The answer lies in the most primitive part of our brain, the amygdala. The amygdala is wired for "fight or flight." It triggers physiological changes such as increased heart rate and more rapid breathing that prepare us to act in the presence of fear-inducing situations. That response kept humans alive millions of years ago when sabretooth tigers were chasing them. Faced with a threatening situation (real or perceived), our amygdala will decide within 12 milliseconds whether we stand and fight or run like hell. To put 12 milliseconds into perspective, the blink of an eye takes about 100 milliseconds. The amygdala fires three and a half times faster than the logical thinking part of our brains. In most emotionally charged situations, we're already feeling before we're thinking. There is even evidence that information about potential dangers in our surroundings can reach the amygdala before we consciously realize there is anything to fear. That means we react to perceived danger before we've had a chance to reflect on what's happening. Our primitive response saves us when we stop running as we reach the edge of a cliff because our brain doesn't want us to take precious time to evaluate our options. But our primitive brain tends to operate the same way in merely upsetting situations as it does in truly life-threatening circumstances. Imagine we hear that a colleague has complained about our performance. In such a case, we tend to react emotionally, perhaps feeling upset or angry, and may find it difficult to objectively evaluate our colleague's assessment of our performance. That's because, in the presence of strong emotions, the emotional wiring of our brain takes precedence over the parts of our brain that process logical thought. What's more, those emotions may lead us to take some unwarranted action before we can think clearly and logically choose our response. It's not a coincidence that the word "emotion" comes from the Latin word "emovere," which means "to move." (See Figure 2.)

However, our natural tendency to first react emotionally to circumstances doesn't mean we are at the mercy of our emotions. Just as we can decide what to think, we can choose how to respond to our

FIGURE 2   *THE IDEAL STATE*

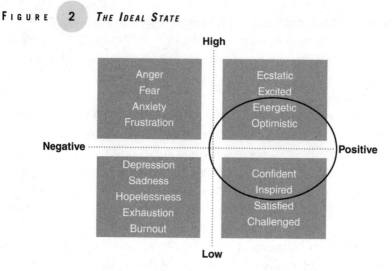

emotions. We can manage our emotions. That's the essence of emotional competence, that is, being able to recognize, understand, and manage our own emotions and influence others' emotions as well.

For instance, we can navigate excessive emotional highs or lows in ourselves by developing the habit of naming them. Labeling emotions is a valuable self-awareness tool. Not only does labeling feelings give us useful information about ourselves, but naming emotions shifts us from a dominant feeling state—in which we might react to our emotions by doing something we later regret—into a thinking mode. By labeling our emotions, we slow down our mind. We create some distance between ourselves and our emotional response. In that space, we can feel less stress, think more clearly, and make better decisions about responding to upsetting situations. That's why we advise our clients to engage in "e-think-motion," our term for activating our capacity for logical thought before we move into action in response to a strong emotion.

Substantial research, such as that conducted by the Korn Ferry Hay Group, reinforces the positive impact of emotional self-awareness on leadership performance. Korn Ferry Hay Group research found that among leaders with multiple strengths in emotional self-awareness, 92% had teams with high energy and high performance. Great leaders create a positive emotional climate that encourages motivation and extra effort, and they're the ones with good emotional self-awareness.

In sharp contrast, leaders low in emotional self-awareness created negative climates 78% of the time.[8]

Recognizing emotions day to day and moment to moment enables us as leaders to choose our response in any circumstance. Emotional self-awareness is vital to a leader's decision-making capability and performance. Once we know how we're feeling, we can begin to reflect on that emotion and proactively choose our response. Responding effectively in the face of strong emotions informs our own behavior and helps others respond more effectively to their own emotions.

Action. The last corner of the experiential triangle is one of "action." Actions can be voluntary or involuntary. For example, blinking or breathing would be examples of involuntary behavior or actions. Speaking or walking would be examples of voluntary behavior. Why is paying attention to our behavior—especially our communication with others—so important? Tom Mungavan, CEO of the executive development firm, Change Masters® Incorporated, cites a classic study by Albert Mehrabian. Mehrabian found that people tend to pay a great deal of attention to how we communicate, for instance, our tone of voice, our facial expressions, and other aspects of our body language, when trying to interpret our meaning. For example, if people sense that what you say and how you say it are inconsistent, they may decide you are not telling the truth. If you want to influence others, you need to be reflective about your communication and ensure that your verbal and nonverbal behavior is aligned.

Getting to Know Your Experiential Triangle. Given the critical importance of self-awareness, how can we cultivate it? One of the most powerful tools we can use to improve self-awareness is the freeze game, which gets its name from the everyday use of the term "freeze" to mean "stop." For example, when children play "freeze tag," a player who is tagged must stop and remain motionless. In our version of the freeze game, we tag ourselves. We stop whatever we are doing to pay attention to our experiential triangle at that moment. The freeze game is a reality check. It's all about taking a break from everyday activities several times a day to focus on what we're thinking, how we're feeling, and what we're doing.

---

[8]Daniel Goleman, "What Is Emotional Self Awareness," Korn Ferry Hay Group, 2019, https://www.kornferry.com/insights/this-week-in-leadership/what-is-emotional-self-awareness-2019.

We perform at our best when we are physically, mentally, and emotionally present. To experience how the freeze game can enhance your self-awareness, take a time out to go through the following exercise.

Play the Freeze Game

1. Say "freeze" and pause

2. Write down
   - What am I thinking?
   - What am I feeling?
   - What am I doing?

3. Are my feelings, thoughts and actions aligned?

4. Is there a better choice for me right now?

How do you take advantage of the self-awareness that results from playing the freeze game? Most importantly, the freeze game gives insight into how aligned your real self is with your ideal self. It can tell you at any given time whether you're acting in tune with your principles, values, and goals.

Playing the freeze game multiple times daily will also help you notice your emotional and physical rhythms—when you're typically feeling good and when you're not. Pay attention to any patterns in your experiential triangle as you move through your day. For instance, the freeze game might help you realize that you often feel sluggish in the morning. You can use that information to make changes that will help you feel more energetic in the morning, such as getting more sleep, improving your diet, or adjusting your exercise routine.

Making the freeze game a consistent part of your life will do more than heighten your self-awareness and improve your attention at the moment. It will also instill a habit of focused reflection that can have profound benefits, especially whenever you are in a highly-charged emotional state. For example, consider Louise Mormon's situation with her mother, Dorothy. After 85 happy, healthy years, Dorothy needed heart valve replacement surgery. While in the hospital, Dorothy contracted MRSA, a serious antibiotic-resistant bacterial infection. She had to be put on a ventilator for months and was slowly dying. Louise was emotionally paralyzed at the thought of losing her mom. Confused and exhausted about what to do, Louise spent a few careful days of thought, rest, and reflection about the situation. After a few days of contemplation, rather than accept the doctors' prognosis and let her mom continue to wither away in the hospital, Louise decided to take a break from her job and bring her mom home to her small town in Ohio. Louise assembled a team of nurses to care for her mom around the clock. Within a few months of proactive care in a healthier, cleaner environment, Dorothy was able to get off the ventilator and begin walking again. Louise told us, "It was the most purpose-driven thing I've ever done in my life. But it took me calming down and getting my head clear, so I could explore my other options." Even in the face of difficult emotions, Louise was able to activate her emotional competence and "choose" her response—one that ultimately saved her mother's life.

Louise's story is only one example of the power of the freeze game. We've taught doctors and nurses to play the freeze game during surgery. Surgical teams we've worked with call it "A Pause for Cause." Any surgical team member can call a "freeze" during surgery. Why would you want your doctor or nurse calling a freeze if you were going into surgery? The answer is simple: One of the most significant risks in surgery is a distracted surgical team, for instance, a team does the wrong procedure or operates on the wrong body part. When coauthor Chuck's daughter was only three years old, she narrowly escaped receiving a lethal dose of anesthesia for a surgical procedure because a distracted anesthesiologist had incorrectly written down her age as being ten years old. That doctor would undoubtedly have benefitted from learning the freeze game.

Triangles of Influence. It's one thing to become more aware of how we think, feel, and act in our life roles. That's clearly important to our ability to modulate our own behavior. But to ensure that those we hope to lead follow us, we also need to become more sensitive about how we affect others' experiential triangles. That's what we mean by triangles of influence: Your experiential triangle influences the experiential triangles of those around you because our emotions are so often triggered by the actions of others. Knowing this allows us to be more thoughtful and proactive about how we influence others (See Figure 3).

Let's say you're about to discuss an assignment with your new employee, Kahlia. You'd like your discussion to result in her feeling positive, confident, and actively engaged in thinking about how to move forward. What do *you* need to think, feel, and do to help create that desired experience for her? For example, you may think about how you want to convey the importance of the assignment. You may want to tap into your enthusiasm about this opportunity for Kahlia or be prepared to express your confidence in her ability to be successful. You may also need to allocate enough time to fully explain the assignment and answer Kahlia's questions.

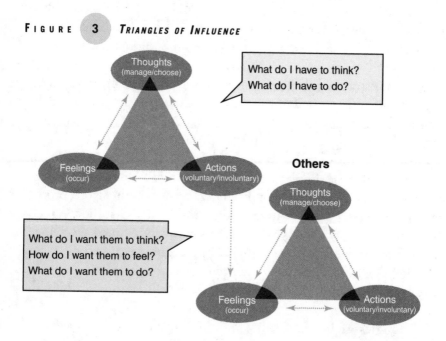

FIGURE 3 TRIANGLES OF INFLUENCE

Earlier, we shared the story of Kathy Fort Carty's leadership epiphany. By having the courage to share their experiences of Kathy's leadership style, Kathy's employees fostered her self-awareness so she could become, in Adam Smith's words, *a spectator of her own behavior.*

Kathy's employees had a personal stake in seeing her grow as a leader. While acting in their self-interest, they also cared deeply for Kathy and wanted the company to succeed. Chuck and his colleague, psychologist Rick Aberman, started working with Kathy and her company in 2005, about 15 years after Kathy Fort Carty started her company. With the support of her leadership coaches, Kathy began to shift her behavior. As Kathy upscaled her leadership effectiveness, her company's growth rate accelerated. Her team noticed the impact of Kathy's behavior on the team and the company's operations. It wasn't much of a stretch for her most talented employees to begin to imitate Kathy's success-promoting leadership behaviors.

The notion that leadership is only a top-down exercise is a dated concept. Today's world demands that we lead up, down, and across, helping one another in our quest for self-awareness. For all of us to make a positive difference in the world today, we must know ourselves. Knowing ourselves better can come from many sources, including our personal awareness and experiences and others' feedback. In a world where change is happening at a dizzying pace and where knowledge and technology have become commodities, developing understanding of who we *really* are is vital for leadership success.

...

We need to cultivate self-awareness to benchmark our real selves against the person and leader we ideally want to be. Self-awareness is essential to understanding whether or not we are living in alignment, that is, whether our behavior is in sync with our goals, and whether the goals we're working toward are consistent with our principles and values. Alignment between values, goals, and behavior is the essence of the principle of integrity. In the following chapter, we'll dive deeper into the next set of leadership essentials, *integrity* and *responsibility*. As you'll discover, integrity and responsibility set the stage for being highly effective and intelligent leaders—leaders who inspire those around them to make a positive difference in our increasingly complex and challenging world.

CHAPTER FIVE

Ignite Integrity and Responsibility

It was a warm New York afternoon in September 2008. Waiting for the meeting to begin, Bill Williams, executive vice president (EVP), President Ameriprise Independent Advisors, looked intently around the boardroom table where he and nine other top executives had gathered. Jim Cracchiolo, Ameriprise chairman and CEO, and Walter Berman, chief financial officer, had just joined the group by video conference. Though Jim wasn't there in person, his trademark quiet intensity immediately filled the room. Jim wanted his team's input on a monumental decision. The "Great Recession," the most catastrophic financial crisis since the Great Depression, was in full swing. The DJIA and S&P indexes were still off at least 50 percent from their late 2007 highs. Financial institutions had bet their balance sheets on shaky mortgage-backed securities, and now the house of cards was crashing down. Investment bank giants such as Lehman Brothers and Bear Stearns had gone bankrupt under the weight of toxic subprime mortgage-based instruments. Global insurance company AIG, deemed "too big to fail," had been rescued from bankruptcy at the 11th hour by a massive federal loan. Merrill Lynch, at its height the world's largest retail brokerage, was swallowed up by Bank of America in a deal heavily subsidized by U.S. government funds.

Like countless other financial institutions, the value of Ameriprise Financial's Money Market Reserve Fund was now threatened by imploding mortgage-backed securities. Americans had thought their money market funds were as safe as bank savings accounts. But they were not. Most assumed, incorrectly, that they couldn't lose money invested in a money market account (MMA.) But the fine print said otherwise. Money market investors, who never imagined their investments could drop below a dollar per share, were at risk of precisely that. In industry parlance, the unprecedented but now likely prospect of money market shares dropping in value below a dollar per share was called "breaking the buck." The Reserve Primary Fund, the storied original money market fund, had already broken the buck and ultimately had to be liquidated. Most other money market funds were in danger of a similar fate.

On the plus side, Ameriprise had no legal or financial obligation to maintain its MMA share value at $1.00. But Jim, Bill, and other Ameriprise execs knew that finances and legal issues were not all they needed to consider in charting a course forward. As Bill explained:

> *Since the founding of our company in 1894 as Investors Syndicate, we had promised our clients that we would stand by them. Our company has always felt responsible for the well-being of our clients. Throughout our 125-year history, we had never been "a day late or a dollar short." Even during the decade of the Great Depression, Investors Syndicate paid out every dollar on its due date, a total of $101 million, to its certificate holders. We had a unique track record of providing service, security, and value to our clients. It made no sense to blow our reputation now.*

Now Jim was asking for each leader's input about whether or not to "break the buck." Bill vividly recalls how the meeting proceeded. "Jim polled each of us, saying, 'I want you to think about everybody—shareholders, clients, advisors, and employees.'"

The consensus of Ameriprise's top team was consistent with the point of view Bill expressed when it was his turn to speak: "We may not be legally obligated to honor the Reserve Fund's share value, but we are morally obligated."

Following the meeting, the company moved quickly to advance $700 million to help their Money Market Reserve Fund clients meet any immediate cash needs. But that wasn't all. Ameriprise leaders also felt responsible for understanding and addressing their advisors' needs. They fast-tracked the development of a host of market volatility resources for advisors to use in helping clients navigate the stresses and challenges of the financial crisis.

Only seven months later, in April 2009, Ameriprise would face an equally fateful decision. With the economy still in free fall, the U.S. federal government was moving ahead with TARP, the "Troubled Asset Recovery Program," intended to prop up the broader financial services sector and dodge the bullet of a catastrophic global economic collapse.

Ameriprise Financial was one of the select financial institutions encouraged to apply for government assistance to stabilize their financial position and boost consumer confidence. To keep its options open, Ameriprise had applied. But by the time TARP funds had been approved and offered, senior Ameriprise leaders had to determine if that was the right path to take. After much discussion among the executive team, Ameriprise declined the TARP program's eye-popping offer of a $2.5 billion loan to subsidize its asset structure. Though Ameriprise's decision was not a shock to industry analysts, the full explanation for Ameriprise's choice was never publicly reported. CEO Jim Cracchiolo cited Ameriprise's confidence in their current capital position and access to potential additional funding sources going forward. Those were legitimate reasons to decline TARP funding, and no doubt Ameriprise's financials contributed significantly to the company's decision to forgo federal government support. But behind the scenes, the decision was more complex and less financially driven. It would have been easy for Ameriprise to accept TARP funds. It would have been tempting to take virtually free money and invest it in a way that enhanced their bottom line. In fact, most financial institutions offered TARP money took advantage of that opportunity. But Jim and his team knew they didn't need the help. As Bill Williams explained: "We knew we could rebound without government assistance. So, to take money we didn't absolutely need would have been a violation of our corporate value of integrity."

A month later, in May 2009, CEO Jim Cracchiolo stood on stage in front of thousands of top Ameriprise performers tapped to attend the company's highly valued annual Circle of Success meeting in

Washington, DC. Jim began his talk with this question: "What would you think if I said we aren't going to accept any government money?" The assembled advisors broke out into deafening applause. They knew that Jim's question signaled a vote of confidence in the health of their company and a commitment to putting clients first. As advisors, they could position the company as being in solid financial territory and, therefore, the most secure place for clients to invest their funds, especially in a highly volatile economic environment.

During the Great Recession, Ameriprise bet on the future. Ameriprise chose integrity over profit when it declined government subsidies it didn't think it needed—even though some market analysts disagreed. The company chose responsibility over financial results when it honored the one-dollar-per-share structure of its Money Market Reserve Fund. Staying true to principles turned out to be not just the right thing to do, but the smart thing to do financially. During the period from just before the start of the Great Recession until 2012, advisor productivity rose 70 percent. Over the same time frame, assets under management for clients increased by 46 percent.

At the time of the 2007–2009 financial crisis, Ameriprise Financial was a new kid on the block. Though it had been in business for more than a hundred years, in its latest incarnation and with a new brand, it didn't have the name recognition it enjoys today. The decisions Ameriprise made during the Great Recession demonstrated both strategic competence and a commitment to moral principles. Those decisions cemented the company's reputation as a trustworthy and reliable financial services company. In the years since, Ameriprise has consistently received awards for high levels of customer service. Ameriprise advisors are frequently recognized for excellence by business publications such as *Barron's* and *Forbes*. And shareholders enjoy excellent returns. In 2021, for instance, Ameriprise's stock price increased by more than 55 percent. Given the vagaries of the economic landscape, every year going forward may not be as profitable. However, Ameriprise's laser-focus on satisfying clients and its commitment to integrity—standing behind what they say and do—is likely to ensure its success, no matter what challenges or crises the future presents. As Bill Williams reflects, "It's easy to do the expedient thing for the short term. It's much harder to do the right thing for the long term. When it comes to the decisions we made in the throes of the Great Recession, I'll never regret that we did the right thing when it mattered most."

INTEGRITY AND RESPONSIBILITY: AN ESSENTIAL PAIR

As we saw in Chapter 3, integrity and responsibility are two of the four universal principles that form our moral compass (Frame 1 of the alignment model). Integrity and responsibility are distinct but intertwined. You demonstrate integrity through your actions, such as telling the truth, standing up for what is right, and keeping your promises. When you have integrity, you also act in concert with the other principles, including responsibility. Responsibility is most importantly about accountability. Effective leaders accept responsibility for their choices, freely admit mistakes and failures, and embrace their duty to serve others. When we think about integrity and responsibility, it's hard to imagine having one without the other. You can see how interconnected these two principles are when you compare the moral competencies associated with integrity and responsibility:

Integrity		Responsibility
Telling the truth	⟺	Admitting mistakes and failures
Standing up for what is right	⟺	Embracing responsibility for serving others
		Admitting mistakes and failures
Keeping promises	⟺	Taking responsibility for personal choices
		Admitting mistakes and failures
		Embracing responsibility for serving others

Leaders with integrity feel a *responsibility* to act with integrity. For instance, they hold themselves responsible for telling the truth, standing up for what is right, and keeping promises. Similarly, it's hard to be responsible without having integrity. It takes integrity to accept responsibility for your choices, admit your mistakes, and commit to serving others. Although integrity and responsibility are separate concepts, they are so strongly related that when we see them in action, we often think of both together as aspects of integrity.

DOUG ON THE CONNECTION BETWEEN INTEGRITY AND RESPONSIBILITY

It is my responsibility to act with integrity. Acting with integrity is much more than not lying. Not lying is as easy as not speaking. I will not have lied if I don't speak, but that does not mean I am acting with integrity. Acting with integrity requires "action." It is a behavior. I tell the truth. I stand up for what is right. I keep my promises. My behavior is in alignment with universal principles and my personal values and beliefs.

INTEGRITY AND RESPONSIBILITY BREED TRUST

Integrity and responsibility would never have emerged as universal principles unless they had a powerful positive impact on our effectiveness in all our life roles. The overarching result of acting with integrity and responsibility is that such actions lead others to trust us. The legendary management theorist Peter Drucker drew the connection between integrity and trust in his 1992 classic *Managing for the Future*. "Trust," wrote Drucker, "is the conviction that the leader means what he says. It is a belief in something very old-fashioned, called 'integrity.' A leader's actions and a leader's professed beliefs must be congruent, or at least compatible."[1] When we trust a leader, we open ourselves to being influenced by them, which leads us to behave in all sorts of positive ways.

As Stephen M. R. Covey, our colleague and bestselling author of *The Speed of Trust*[2] shared in a personal conversation with us, "The first job of a leader—at work or at home—is to inspire trust. It's to bring out the best in people by entrusting them with meaningful stewardships, and to create an environment in which high-trust interaction inspires creativity and possibility." Covey cites a recent Watson Wyatt study showing that high-trust companies outperform low-trust companies by a whopping 286 percent. Sadly, as Covey pointed out, trust in organizations is spiraling down in most parts of the world, a trend Covey shared with us in pointing out the results of the last few annual

[1] Peter Drucker, *Managing for the Future* (London: Routledge, 1993).
[2] Stephen M. R. Covey, *The Speed of Trust* (New York: Free Press, 2018).

Edelman Trust Barometers. Disturbingly, the 2022 Edelman survey concluded that "distrust is now society's default emotion." The Edelman researchers summarize the impact of low trust in this way:

> *Nearly 6 in 10 [survey respondents] say their default tendency is to distrust something until they see evidence it is trustworthy. Another 64% say it's now to a point where people are incapable of having constructive and civil debates about issues they disagree on. When distrust is the default— we lack the ability to debate or collaborate.*[3]

Why is this finding so critical to leadership effectiveness? If you are not a trustworthy leader, then followers won't collaborate with you in service of a positive purpose. You won't be able to influence others in the direction you intend. So, what's the antidote to this pervasive decline in trust? As successive Edelman surveys consistently find, integrity and other aspects of ethical behavior are the strongest drivers of trust.[4]

It's worth keeping in mind that trust is a two-way street. As a leader, you need to be seen as trustworthy, and you also need to trust those around you. In the words of legendary leadership expert Warren Bennis, "Leadership without mutual trust is a contradiction." Stephen M. R. Covey agrees, reminding us that "Whether you're in an office, on a sports team, in a community, or a member of a family, if you can't trust one another there're going to be problems. Nothing works without trust." Leaders can't make a positive difference without trust, and trust simply doesn't happen unless a leader demonstrates integrity and responsibility.

Numerous surveys confirm the importance of integrity and responsibility. For example, 75 percent of employees in a 2016 Robert Half Management Resources survey cited integrity as the most important attribute for business leaders. Given the importance of integrity, several 2020 Gallup Surveys in Europe and the United States offer cause for concern. Less than half of employees in Europe and one-third of work-

---

[3] 2022 Edelman Trust Barometer, Edelman, https://www.edelman.com/trust/2022-trust-barometer.
[4] Ibid.

ers in the United States believe their employer "would do what is right" if an employee raised a concern about ethics and integrity.

The solution? Make every day a day when you do your best to act responsibly and with integrity. When followers trust that you will do the right thing, they are more likely to be engaged. By promoting a culture of integrity and responsibility, you will dramatically increase your ability to influence others to do what together you have set out to do.

TELLING THE TRUTH

The key to integrity is your willingness as a leader to tell the truth. Chuck refers to this aspect of integrity as "accurately defining reality," that is, "telling it like it is." It's a shame we need to qualify the concept of "defining reality" with the adjective "accurately." "Accurate" and "reality" should be redundant. When it comes to speaking the truth, we've long had people such as flat Earthers and holocaust deniers who insist their views are factual. But today, across the globe, truth and belief have become conflated. It's as though the entire planet is suffering from a massive case of confirmation bias. Rather than look for what is objectively true, we increasingly seek out information sources that reinforce our individual prejudices. In the current hyper-partisan environment in the United States, for example, even quantifiable data becomes politicized. For example, a year after the January 2021 inauguration of U.S. President Joe Biden, 35 percent of Americans continued to believe that the election was fraudulent, despite no evidence of widespread voter fraud.

Public figures these days toss around terms such as "alternative facts" and "fake news." As authors, we've never before seen a time when so many public leaders have been so willing to "make things up," twisting or distorting reality for their political benefit. Always, but especially when times are tough, leaders need to be able to tell hard truths while still providing people with genuine reasons for hope and optimism. When we deny people the truth, we're depriving them of the information they need to make good decisions about how to deal with a given situation. It is during times of adversity that you can have the most positive impact as a leader. That's because it can be tough for people to make good choices during periods of crisis and uncertainty. When leaders tell the truth and accurately define reality, they help people cut through all the confusion and see more clearly.

CHUCK: ACCURATELY DEFINING REALITY

As part of an organizational change in the financial services company where Doug and I worked at the time, I was part of a group of people about to assume newly created regional executive positions. The new role included more responsibilities than most of us had held previously. We viewed the role as a promotion, with significant added pressures and expectations. Therefore, many of us anticipated a commensurate significant increase in compensation. When our offer letters came, we were underwhelmed by the new compensation plan. Believing it was unfair, we began to challenge the new executive comp plan. Many of us emailed and asked for private meetings with Doug, my leader at the time, so that he would hear and understand our perceived grievances. Over the next few weeks, Doug patiently took our calls, answered our questions, and responded to emails, hoping they would give us the needed answers and help us move on from this issue. Sadly, that wasn't the case.

Finally, Doug called us together for a meeting with his brilliant controller, Jim Jensen. Jim arrived well prepared and explained to us how the company made money. He walked us through where every dollar went from the time it came in the door to our company. After about 90 minutes at the whiteboard giving an utterly transparent explanation of the financials, Jim put his marker down. The room was quiet. You could hear a pin drop. Then someone in the room raised his hand and said, "Thank you, Jim. This comp plan makes complete sense now."

Instead of getting angry or taking it personally, Doug, acting with integrity, responsibility, and complete transparency, stood his ground. He accurately defined reality for us, completely diffusing the compensation issue. We could let go of any resentment and move forward to succeed in our new jobs. In the years since, I've often considered this experience a great illustration of how telling the truth as a leader, even if painful, can foster trust and maintain engagement with those we need to influence.

The story Chuck tells about Doug's response to his new regional executives' dissatisfaction with their compensation plan demonstrates that leaders with a reputation for being honest generate a powerful climate of trust. People who work for honest leaders relax because they can safely assume there won't be hidden surprises coming out of the organizational woodwork. People accomplish more and can work with greater creativity when they don't have to waste energy watching their backs. People will always be inspired and energized by a leader they trust to be straight with them, especially during stressful times.

STANDING UP FOR WHAT IS RIGHT

Taking principled stands is the hallmark of an effective leader. Unfortunately, when it comes to doing the right thing, negative examples are all too common. Doug's previous books, *Moral Intelligence*[5] and *Moral Intelligence 2.0*,[6] chronicle numerous failures of leadership integrity and responsibility, ranging from the 2001 Enron scandal to the tactics of the Wall Street firms that precipitated the Great Recession of 2008–2009.

But there are also heartening examples of standing up for what is right, often from the ranks of U.S. military officers. For instance, on March 24, 2020, in the early days of the novel coronavirus pandemic, a few cases of COVID-19 were diagnosed among the crew of the USS *Theodore Roosevelt,* a nuclear-powered aircraft carrier deployed in the Western Pacific Ocean. Within a few days, dozens of sailors were sick, forcing the ship into port in Guam. As COVID-19 infections skyrocketed, Captain Brett Crozier, *Roosevelt's* commander, was disturbed by what he saw as his command's failure to move quickly enough to mitigate the outbreak. On March 30, he sent an email memo to a relatively large number of Navy officials, warning that "decisive action" was required to prevent onboard deaths from COVID-19 and once again asking permission to isolate most of his 5,000-member crew onshore.

---

[5] Doug Lennick and Fred Kiel, *Moral Intelligence: Enhancing Business Performance and Leadership Success* (New York: Wharton School Publishing, 2005).
[6] Doug Lennick and Fred Kiel, *Moral Intelligence 2.0: Enhancing Business Performance and Leadership Success in Turbulent Times* (New York: Prentice Hall, 2011).

"We are not at war. Sailors do not need to die. If we do not act now, we are failing to properly take care of our most trusted asset, our sailors," Crozier wrote.

Crozier's email was immediately leaked to the *San Francisco Chronicle*, which published the email and suggested that the Navy was not responding adequately to the crisis. Only two days later, on April 2, Acting Secretary of the Navy Thomas Modly fired Crozier, claiming that the captain exercised "extremely poor judgment" by sending the memo in a way that exposed it to being leaked.

From media reports, it seems that Captain Crozier knew that his choice to communicate via unclassified email to a group of influential senior naval officers would put his career at risk. Despite that, he felt morally obliged to speak out to convey the sense of urgency he felt about the well-being of thousands of sailors. Crozier's decision to stand up for what he believed was right demonstrated integrity and responsibility. Though Crozier's actions ultimately derailed his naval career, they reinforced his sailors' belief that he cared deeply about them. The crew of the *Roosevelt* considered him a hero, and after he was relieved of command on April 3, 2020, they famously gathered on deck to support him with chants and cheers as he left the carrier. In the wake of Crozier's email, support poured in from colleagues, including this email:

> *"You restored my faith in what it means to be a [commanding officer]," an auxiliary division officer wrote to Crozier on April 2 [2020.] "I came from a pretty bad command climate on my previous ship and after 12 years in the military was set on getting out after this tour. You restored that."*[7]

Captain Sully Sullenberger, widely regarded as a hero for successfully landing a disabled plane on the Hudson River in 2009, saving the lives of all 155 passengers, tweeted this about Crozier's actions and their aftermath: "I am saddened but heartened by the story of Captain Brett Crozier, USN. His moral compass points to True North.

---

[7] Gina Harkins, "As the Navy Moved to Fire Capt. Crozier, Other Leaders Rallied Around Him," *Military.com*, May 10, 2021, https://www.military.com/daily-news/2021/03/10/navy-moved-fire-capt-crozier-other-leaders-rallied-around-him.html

I commend him for putting the welfare of his crew above his career. What he did is something I hope I would have done."

Chairman of the Joint Chiefs of Staff, General Mark Milley's actions in the months following the November 2020 presidential election offer another example of the consequences of taking a principled stand. Reports indicate that Milley and other top military leaders became concerned about the possibility of a coup when then-President Trump lost the election but refused to accept its results. Trump claimed that the election results were fraudulent and repeatedly suggested that violence might be necessary to keep him in power. The January 6, 2021, riot at the U.S. Capitol was widely regarded as an attempt to overthrow the election results by disrupting the congressional process for certifying Electoral College results. Watching the violence on the Capitol that day intensified Milley's fears.

According to accounts in Bob Woodward's book *Peril*, Milley took steps to block the president from launching a potential unwarranted nuclear strike or ordering the military to keep him in power somehow. When Milley's actions were revealed, they prompted strong reactions, largely along partisan political lines. Some condemned him as a traitor, noting that as commander-in-chief, the president has sole authority to order the use of nuclear weapons as he sees fit. Others hailed Milley as a patriot who had protected the country from nuclear catastrophe.

Milley's and Crozier's respective decisions to do the right thing as they saw it remind us that practicing integrity and responsibility is not easy and may not benefit us personally. Milley's actions tarnished his reputation in some quarters, fueling calls for his resignation. Crozier's actions led to his being relieved of command of the carrier *Roosevelt* and declared him ineligible for any future command positions.

Though standing up for what is right may entail risks, it's essential as a leader to consider the risks of failing to stand up for what is right. If Crozier had not been forceful in alerting U.S. Navy higher-ups of conditions on the *Roosevelt*, likely, far more sailors than the one who tragically died from COVID-19 on his ship would have lost their lives. Had Milley failed to do what he could to limit the likelihood of ill-considered decisions by an outgoing American president, people in the United States and across the globe might be far less safe today.

As Captain Crozier's and General Milley's stories illustrate, you'll probably never get 100 percent approval from others when you take a principled stand. As we've noted, people differ in their perspectives about what is true or the right thing to do. But if you want to be an effective leader, the only choice you can make is to act with integrity, having searched for the truth and gathered as much accurate information as you can. Having done that, you will always reap the intrinsic reward of knowing that you did your best to do the right thing. Your integrity and commitment to responsibility are yours, as shown by what you do.

In contrast to Crozier and Milley, leaders who ignore the principles of integrity and responsibility are powerless to influence others positively. As leadership expert George Bradt points out:

> *Nothing kills credibility faster than not practicing what is preached. A leader underscores discipline and timeliness yet shows up late for meetings. Or a leader proclaims people to be the most important assets, then instigates layoffs to boost profitability.*[8]

Bradt underscores the need for leaders to recognize that the spotlight is always on them. As a leader who is often a person with considerable position power, your actions are always subject to extreme scrutiny.

Wherever you lead, whether in a for-profit, nonprofit, government, or community organization, you have an opportunity to increase your impact as a leader dramatically—and stand out from the pack—by acting with integrity and responsibility. That doesn't mean you will always be rewarded in conventional ways for acting with integrity. Captain Crozier's firing is only one example of the punishment you may suffer when you choose principle over politics. But those sailors who cheered Crozier at arguably the lowest point in his career learned the lessons of integrity and responsibility that their commander modeled.

Making a principled stand can be challenging when it comes to your unique leadership environment. In many organizations, there may be considerable pressure to agree with popular positions. People who take unpopular stands may risk their career advancement, their reputations, or their livelihoods. Demonstrating integrity and responsibility means accepting the risks of standing up for what is right because the moral consequences of looking the other way are unacceptable.

---

[8] George Bradt, "Practice What You Preach or Pay the Price," *Forbes* (April 10, 2013), https://www.forbes.com/sites/georgebradt/2013/04/10/practice-what-you-preach-or-pay-the-price/.

DOUG: STANDING UP FOR WHAT IS RIGHT

When I first became a senior vice president within the American Express Companies, I was 36 years old and at the time, the youngest senior executive in the corporation. This was a big step up for someone who didn't even have a college degree. I was scared from time to time. I was intimidated from time to time. But I believed in myself and thought I could work effectively with my older colleagues and direct reports to get the job done.

Early in my first year, I was on a business trip with one of my more experienced peers. On the flight to our destination, he turned to me and asked, "Doug, do you want to know the secret to success around here?" I said, "Sure!" I was thrilled he wanted to help me.

He said, "When you see a parade, jump in front of it and act like you've been leading it all along." Though I was appalled, I didn't say a thing. I knew it was wrong to take credit for someone else's good work, but for some reason, I just nodded and said nothing. I did not stand up for what is right.

Over the next few weeks, I kept thinking about that incident. I felt uncomfortable and worried that my silence had been misinterpreted as approval. Finally, I approached my colleague about my concern. I told him that I hoped I would never take credit for someone else's good work, and I wouldn't stand by and watch anyone else do that either. Of course, he agreed with me. What else could he do? More importantly, I noticed that after our conversation, he found opportunities to give credit to others for their accomplishments instead of always taking credit himself. Even if my peer had not changed his MO, I would have felt better knowing I took a principled stand. But seeing him try to share credit with others was the icing on the cake.

KEEPING PROMISES

Keeping promises is a hallmark of integrity because it shows that followers can trust us to do what we say we will do. Keeping promises to those we lead builds loyalty and inspires them to give their best efforts to our shared mission. As Stephen M.R. Covey reminds us, "We judge ourselves by our intentions but others by their behavior. This is why one of the fastest ways to restore trust is to make and keep commitments—even very small commitments—to ourselves and to others."

RESPONSIBILITY

Being responsible means taking responsibility for personal choices, admitting mistakes and failures, and embracing responsibility for serving others. Being responsible doesn't mean an individual leader can control a situation completely. It does mean holding oneself accountable for the actions one takes and committing to do the right thing as best as humanly possible, even in the face of obstacles or extenuating circumstances. U.S. President Harry Truman famously kept a plaque on his desk with the words "The Buck Stops Here." He referred to it several times, notably during his presidential farewell address:

> *The greatest part of the president's job is to make decisions—big ones and small ones, dozens of them almost every day. The papers may circulate around the government for a while, but they finally reach this desk. And then, there's no place else for them to go. The president—whoever he is—has to decide. He can't pass the buck to anybody. No one else can do the deciding for him. That's his job.*[9]

That the expression "the buck stops here" has survived nearly 70 years is a testament to the importance of responsibility. That we need the reminder indicates how difficult it can be to live in alignment with the principle of responsibility.

Lack of responsibility is nothing new. But the scale of irresponsibility—across all sectors of society in recent years—is staggering. Leaders' sense of responsibility has become warped. The news is full of headlines such as these that document a pervasive responsibility gap among leaders at the highest levels:

Wells Fargo CEO blames employees, not company culture, for scandal

Boeing's new CEO stopped short of accepting blame for the fatal 737 Max crashes and dodged a question about whether US pilots could have avoided them

Fayette Regional [Hospital] to Lay Off 49; CEO Blames Obamacare

[9] "A Presidential Farewell: Truman's Farewell Address to the Nation," *Tru Blog*, accessed April 6, 2022, https://www.trumanlibraryinstitute.org/farewell-address/.

Toll Brothers gives disappointing guidance; CEO blames media for housing slowdown

Facebook is defending its algorithms. Critics aren't buying it.

As the previous headlines illustrate, accepting responsibility is frequently challenging for individual leaders and their organizations. When leaders don't acknowledge responsibility for their decisions, mistakes, and most importantly, others' well-being, everyone suffers. Followers disengage, and leaders lose credibility. Fortunately, we can learn lessons of responsibility from many exceptional leaders. Manny Padro, a financial services business owner, and Don MacPherson, cofounder of Modern Survey and founder of 12 Geniuses, exemplify the principle of responsibility through their respective work with disadvantaged teenagers. Joanie Goulart demonstrates the principle of responsibility through her career devoted to serving the housing needs of homeless and low-income individuals. Mary Lennick embodies responsibility through her leadership of an innovative private foster care organization. Leaders such as Manny, Don, Joanie, and Mary rarely make the headlines. Still, they have embraced the principle of responsibility by serving those too often neglected by mainstream society. It may be challenging to accept responsibility, but the rewards are worth it. We may embrace integrity and responsibility because it's morally right, only to discover that our commitment to integrity and responsibility is also the smart thing to do for our organizations and followers. As Stephen M. R. Covey notes, "Where high trust exists [a product of demonstrating integrity and responsibility], things move faster and are cheaper."

ADMITTING MISTAKES

An online survey conducted by Dale Carnegie Training in 2016 of nearly 3,100 employees across 13 countries found that "admitting when they are wrong" produced the most significant gap of any leadership behaviors in terms of the difference between its importance to employees and its consistent performance by supervisors. Eighty-one percent of respondents said that having a leader who will admit to being wrong is important or very important to inspire them to give their best efforts at work. Still, only 41 percent said their supervisors could be trusted to do so consistently—a gap of 40 percent."

CHUCK: LEADING BY EXAMPLE

As a newly minted leader at American Express, I wanted to get off on the right foot in leading my team. At 28 years old, I was promoted to lead what had been a group of 20 former peers. While I had previously served in leadership roles in school, sports, and previous part-time jobs, this would be my first leadership role at American Express. Each Monday at 9 a.m., we held a district meeting for all members, where we talked about results from the previous week, updated the team on any company topics, and discussed our focus for the upcoming week. This particular Monday was going to be the first district meeting where I led the group since my promotion, so I had gotten to the office early to prepare and get the meeting started promptly at 9 a.m.

I had prepared the agendas, had copies for everyone, and arrived at the training room at about 8:55 a.m. Sitting at the front of the room, nervously checking my watch, I noticed that the clock struck 9 a.m., and I was still the only person in the room. After about five minutes, a few people started to amble into the room, with more coming in over the next 15 minutes until we had everyone finally assembled at about 9:20 a.m. By this time, I was fuming. This was not the start I had expected, and I knew I had to reset expectations for everyone so we would have timely meetings. Taking a deep breath, I asked the group what time the meeting was scheduled to start. "9 a.m.," everyone responded. "What time is it now?" I asked impatiently. "It's 9:20," someone replied. "From now on, this meeting will start promptly at 9 a.m.!" I insisted.

One of my good friends and former colleagues raised his hand from the back of the room.

"What?" I snapped, feeling a bit irritated.

"You were always late for this meeting before you became a manager. What's the big deal with being on time now?" my former peer inquired.

It was then that I learned one of my most important lessons as a new leader: my behavior was now under a heightened level of scrutiny, putting added emphasis on "leading by example." Even when I didn't think people were noticing, my behavior was noticed, even for something as simple as being on time for a meeting. It made me realize the significance of always acting with integrity.

Admitting mistakes makes sense, not only as a moral imperative but a practical one. Covering up mistakes violates not only the principle of responsibility, but also puts our integrity at stake. When we refuse to acknowledge mistakes, we waste time and energy and often make a situation far worse than it needs to be. As logical as it seems from a leadership perspective to admit our mistakes, there are powerful psychological and neurological obstacles to doing so. Leadership development consultant Michael Timms points out that recent research studies reveal that humans are "wired to blame." Timms summarizes the research on the origins of blame in this way:

> *We are all naturally wired to blame other people or circumstances when things go wrong. These propensities are partially psychological, driven by something called the fundamental attribution bias. We tend to believe that what people do is a reflection of who they are, rather than considering there may be other factors (social or environmental) influencing their behavior.*
>
> *This is why when major workplace disasters are reported in the news, "human error" is often the first, and sometimes only, explanation provided, ignoring the systemic factors that led to the failure. It also feels the most satisfying. If someone else is to blame for our problems, then they need to change—not us.*[10]

Despite our ingrained tendency to blame others when things go wrong, it's clear that playing the "blame game" never turns out well. For instance, aerospace company Boeing's executives, employees, and shareholders discovered the painful costs of covering up mistakes in the wake of two fatal 737 MAX 8 plane crashes caused by faulty software. Boeing's leadership's failure to accept responsibility sent exactly the wrong message to their employees about the importance of responsibility. Dennis Muilenburg, the CEO who headed Boeing at the time of the two fatal crashes, was fired for helping cover up technical problems that led to the crashes while blaming the pilots. By March 2020, Boeing had a new CEO, but the culture of blame and aversion to taking responsibility continued. In an interview, Boeing chief executive David Calhoun, who had publicly praised former CEO Dennis Muilenburg before his ouster, downplayed board responsibility for the crisis and largely blamed his predecessor.

[10] Michael Timms, "Blame Culture Is Toxic. Here's How to Stop It," *Harvard Business Review* (February 2, 2022), https://hbr.org/2022/02/blame-culture-is-toxic-heres-how-to-stop-it.

"It's more than I imagined it would be, honestly," Calhoun said. And it speaks to the weaknesses of our leadership." He claimed predecessor Dennis Muilenburg had ramped up Boeing's plane production too quickly. "I'll never be able to judge what motivated Dennis, whether it was a stock price that was going to continue to go up and up, or whether it was just beating the other guy to the next rate increase," Calhoun said. Calhoun went on to deflect blame to the former CEO: "If anybody ran over the rainbow for the pot of gold on stock, it would have been him".[11]

The Boeing MAX was grounded in March 2019, though by November 2020, it was cleared to operate again by the U.S. Federal Aviation Administration. In addition to the devastating loss of 347 lives, financial losses from the MAX crisis were estimated to be at least $23 billion.

Clearly, failure to take responsibility for personal or organizational choices can result in devastating consequences. Beyond the catastrophic loss of life and the crippling financial impact of disasters such as the twin Boeing MAX tragedies is the negative modeling by organizational leaders, who could have chosen to respond in a high-integrity way that inspired confidence rather than cynicism in their workforce.

In contrast, admitting when you are wrong builds trust and reinforces followers' perceptions of your integrity. It's rarely worth trying to cover up a mistake. Typically, by the time leaders realize they've made a mistake, others have noticed too. Leaders who fail to admit they were wrong leave followers feeling that their leaders consider being right more important than being honest. Taking responsibility demonstrates that a leader values integrity over the easier paths of making excuses or hoping their mistakes won't be exposed.

Admitting your mistakes as a leader does more than build your credibility. It helps enhance your organization's culture in several ways. First, leaders who admit mistakes model the principle of responsibility for others. Admitting your mistakes shows people that they too can be open and honest in admitting their mistakes.

---

[11] Natalie Kitroeff and David Gelles, "'It's More Than I Imagined': Boeing's New CEO Confronts Its Challenges," *New York Times* (March 6, 2020), https://www.nytimes.com/2020/03/05/business/boeing-david-calhoun.html.

Another advantage of admitting that you have screwed up is that it often prevents someone else from being blamed for your mistake. It's common in organizational hierarchies for junior staff to take the fall for their senior managers. Few things are more demoralizing to team members than unfair criticism. Admitting mistakes also can strengthen your bond with those you lead, who then feel that you are more approachable by virtue of your admission of fallibility. Finally, admitting mistakes communicates a strong message that learning is valued. It says, "We all make mistakes. We know that mistakes and failures are necessary on the road to success. We expect you to learn from your mistakes, and in the future, we hope you will make new mistakes, not repeat old ones."

By admitting mistakes, you encourage others to take smart risks, fostering innovation and superior performance. As jazz legend Miles Davis once said, "When you hit a wrong note, it's the next note that makes it good or bad."

SERVING OTHERS

All effective leaders embrace responsibility for contributing to the well-being of others. Serving others is not a "nice to do"; it is a "need to do." Followers don't exist to serve you. You exist as a leader to help those around you be the best they can be. The best way to influence others is to help them grow their skills and give them the resources they need to successfully accomplish the mission you both share.

Terry Rasmussen is the CEO of Thrivent, a Fortune 500 diversified financial services organization. Cultivating strong followership is an important part of Terry's leadership philosophy. In her mind, that means listening to and supporting her people and engaging their best efforts. The value of Terry's efforts to engage her people's best efforts was tested in 2020 when Thrivent was about to embark on a sweeping strategic transformation that would challenge many long-held practices and routines at the company. Employees liked doing things the way they always had. Some resisted change. Just as field and corporate leaders were gathering in Scottsdale, Arizona, to roll out a new, digital-first business model, COVID-19 surfaced and started rapidly spreading across the United States. Terry wasn't the only CEO to wrestle with how to respond to the pandemic. But she was probably one of the fastest to decide how to deal with it. Flying back home from Scottsdale to Minneapolis, it took her less than three hours to decide that Thrivent would close its offices and shift employees to home-based remote work. As Terry recalls:

> *The pandemic forced a re-prioritization. It moved employee safety to the top of our list. We formed two SWAT teams to plan the transition from office to home-based work. Within a few days we had 2,200 people working from home and were feeling confident. Three weeks later we had all 7,000 employees—advisors, corporate workers, product people, and technology people—working from home. Though we made our decisions based on our responsibility to put employees first, our decisions led to an unplanned benefit. Moving to remote work accelerated our strategic plan by 18 months. Part of our plan had included becoming more digital and doing more work that didn't depend on face-to-face interaction. We had expected to gradually ease into this change. But the pandemic didn't give us a choice. We had to do it in days and weeks rather than months.*

Terry's rapid action to ensure her people's safety didn't go unnoticed by Thrivent employees. They widely interpreted her actions as proof that she really cared about them. From a business perspective, it also helped employees reframe the company's strategic shift from an unwelcome change to a necessary step to protect the health and safety of Thrivent's employees and clients.

Terry's story underscores that serving others is not just about being responsible. It is also a matter of compassion. By serving others, you communicate that you care about them and want to help them achieve their goals, not just contribute to your own objectives. And since we're all wired to depend on one another for survival, serving others also demonstrates to those around you how they can contribute to the well-being of others.

Accepting responsibility for serving others is also a secret weapon for leaders who want to promote high performance among their work-forces. Kim Shankle, chief human resources officer for the nonprofit American Society for Microbiology, has discovered that secret. In her role, she is part of a leadership team that deals every day with the growing challenges of meeting its mission while remaining financially sustainable. To master that challenge, Kim embraces her responsibility for serving others. As she sees it,

I'm a big proponent of servant leadership. As leaders, we need to close the gap between words and behavior. Traditionally, leadership has been very "I-focused." We need to change from a top-down model of leadership to one in which we serve those we lead. An important part of that is understanding how effective I am with my people. So, my question to everyone is "What am I doing or not doing to help you be successful?" Beyond that, I make sure that I don't take people's efforts for granted. I'm grateful for what they do to contribute to our mission. I always say, "Thank you."

To make their organizations successful, leaders need committed team members. One of the best ways to encourage people to unleash their talents and creative energy in service to their organization is for their leaders to serve them. Most people don't need to be coerced into doing their best work for their organization. Left to their own devices, most team members will spontaneously contribute to your organization as their way of growing and succeeding in life. Therefore, one of the best ways to inspire strong performance is for leaders to serve those around them, in effect telling them:

I know that what you are capable of producing and what you want to produce is far greater than what our organization needs in order to succeed. So, my opportunity as your leader is to serve you as you do what you want to do, which I already know goes beyond what I need from you. My goal is to serve your needs, help each of you be as successful as you want, and help you get out of life what you want. If I can help you accomplish what you want, I know our team will do very well.

...

Leadership integrity and its companion, responsibility, stand out as an unparalleled driver of positive performance by employees, teams, cast members, children, and everyone else you hope to influence. When you have integrity and are responsible, people around you know they can count on you. They can trust you to be honest, stand up for what is right, do what you say you'll do, and help them get what they want and need for themselves. That said, moral competencies such as integrity and responsibility are only the beginning of the essential "soft skills" needed to positively influence others. In the next chapter, we'll make the case for the importance of two key emotional competencies: empathy and compassion.

EXERCISE: ASSESS AND STRENGTHEN YOUR COMMITMENT TO INTEGRITY AND RESPONSIBILITY

The following statements represent some of the critical competencies related to the principles of integrity and responsibility.

Take a few minutes to think about how well each statement reflects your behavior as a leader.

What changes could you make for any statements that don't consistently represent your behavior that would strengthen your competence in that area?

Integrity

1. I tell the truth unless there is an overriding moral reason to withhold it.
2. I respectfully deliver truthful messages.
3. I challenge someone if I see them doing something that isn't right.
4. If I knew my organization was engaging in unethical or illegal behavior, I would report it, even if it could hurt my career.
5. When I agree to do something, I follow through.

Responsibility

1. When I make a decision that turns out to be a mistake, I admit it.
2. When I make a mistake, I take responsibility for correcting the situation.
3. When things go wrong, I do not blame others or circumstances.
4. I pay attention to the development needs of my team.
5. I spend a significant amount of my time providing resources and removing obstacles for my team.

CHAPTER SIX

Embrace Empathy and Compassion

Michael Brindisi first learned compassion from his father. He grew up in a modest Italian neighborhood of well-kept row houses in inner-city Philadelphia. When it snowed, which wasn't that often in Philly, Michael's dad would eagerly grab his shovel and clear their front walkway. Then he'd shovel out the walkways of four or five nearby houses. Michael's mom cared deeply about her husband and used to worry that he would overexert himself. She'd ask him, "Why did you do all that shoveling?"

Michael's father gave the same answer every time: "Because I can." Today, Michael is the long-time CEO and artistic director of the prestigious Chanhassen Dinner Theatres (CDT) in greater Minneapolis, the largest professional dinner theater in the United States. CDT offers an appealing menu of Broadway musicals, comedy, cabaret, and concerts, paired with an upscale dining experience. Chanhassen is a special place, and not just because of the caliber of its productions and performers, some of whom have become famous after working at CDT. For example, two-time Golden Globe winner Amy Adams spent three years at Chanhassen before launching her Hollywood career. The heart of Chanhassen is a core group of people who have stayed with CDT for years. Chanhassen is a hard place to leave. As Amy Adams noted when she left Chanhassen:

> There were times when I first arrived in Los Angeles where I would pine for that time when I knew exactly what was in front of me, and every day was the same. I really loved that security and schedule. The people I worked with there were also a great family to me. They spoiled me, and then I come out to Los Angeles and whew!

Typical of the career trajectory of many marquee Chanhassen actors is the journey of another leading actor who left to work on Broadway for a while but came back, drawn by the distinctive, stable, and compassionate atmosphere of CDT. Culinary staff also tend to have long careers with CDT. The head bartender has been there for more than 30 years. Many wait staff are second-generation employees who followed in their parents' footsteps. At Chanhassen, people feel that they are more than employees—they feel like valued members of a family. It's the kind of place where people are loyal to the organization and do their best to wow their audiences. CDT employees create an experience that brings customers back time and again.

What's Michael's contribution to all this? People know him as an empathetic and compassionate person. Even though Michael is CEO, people at all levels come to him to discuss serious personal challenges, such as dealing with an unplanned pregnancy, how to help a child with a life-threatening illness, or overcoming thoughts of suicide.

"I understand them," Michael says. "I am intuitively empathetic, and I like that about myself. And I learned this as a kid from the way my father took care of people in our neighborhood."

"There are lots of things I don't like about myself," Michael adds, with characteristic modesty. "But being empathetic feels natural. I would do it even if it didn't help CDT be more successful."

Over the years, Michael has demonstrated empathy and compassion by helping people with mental health or substance abuse problems get the professional help they need. He's kept people on the payroll when they ran into tough times. In 2020, when the coronavirus pandemic forced the theater's closure, Michael spearheaded the decision to continue to pay for employees' health insurance and created a fund to help employees offset their loss of income. These decisions were financially costly, but to Michael, they were no-brainers—in each case, he believed it was the right thing to do. Michael actively cares about people, and his people respond to his compassion with loyalty, longevity, and positive performance.

Michael has practiced empathy and demonstrated compassion for so long that it may seem to the rest of us that it's easy for him. But that's an illusion. We all have an inborn capacity for empathy and compassion, but it's a capacity that needs to be developed with the help of role models like Michael's dad and strengthened through practice. As Michael's story illustrates, practicing empathy and compassion is a smart investment because the ability to be empathetic and compassionate improves our communication and strengthens our connection with those we hope to influence. That in turn, leads to a whole host of positive leadership outcomes. But before we discuss the key role of empathy and compassion in our work as leaders, let's clarify what empathy and compassion are all about.

EMPATHY AND COMPASSION: AN ESSENTIAL PAIR

There are many definitions of empathy and compassion. Some experts think of empathy and compassion as part of the same human capacity. Others may use the terms "empathetic" and "compassionate" interchangeably. We believe that can be confusing. In our view, empathy and compassion are distinct but closely related skills. Empathy is the ability to understand and appreciate what others are thinking, feeling, and doing—and why. In Chapter 4, we introduced the idea of "triangles of influence" to emphasize the value of paying attention, not just to our own experiential triangle, but to that of others we hope to influence. Another way to think of empathy is that it is shorthand for accurately recognizing the experiential triangles of others. When leaders show empathy, followers typically sense their leaders "get them." Some people describe their experience of being with an empathetic leader as a feeling of "being seen." Leaders who empathize with their followers are far more likely to influence others to pursue a shared worthwhile purpose.

Compassion, on the other hand, involves taking the next step—using what we have come to empathetically understand about others to show that we care about them concretely. Zach Mercurio, a leadership expert and author, aptly describes compassion as "empathy in action." We can have empathy without compassion. It's possible to fully understand how someone else experiences a challenging situation without taking steps to help. However, it's hard to imagine compassion without empathy. We need to put ourselves in another's shoes to envision what it's like to be them if we want to make good decisions about the most effective way to show that we actively care about them. Psychiatrist Helen Reiss explains how empathy drives compassion and the incredible power of the connection between the two:

> There are two important reasons why your brain is primed to experience the pain of others: to teach you what to avoid and to motivate you to help the injured person, whether their pain is physical, psychological, emotional, or to some degree of all of these. One byproduct of helping others is that it also inspires others to help in return. Helping others feels good. This is considered the basis for collaboration, cooperation, and reciprocity in human relationships.[1]

Apart from the general survival value of empathy and compassion, empathy and compassion combine to increase your leadership influence dramatically. Empathy paired with compassion is the glue that binds leaders and their people together in positive, productive relationships. According to Helen Riess, "Neurobiology seems to predispose us to a preference for leaders who above all express empathy and compassion."[2] People you want to influence can tell if you're able to put yourself in their shoes and take an active interest in their concerns. When followers see that you understand and actively care about them, they are far more likely to trust you. And when followers trust you, they feel safe. They don't need to fear being judged harshly or punished. In that safe and trusting space, followers are free to absorb information, get unstuck, and identify the best ways to move forward.

We've adapted Reiss's explanation of the empathy-compassion connection to create the "empathy compassion pathway," which illustrates how a leader can activate empathy and compassion to influence followers.

---

[1]Helen Riess, *The Empathy Effect: Seven Neuroscience-Based Keys for Transforming the Way We Live, Love, Work, and Connect Across Differences* (Boulder, CO: Sounds True, 2018).
[2]Ibid.

The Empathy Compassion Pathway

Leader understands the challenging experience of their followers

Leader helps their followers address the challenging experience

Followers feel understood and supported by their leader

Followers and leader move forward with a shared
understanding and a sense of purpose

Think of the empathy compassion pathway as a Google Map with driving directions that show you how to use empathy and compassion to reach an important destination—the results you hope to achieve with the help of your followers.

Step 1: You Understand the Challenging Experience of Your Followers

Though negative reactions to difficult situations aren't inevitable, it's common for adverse circumstances to lock followers into highly charged emotions, irrational thinking, and unproductive behavior. Whenever a follower is stuck in such a state, progress toward the goals you and they share is virtually impossible. Fortunately, you have a powerful tool for helping followers get unstuck. As our colleague, psychologist Rick Aberman, has taught us, people have a deep need for us to understand them emotionally. To Rick's insight, we would add that people want us to understand not just how they feel but also what they think and why they behave as they do in their current situation. Empathy doesn't necessarily mean that we agree with others' perspectives or actions, nor do most people expect that from us. They do expect us to be able to envision the world from their point of view. And when we communicate that understanding effectively, people are more open to moving forward and exploring solutions. So, the first step of the empathy compassion pathway is to demonstrate that you understand a follower's challenging situation from their unique perspective. That's the essence of empathy—your awareness of another person's experiential triangle of thoughts, feelings, and behavior.

Jen des Groseilliers is an excellent example of how a leader can tap into empathy and compassion to help her people up their game. Jen has a well-deserved reputation as a high achiever. In college, she was a Division I basketball player. She earned a law degree before fast-tracking her way through increasingly demanding leadership positions in the financial services industry. Currently, Jen is chief of advisor experience and a partner at WestPoint Financial Group, a division of MassMutual. It's a big job spanning four Midwestern states, and she excels in that role while at the same time prioritizing family life with her spouse and their three children. As Jen developed her leadership skills over several years, she discovered that empathetic listening was a differentiator in contributing to her leadership effectiveness. Jen recalls this experience of using empathy and compassionate coaching to help several team members get back on track:

> In my role as partner, I was assigned several people to work with follow-ing a reorganization. These were people at risk because they were not seen as performing at a level that would justify keeping them on board. One had been displaced, so was especially vulnerable. I felt for the situations they faced. I took the time to listen to them, hoping they would let their guard down and let me know who they really were. I got to know them and thereby recognize their power and potential to grow and contribute. In my work with them, I began with a discussion of their values. Later they let me know that the time I spent listening and focusing on their values showed them I really cared. I respected them and in turn they respected me. Today, both are high contributors. They had always been technically strong, but through our work together, they have now become much better people leaders.

For empathy to be practical, your understanding of another's experiential world needs to be accurate. And that's exactly what Jen aimed to achieve. It's easy to assume that someone going through a rough patch is having the same reactions as you would in a similar situation. Jen avoided a common but dangerous assumption that could have derailed her communication with the people she most needed to influence to ensure success in her new role. Jen used her empathetic skills to understand as accurately as possible what her followers were going through. Jen relied on two main techniques, which you can use to enhance your leadership effectiveness.

First, *practice active listening.* Many of us aren't good listeners. Instead of paying close attention to what someone else is saying, we "listen to reply," that is, we listen just enough to start thinking about what we want to say in response. Maybe it's because we're eager to tell our own story of a similar experience. Or perhaps we think we can help the other person by offering some well-meaning advice. However, when we're too quick to change the focus of the conversation to ourselves and our ideas, the person trying to communicate with us won't feel understood.

In contrast, active listening is a type of listening in which you pay close attention to what another person is saying. You concentrate only on trying to understand what the person is communicating. When you're actively listening, you speak for two reasons: to check whether you accurately understand what another is trying to express, and to let that person know that you care enough to pay attention and want to understand what's going on with them. When someone is telling you about their experience, periodically summarize what you have heard them tell you about how they are reacting to a situation. Then follow up with a question such as "Do I have that right?" At that point, your follower can confirm or clarify what they are experiencing.

Jayden is proud to be the first person in his family to earn a graduate degree. After he completed his MBA, he was hired as a management trainer by a large telecommunications company. Eager to boost his leadership credentials, Jayden attended an out of state seminar on emotional intelligence. He knew his wife, Keisha, had faced a very challenging week with their two young children while he was away. As soon as Jayden walked in the door to their home in central New Jersey, his wife started filling him in. After four exhausting days taking care of sick kids, Keisha was depleted. Usually, Jayden would have made several "helpful" retroactive suggestions. This time, he decided to practice active listening, a technique he had just learned at the seminar. As Keisha spoke about her difficult week, Jayden listened quietly, occasionally adding his summary of what he thought he'd heard her say during the previous few minutes. After going back and forth a few times, Jayden said, "Wow, it sounds like you felt pretty frustrated that I wasn't around to help."

His wife promptly responded, "I know exactly what you're doing, Jayden. But keep on doing it!"

Jayden's first real-life attempt at active listening was a little awkward, but his wife immediately noticed the difference in his communication and liked how it felt. Today Jayden excels as a leadership trainer and coach. Whenever Jayden tells his active listening story to learners, he always adds "You don't even have to be great at active listening for it to be effective. You just have to try."

The second technique for developing and demonstrating empathy is to *ask open-ended questions*. Asking open-ended questions is both challenging and critical to your leadership effectiveness. Ben Benjamin, a communications consultant, and coauthor of the book *Conversation Transformation*, underscores the importance of asking open-ended questions: "Everybody who talks communicates," says Benjamin, "but most people communicate badly most of the time."[3]

According to Benjamin, one of the most common mistakes leaders make is asking leading questions, like: "Do you really think people will buy that product?" or "This is what our main focus should be, right?"

In Benjamin's view, such questions leave a follower with two bad options—give the leader the answer you think they want, even though it doesn't represent your views, or accept the risks of giving a leader an answer you know they don't want to hear. In contrast, open-ended questions help you learn more about an individual. When you ask open-ended questions, you ask them with the genuine intent to understand. You ask them in a neutral way, without verbally or nonverbally suggesting that you are looking for a certain kind of answer. Open-ended questions are those that cannot be answered with a yes or no response. "Did you try talking to your teammate about this?" is an example of a closed-ended question because it's easy to answer with a yes or no. It's also a leading question since it suggests that talking to the teammate is an action you would recommend. Asking open-ended questions is both an art and a discipline. It's an art because it takes careful thought to frame questions in a way that encourages people to be thoughtful about their situation. It's also a discipline because it requires that you put aside your biases and assumptions about another person's

[3]Ben Benjamin, Amy Yeager, and Anita Simon, *Conversation Transformation: Recognize and Overcome the 6 Most Destructive Communication Patterns* (New York: McGraw Hill, 2012).

situation and how they should handle it. When crafting open-ended questions, begin your questions with:

What…
How…
Where…
When…
Can you tell me more about…
How did you feel when…
What options did you consider…

When you begin your questions with openers such as these, it's much harder to ask nonempathetic questions. For example, imagine how you would feel if someone asked, "Why did you do that?" Depending on the vocal tone of the person who asked you that question, there's a good chance you might feel criticized and might respond defensively. Think instead about your reaction to someone asking you a question like "How did you approach this situation?" You'd be much more inclined to think that the questioner was interested in your experience and wanted to encourage you to be reflective about your behavior. Open-ended questions, delivered with a supportive nonverbal tone, create an environment of acceptance, understanding, and respect.

Despite the importance of active listening and asking open-ended questions in communicating empathy and compassion, there are times as a leader when it's helpful to offer opinions and suggestions to your followers. Recent research indicates that employees, especially millennials, expect and appreciate your insights and advice. That said, many leaders are too quick to give advice, potentially robbing followers of the opportunity to be more independent and empowered in their work. So, instead of defaulting to a leadership style in which you feel responsible for directing others in how to solve a problem, help them explore their situation by asking open-ended questions. The more you use open-ended questions, the more you communicate understanding to your followers and confidence that they can, with your support, deal with any challenging situations they may face.

Step 2: You Help Your Followers Address Their Challenging Experience

To be an influential leader, you need to translate your empathetic understanding of a follower's experience into compassionate action. If you succeed in carrying out Step 1, followers will recognize that you understand the situation they face. However, that's not enough. To be an effective leader, followers need to see that you understand their situation *and* are willing to support them in improving it.

There is no better model for translating empathy into compassionate action than Yorgina Ureña, who founded Jaco Impact in 2017 to serve a variety of community needs in Jaco, a popular tourist destination on the Central Pacific Coast of Costa Rica. Through Jaco Impact, Yorgina and her volunteers organize environmental projects, including beach cleanups, offer educational programs such as English lessons for local children, conduct workshops in job search skills, and promote the work of local artists and artisans through consignment sales at Jaco Impact's storefront. Even in this popular beach town, unemployment is high, especially since the beginning of the coronavirus pandemic and the damage caused by two hurricanes that struck the area in late 2020. During these crises, Yorgina and Jaco Impact became a clearinghouse for donations of food, clothing, and household items to help people in need.

"In the beginning," Yorgina recalls, "I gave away everything for free. Then I thought, 'I'm doing it wrong. The poor expect the government or someone just to give them what they need. That is keeping them poor in their minds.'" So Yorgina changed her approach.

"Now, whenever someone asks me for something, I tell them, 'If you want something, you need to do something. If you want a bag of food, you need do something like help clean the office or volunteer for a shift at the store.'"

Yorgina has seen a change in the people she serves since she began to ask them to give their time in exchange for what they received. "It helps them feel important," she explains. "It's changing their mindset. They feel better about themselves because they are making a contribution."

Jaco Impact and the community it serves both benefit from Yorgina's recognition that compassion and charity are not the same. Similarly, compassion does not necessarily mean solving someone's problem for them. In many instances, the most compassionate thing you can do is to encourage your followers to take the lead in figuring out how to solve their own problems or achieve their goals. That is why, in step 2 of the empathy compassion pathway, just as in step 1, asking questions is typically more helpful than giving advice. Questions such as "What do you think might improve this situation?" set the stage for helping someone move forward in a more positive direction. If your follower struggles to come up with ideas, then it's time to suggest some options. When sharing your thoughts as a leader, the compassionate approach is to suggest possibilities rather than dictate solutions. For example, there is a big verbal and nonverbal difference between saying, "What if we met for 10 minutes every morning for the next week to review your goals for the day?" versus "I want to review your goals every morning in my office."

Step 3: Your Follower Feels Understood and Supported by You

In step 1, you've demonstrated empathy. In step 2, you've shown compassion. You've let your followers know that you care enough about them to take concrete action to help. If you've taken time to show empathy and compassion using the suggestions in steps 1 and 2, step 3 usually naturally follows; and your followers likely feel understood and supported by you. But empathy and compassion's impact on followers can go far beyond that. Vanessa Druskat, associate professor of organizational behavior at the University of New Hampshire, has researched the factors that differentiate the highest performing leaders from those at average levels. Her studies show that elite leaders are empathetic and compassionate. Such leaders create "cultures of belonging," environments in which people feel understood and valued. In cultures of belonging, followers feel free to fully be themselves. They feel worthy no matter how different they are from typical employees. Those feelings of being understood and valued fuel a positive connection between followers and leaders.

Step 4: You and Your Follower Move Forward with a Shared Understanding and a Sense of Purpose

Step 4 of the empathy compassion pathway happens when a leader's empathy and compassion translate into sustainable performance gains. Over time, everything you do to show followers that they are understood and valued fuels a positive connection between you and your followers. When it comes to influencing others in pursuit of a meaningful purpose, step 4 is your payoff for being empathetic and compassionate.

At Chanhassen Dinner Theatres, CEO Michael Brindisi takes advantage of the empathy compassion pathway to create alignment throughout the organization, thus building commitment to its mission and enhancing performance across all functional areas. Michael routinely uses his empathetic and compassionate instincts to help those around him. It helps Michael feel good. But Michael isn't the only one who feels good. His empathy and compassion make others feel good too, inspiring people at all levels to perform at their best in the roles they fill. In the lean times of the pandemic, CDT could easily have lost the people it would need most when operations resumed. Across the food services industry, for instance, business owners have struggled to rebuild staff as pandemic restrictions have eased. But thanks to Michael's empathy and compassion, most employees remained loyal and were more than ready to resume their roles as soon as circumstances allowed. Michael's goal of a profitable reopening of CDT would not have been possible had he not demonstrated empathy and compassion to his employees before and throughout the pandemic crisis.

EMPATHY, COMPASSION, AND LEADERSHIP PERFORMANCE

A leader's empathy and compassion help create the emotional energy an organization needs to engage the discretionary efforts of those who work with that leader. By discretionary efforts, we mean the actions people take that go above and beyond what is required to satisfy their jobs' baseline requirements. Discretionary efforts, often referred to as "best efforts," of followers create a level of productivity that translates into exceptional organizational performance. When members of your organization think you understand their emotional state and care about them, they become highly motivated to do whatever they can to support you as their leader and help the organization succeed. Empathy and compassion are also trust-builders that help people feel safe when facing challenges and taking risks. What's more, empathetic and compassionate leaders are simply more likable, a quality that research has found is strongly correlated with leadership effectiveness.

Tami Pinchiaroli is a senior leader who consistently leverages empathy and compassion to inspire high performance in her organization.

When the novel coronavirus pandemic first arrived in mid-March 2020, her Fortune 100 company directed all employees to work from home unless they were critical to onsite operations. Tami had to move quickly to establish a new normal for her team of finance managers and analysts located in various locations across the globe. In some ways, the transition to telecommuting seemed easy. Tami's team was already geographically dispersed, so most people were used to communicating virtually with their colleagues as needed. But Tami knew that her team's home situations were far from easy. Most didn't have a dedicated workspace. Many were parents who suddenly had children underfoot or needed to help with distance learning. Grocery shopping became a nightmare because of shortages of food and other essentials. And everyone feared that they or family members might catch a deadly virus.

With those challenges in mind, Tami took a few critical steps. First, she established daily team meetings via the Zoom teleconferencing app. Under normal circumstances, people didn't interact daily. Now everyone across her organization got a chance to communicate with and see one another every day, even if they didn't report directly to Tami. Tami also tried to inject some fun into their meetings. Each day a volunteer began the team meeting with a quick activity, such as asking people to share their recommendations for a "guilty pleasure" TV show to binge-watch. She also made a point of, in her words, "overcommunicating," (though in our view, it's virtually impossible to overcommunicate). Tami wanted to be sure that everyone had the same information.

Finally, Tami was determined to support her team in dealing with the stresses of the quarantine environment. She encouraged people to set boundaries between home and work life. She told her team, "Just because you're working at home doesn't mean you should be working all the time. Set your business hours and go off duty like you would if you were in the office."

Tami also was an advocate of flexible work/life scheduling. She told people with children to take the time they needed during regular business hours to address kids' needs. She suggested that if it worked better for them to go grocery shopping during business hours, when schedules permitted, they should feel free to do that as long as they communicated with their leader for awareness. Tami reinforced that people were accountable for their work results, not for being at their computers every minute of the business day. She also encouraged leaders on her team to show compassion to their employees in dealing with the challenges of the new normal. Tami's leadership in the face of the pandemic is emblematic of step 4 of the empathy compassion pathway. Tami's steps sealed her team members' loyalty and engagement during an unimaginably stressful time.

When asked where her empathy and compassion come from, Tami says, "What's most important to me is health and family. If you have those two, everything else comes together. Work can wait."

At this book goes to press, most of Tami's team have returned to their offices on a hybrid schedule. Though they rarely saw one another in person for several years, thanks to Tami's compassionate approach throughout the pandemic, the people she leads are closer, more empowered, and more productive than ever.

DOUG AND CHUCK: EMPATHY AND COMPASSION

It's one thing to feel empathy for the circumstances of others. It's quite another to do something about it. Since the founding of our company, think2 perform, we've sought to make the world a better place through our work. But several years ago, we realized that our staff demographics—mostly older, white, and male—could limit our impact.

We were empathetic about the challenges many communities face when excluded from full participation in society or having less access to professional opportunities. But it has taken us some time to translate our empathetic instincts into compassionate action. For instance, on the product side, we now offer a Spanish version of our popular "Values Cards." Our community outreach has strengthened from charitable contributions to life-changing programs for underserved groups. The think2perform Research Institute, a nonprofit organization whose research is available to anyone in the world for free, has launched a Future Leaders Academy, which teaches real-world leadership skills to high school and college students from predominantly minority communities. think2perform, our for-profit business, will offer paid internships to some of the young adults who graduate from the Leadership Academy. It's a win-win: participants benefit from exposure to a high-performing business culture, and we fill our job pipeline with talented and diverse candidates.

We believe that our efforts to support diversity, equity, and inclusion represent compassion in action, thus expanding our positive impact on the world. But we're not content with what we've done so far. We are constantly looking for new ways to make a positive difference through empathy and compassion.

EMPATHY, COMPASSION, AND THE BOTTOM LINE

Our beliefs about the impact of leaders' empathy and compassion on their organizations' performance come partly from decades of first-hand experience coaching thousands of leaders. But the significance of the empathy compassion pathway as a differentiating leadership essential has also been validated by many quantitative research studies.

In 2000, American Express Financial Advisors (now Ameriprise) commissioned a comprehensive independent evaluation of the business impact of the company's emotional intelligence (EI) development programs. The effect of EI training on financial advisors was impressive. In market groups participating in the training, revenue generation, client acquisition, and additional business from existing clients increased dramatically. What's more, empathy was the emotional competence that improved the most following training and therefore deserves much of the credit for improving business results in such a significant way.

Another study, the "Global Empathy Index," last conducted in 2016, makes a compelling case for the impact that empathetic and compassionate leadership can have on business profitability. The Global Empathy Index measured the extent to which corporations demonstrated empathy and compassion in their communications to employees, customers, and the public via social media. Results indicated that the top 10 scoring companies in the Global Empathy Index increased in value more than twice as much as the bottom 10 and generated 50 percent more earnings (defined by market capitalization).[4]

In *Return on Character: The Real Reason Leaders and Their Companies Win,* author Fred Kiel[5] describes his research demonstrating the impact of a leader's compassion on various organizational performance measures. In Kiel's study, leadership behaviors based on the four principles (integrity, responsibility, forgiveness, and compassion) are the behaviors most appreciated by employees and make the most difference in the levels of workforce engagement that drive an organization's financial results. Interestingly, while leaders of companies with outstanding financial performance were high in measures of all four principles, *leaders of*

---

[4]Belinda Parmar, "The Most (and Least) Empathetic Companies," *Harvard Business Review* (November 27, 2015), https://hbr.org/2015/11/2015-empathy-index.

[5]Fred Kiel was Doug Lennick's coauthor for *Moral Intelligence* and *Moral Intelligence 2.0.* The four principles studied in Fred Kiel's research on leaders' character originated from Doug and Fred's work on the foundational principles of moral intelligence.

companies with the weakest return on assets were rated by employees as especially low in compassion.[6] Kiel's findings suggest that, while all moral competencies are essential, compassion may be the most significant contributor to an organization's productivity and performance.

Alan Jope, CEO of Unilever, would agree. As Jope explains, "We believe that if we look after our employees and our customers, if we worry about society and the planet, if we take care of our supplier partners, then our shareholders will be well rewarded."

Several qualitative surveys underscore the relationship between leadership empathy and compassion, employee engagement, retention, and business performance. For instance, the fifth annual Businessolver survey, *The 2020 State of Workplace Empathy*, gathered input from employees and leaders at varying organizational levels. Some of the most intriguing survey findings include the following:

- Three-quarters of employees believe an empathetic organization inspires more motivated employees, compared to two-thirds who said the same only a year earlier.
- An empathetic workplace plays a key role for employees considering where they would take employment, their salary, their work effort, and whether they will stay at their current organization.
- Three-quarters of employees said they would work longer hours for an empathetic employer, and 80 percent said they would switch companies for equal pay if the employer were more empathetic.
- Of Gen Z employees, 83 percent would choose an employer with a strong culture of empathy over an employer offering a slightly higher salary.[7]

Finally, the Center for Creative Leadership analyzed data provided by 6,731 managers from 38 countries to understand the impact of empathetic leadership on a leader's job performance. In reviewing the survey findings, we noted that CCL includes the notion of compassion as part of its definition of empathetic leadership. The CCL study found that the managers rated highest in empathetic leadership by their direct

---

[6]Fred Kiel, *Return on Character: The Real Reason Leaders and Their Companies Win* (Boston: Harvard Business Review Press, 2015).
[7]Businessolver, *2020 State of Workplace Empathy: Executive Summary,* 2020, https://www.businessolver.com/workplace-empathy-executive-summary.

reports were the same leaders rated as the best overall performers by their managers.[8]

BARRIERS TO EMPATHY AND COMPASSION

Given such strong evidence of the positive contribution of empathy and compassion to a leader's effectiveness, you might wonder why many leaders seem so lacking in empathy and compassion. It turns out that some leaders believe that empathetic and compassionate responses could be viewed as a sign of weakness or lack of leadership competence. According to Helen Riess, a psychiatrist, and author of *The Empathy Effect*, "Leaders with tough and curt attitudes may believe they are projecting authority. Surveys of business leaders find that almost 40 percent worry about being too nice, and more than half think they need to flex the muscle of their authority to stay on top."[9] The most recent research shows a dramatic increase in leaders' reluctance to demonstrate empathy. For instance, the *2021 State of Workplace Empathy* survey found that 68 percent of CEOs fear being less respected if they show empathy in the workplace, a 30-point increase from the previous year's survey. This gap between the leadership empathy followers need to perform at their best and what leaders are willing to provide is both disturbing and unwarranted.

Riess debunks the conventional wisdom that leaders can't be both empathetic *and* competent. She argues—backed by research evidence—that empathetic leaders are viewed by those around them as more competent than nonempathetic leaders.[10]

In some cases, leaders have a different concern. They fear that being empathetic and compassionate might make it harder for them to hold their followers accountable when they do not meet expectations. However, holding people accountable and being empathetic or compassionate are not mutually exclusive. Influential leaders understand

---

[8]William A. Gentry, Todd J. Weber, and Golnaz Sadri, "Empathy in the Workplace A Tool for Effective Leadership," *Center for Creative Leadership*, https://cclinnovation.org/wp-content/uploads/2020/03/empathyintheworkplace.pdf?webSyncID=334b25b5-93e5-4ee4-40e3-4e74063d531b&sessionGUID=d4b55505-37aa-cb8b-3b8b-8001e53b69cc.
[9]Helen Reiss, *The Empathy Effect* (Boulder, CO: Sounds True, 2018).
[10]Ibid.

that most people want to do a good job, despite difficulties that may get in the way of succeeding. One of the most compassionate things you can do as a leader is to help others remove the obstacles to their ability to perform as well as they would like—and that begins with empathy.

As an example, let's say that a direct report is chronically late for work because one of her children has regular morning tantrums. You may understand why it's difficult for your employee, but you don't need to sympathize with her or think it's ok for her to be late so often. You can hold her accountable for showing up on time without being a "mean boss." In fact, being empathetic in that situation can set the stage for improving her performance as well as yours. For instance, you might meet with your employee to coach her about her lateness. You begin the discussion with empathy by recognizing out loud how you think she might be feeling. You let her know that you understand the difficulties she is having at home and that you'd like to work with her to figure out a way she can manage the situation so it doesn't negatively affect her job. Together you brainstorm changes she could make to routines at home that would allow her to get out of the house on time. You also might offer to adjust her work schedule to begin and end her workday an hour later. Whatever solution you choose, tapping into your empathy and compassion demonstrates that you are concerned enough to care about her professional performance, not only her personal difficulties.

EMPATHY AND COMPASSION BEGIN AT HOME

The first step in cultivating your capacity for empathy and compassion toward others is to have empathy and compassion for yourself. Self-empathy may sound like a contradiction in terms since empathy, by definition, is a capacity for understanding others. One way of thinking about self-empathy is to see it as a form of self-awareness. When you are empathetic and compassionate toward yourself, you are aware of your thoughts, feelings, and behavior, and you understand your experiences objectively without judging or blaming yourself. Just as leading yourself is critically important to effective leadership of others, self-empathy is an important first step to demonstrating empathy toward others. We need to begin with empathy and compassion for ourselves if we hope to have the emotional energy to be empathetic and compassionate towards others. It's like the pre-flight instructions airplane passengers are given in the event of a cabin depressurization: *When you see the oxygen masks come down, put yours on first, before helping others with theirs.*

CHUCK: DEVELOPING EMPATHY

"Emotions are stupid" was a phrase I often heard around my house growing up. My dad was a brilliant, successful aerospace engineer with a master's degree in mechanical engineering. Everything was a math equation to my dad, and logic was valued above all else. He saw emotions as something for weak people who couldn't cope. Those were the messages that I grew up with, and they shaped how I dealt with my own emotions as well as the emotions of others.

I found empathy challenging when I was promoted to a leadership role early in my career. If members of my team became emotional, I flat out didn't recognize what they were feeling or know how to help them. So, they either stayed emotionally stuck or turned to someone else for support. It took some time to recognize that I needed to develop my capacity for empathy if I wanted to lead others effectively. Empathy, I realized, wasn't sympathy. It was understanding what it was like to be in other people's shoes. Once I learned how to recognize and acknowledge others' emotions—not an easy task—I was able to help them deal with whatever was holding them back.

Empathy is like a second language to me. I wasn't born speaking it, but with practice, I've become more fluent. And because I had to learn that emotions aren't stupid, when I see others who find empathy as challenging as I once did, I get it! I empathize with them, and I think I'm a better coach to them because I know firsthand what it takes to become an empathetic leader.

ENCOURAGING EMPATHY AND COMPASSION IN OTHERS

As a leader, your ability to influence others increases greatly when you become a role model for others. The more consistently you demonstrate empathy and compassion to others, the more likely they are to follow your example and be empathetic and compassionate themselves.

FOSTERING A CULTURE OF EMPATHY AND COMPASSION

- When you see a follower acting without empathy toward someone, ask that follower what the other person might be feeling. If needed, share your ideas about what you think that other person might be feeling or experiencing.
- Offer training or other resources, for instance, a workshop on empathetic listening.
  - Devote periodic team meeting time to empathy development, such as watching Helen Reiss' YouTube video on empathy,[11] and discussing how to strengthen empathy in the team.
  - Teach those you lead how to play the freeze game[12] to develop more awareness of their own and others' thoughts, feelings, and behavior.
  - Teach those you lead to use the empathy-compassion pathway to guide their interactions with others.

...

It's impossible to overstate the importance of empathy and compassion to your effectiveness as a leader. We've all had experiences with leaders who see us as commodities to be used, not as human beings who deserve understanding and compassion. We know the difference between leaders who care about us and those who don't. And if we're honest, we know the difference between how much or little effort we make in our work life depending on whether or not our leader treats us with empathy and compassion. Empathy and compassion have always been valuable leadership qualities, but today they are needed more than ever. Seismic changes over the last 20 years in the expectations of followers, shifting workplace demographics, the global shortage of workers with next generation skills, and disruptive technologies, among many other forces, all demand that leaders cultivate compassionate relationships with their most precious resource—the people they need to help them accomplish their purpose. Richard Leider, best-selling author and one of America's preeminent life and leadership coaches, emphasizes the urgent need for empathy and compassion: "The premium in today's world is on empathy and compassion. Compassion is the soul of purpose, because the primary reason for our existence is to grow and give."

[11]Helen Riess, *The Power of Empathy: Helen Riess at TEDx Middlebury*, 2013, https://youtu.be/baHrcC8B4WM.
[12]See Chapter 4

CHAPTER SEVEN

Decide Wisely

Mountaineer Chris Klinke and his two Nepalese Sherpas, Dawa and Temba, had spent the night at Camp 2 on Cho Oyu, at an altitude of 23,000 feet. Chris gazed intently at the imposing summit looming 4,000 feet above them. By the movement of the clouds at the top, Chris could see that high winds were gusting. Cho Oyu is the sixth highest peak in the world, rising 26,795 feet (8,188 meters) above sea level. In the Tibetan language, Cho Oyu means "Turquoise Goddess" and is considered the "easiest" of the 8,000-meter peaks to climb. It was late in the climbing season of 2005. Only a few days earlier, Chris had reached the northwest peak of Shishapangma—a "false summit" at 8,013 meters—only to abandon the quest to reach the "true summit" 14 meters (46 feet) above because of deadly avalanche conditions. This was Chris's first trip to Nepal, and he was hungry to reach the actual summit of an 8,000-meter monster. Cho Oyu was his last chance for this season.

Chris and his team had been pushing hard. They had even skipped a day of rest to take advantage of good weather and maximize the time they had left since the window for safe climbing was closing quickly. Earlier that morning, they had decided to summit Cho Oyu from Camp 2 and climbed on for more than four hours. Initially, winds had been blowing from the northeast, which afforded them some protection, but the direction was changing quickly. Now they were battling brutal gusts of 60–70 mph. With air temperatures already below zero degrees Fahrenheit, the wind chills were –30 to –40 degrees F.

"Cold like that is uncomfortable, but wind gusts at that speed will kill because they suck the warmth right out of your body," Chris explained as he recalled that day.

Chris had carefully chosen his Sherpas. Dawa was a veteran guide with 20 years of climbing experience. Temba, a younger guide, was unusually talented and eager to gain experience climbing 8,000-meter peaks. This was Temba's first time above 7,000 meters, so he was pushing hard to continue. Dawa was in a hurry because Dawa was always in a hurry. The team hadn't brought a stove or tents because they were expecting to summit and return to Camp 2 on the same day. But the high winds now threatened that plan. As the three men struggled mightily to reach Camp 3, on the ridge just below the summit, they saw a lone tent left behind by an earlier expedition. It was stocked with food, a stove and gas, and would give them shelter from the bone-chilling wind and a chance to warm up.

Chris, Dawa, and Temba clipped their gear to their ice axes, and then into the ice, to prevent losing anything to a random gust. Then they huddled inside the tent as the winds howled outside its paper-thin nylon walls. Without a radio and with no other climbers in the area who could help them if needed, Chris began to think through their options. "If things go south, what can we do? If one of us falls, can the other two get him down?" There was a language barrier too. Chris knew only a few words of Nepali, and the Sherpas could speak only a bit of broken English. The three waited anxiously for the winds to calm down, but unfortunately, they never did.

Based on his years of experience, Dawa was convinced they could summit that day and that waiting would only cost them precious time.

"Now is the time to go," Dawa urged.

With Temba eager and Chris agreeing somewhat hesitatingly, Dawa cautiously stepped out of the tent first, with Chris behind him and finally, Temba joining them. As Temba took his last step out of the tent, a violent blast of wind ripped the tent from its stakes and sent it flying over the ridge into the vast valley 10,000 feet below. Should something go wrong on the push to the summit, the last possible option for shelter was now gone.

Renowned American high-altitude mountaineer Ed Viesturs' words echoed in Chris's head: "Trust your voice..." Having summited all fourteen 8,000-meter peaks without oxygen, Ed had emphasized to Chris the costs of making the wrong decision while on the mountain. With no shelter, heat, or extra water, Chris made the difficult decision to turn around and return to Camp 2, much to the dismay of his trusted Sherpas. Days later, safely back in Kathmandu, Chris learned that a team on Shishapangma at the same time that Chris and his team were battling the same weather system on Cho Oyu, had become trapped because the winds were so strong. Pinned down in impossibly frigid conditions, several members of that team lost toes and fingers to severe frostbite.

Chris's decision to resist the lure of the Cho Oyu summit undoubtedly kept the team from injury and may very well have saved their lives. Chris's experience validates the value of wise decision-making to successful leadership, especially when the stakes are high.

DECISION-MAKING IS A FULL-TIME JOB

Researchers have estimated that we average a jaw-dropping 35,000 decisions each day. That's 245,000 decisions per week and more than 12 million decisions per year. We make most of these decisions from habit and rarely give them a second thought. Studies have found that about 40 percent of what we do every day is automatic rather than the result of conscious decisions. Some choices don't matter that much, such as whether you put on your new black shoes or your favorite old brown ones. However, other decisions we make day to day can have a big impact on the direction our lives take, for good or ill. Reaching for a few cookies whenever you feel stressed can eventually threaten your health while reaching for your running shoes each morning when you wake up would likely have the opposite effect. If 40 percent of what you're doing daily is habitual, 60 percent of your daily activities are intentional. In other words, you spend more than half your time doing things you have consciously decided to do moment to moment.

Many of those thousands of intentional decisions are visible to those around you. Your influence as a leader, then, depends greatly on others' response to the decisions you make—and the way you make them. In the context of the alignment model, decisions and their consequences are part of Frame 3, your behavior. And as you've seen, human brains are wired so that your behavior—your experiential triangle—strongly affects the experiential triangles of those around you. Make wise decisions, and the right people will follow you. Make poor decisions, and good people will run the other way. That's why all those decisions you make *on purpose* need to be made *with a purpose*. And that purpose ideally is a positive one, driven by principles and worthwhile values.

OBSTACLES TO DECIDING WISELY

Pick up a newspaper, check your Twitter feed, or watch a cable news channel. Most news is bad news, and most of the worst news falls into one of two categories—natural disasters or poor decision-making. One could even argue that some so-called natural disasters result from faulty leadership decisions. For instance, increasingly frequent and damaging wildfires in the western United States result significantly from inadequate social policy related to climate change. Whether it's the latest surge of a global pandemic, a fatal Florida condo collapse, or dysfunctional partisan battles in the U.S. Congress, these and so many other crises could have been prevented or mitigated by wise leadership decision-making.

Why is poor leadership decision-making so rampant? As we've seen in Chapter 1, "Everyone Is a Leader," there are cases in which leaders simply have bad intentions. Leaders with values or goals that are not aligned with universal principles are responsible for the worst of human-caused disasters, both past and present. However, if you're reading this book, you're not that kind of leader. Like most leaders we work with, you're probably well-intentioned and have good values. But still, you're human. Like all of us, you make mistakes, and some of those mistakes include faulty decisions. So, increasing your leadership effectiveness includes developing greater self-awareness about your decision-making strengths and weaknesses. Understanding what can get in your way regarding sound decision-making is key to your positive influence as a leader. Poor decisions result from two main traps: strong emotions and mental biases.

EMOTIONAL LANDMINES

Making choices we later regret usually involves high-energy emotions, such as fear, anger, or excitement. Noticing that we're experiencing strong emotions, for instance, with help from playing the freeze game, is a sure sign that the quality of our decision-making may be at risk. It's natural to respond emotionally to stressful circumstances. Severe stress typically activates a "fight-or-flight" response, temporarily disabling the logical part of our brain so essential to making intelligent decisions. As we've already seen, a fight-or-flight response is a good thing when we're in physical danger because it allows us to get out of harm's way immediately. But the stresses we experience in today's world are rarely the result of life-and-death situations. In most stressful situations, we do have time to evaluate a situation objectively and decide on a wise response. Unfortunately, we're programmed to respond in fight-or-flight mode whenever we feel threatened, even when there are no prehistoric woolly mammoths around about to attack us. Today's woolly mammoths may take the shape of a critical boss, a nonproductive employee, a sports team member's injury, or a family member's addiction.

Whenever we're feeling strong emotions, the part of the brain we need to think clearly about what's happening is not operating. It doesn't work. In PET brain imaging, the part of the brain that mediates emotional responses looks bright. On the other hand, the part of the brain involved in objective decision-making looks dark. That's because your emotional brain has disabled your logical brain. So, when facing a stressful situation, you overreact or respond illogically. In short, you make a poor decision.

PREVENTING EMOTIONALLY DRIVEN DECISIONS

Playing the freeze game several times a day and whenever you're in a stressful situation is the best first step to preventing poor decisions. As soon as you realize you're in a stressful situation, pause what you're doing, play the freeze game, and get a handle on what you're thinking, how you're feeling, and what's happening with you physiologically. As you learned in Chapter 4 on self-awareness, the freeze game takes a minute or less. A key benefit is that it slows down your response to a stressful situation by giving you something else to do rather than reacting prematurely or irrationally to the problem at hand. Later in this chapter, we'll present a unique model of decision-making that will enhance your ability to overcome irrational decision-making and empower you to make wise, values-based decisions.

TIPS FOR PREVENTING EMOTIONALLY DRIVEN DECISIONS

- When in a stressful situation, pause to play the freeze game. This allows you to notice emotions that may drive unwise decisions. The freeze game also helps delay your initial response, so you have time to respond most rationally and productively.
- To feel calmer in a stressful situation, focus on your breathing for a minute or two. Breathe slowly and deeply, following your breath as you inhale and exhale.
- Once you feel calmer, work consciously to engage the logical part of your brain. Remind yourself that your initial emotional reaction to a challenging situation is not necessarily what should dictate your response.

MENTAL BIASES

A second barrier to wise decision-making stems from mental biases. Mental bias, also called cognitive bias, refers to the tendency to make decisions that are not logical, that is, not grounded in the objective and particular facts of the current situation. Biased choices are those made based on programmed ways of responding to seemingly similar situations. Everyone has mental biases. And they're not necessarily bad. They are shorthand principles that the brain uses to manage the thousands of decisions and actions we take in any given day. For instance, we may have a mental bias that "people are trustworthy." This principle allows us to deal with people efficiently. By assuming that we can trust most people, we feel confident about answering the door, working on a project with a fellow employee, eating food prepared by others, and so on. Imagine how exhausting it would be if every time you met another person, even someone you knew, you had to figure out whether that person could be trusted. Your daily life would probably collapse under the strain of gauging each person's trustworthiness from scratch. So, for the most part, our mental bias that "people are trustworthy" is highly functional—even though it's not entirely true.

Other positive biases are not so helpful. For example, when Kathy Jordan was in high school, she attended a National Science Foundation program at Hahnemann Medical School in Philadelphia. Out of the 50 participants, Kathy was one of two who attended Catholic high schools. Most participants happened to be Jewish. Based on her experience in the program, Kathy came to believe that Jewish people were much smarter than people from other ethnicities. Twenty years later, when Kathy was co-teaching a leadership program with Perry London, a noted psychologist who had emigrated from the United States to Israel, Kathy mentioned her belief that Jewish people were unusually intelligent. When Perry heard that, he chortled.

"I've lived in Israel for 20 years," he said. "Jews aren't any smarter than anyone else."

That was a lesson to Kathy that even positive biases are often flawed.

Many mental biases are outright harmful. For example, racial bias is an incredibly toxic influence on decision-making. Take this analysis reported by NPR:

> . . .*Yara Mekawi of the University of Illinois and her colleagues found two main things: "First, people were quicker to shoot black targets with a gun, relative to white targets with a gun. And . . . people were more trigger-happy when shooting black targets compared to shooting white targets."*[1]

We need to be aware of our biases to make wise decisions. Unrecognized mental biases allow us the delusion that we're making an objective decision when, in fact, we're not. Mental biases can cause us to ignore important data, attach too much importance to certain data, or encourage us to make decisions based on misguided beliefs about ourselves, our followers, or the situation we're in. To factor in the impact of mental biases on our choices, it's important to explore how biases can affect the accuracy of our decision-making. The more self-aware we are of the biases that influence our leadership choices, the

---

[1] NPR Staff, "Shooters Quicker to Pull Trigger When Target is Black, Study Finds, *NPR,* April 15, 2015, https://www.npr.org/2015/08/29/435833251/shooters-quicker-to-pull-trigger-when-target-is-black-study-finds.

more we can counter the harmful effects of biases on our leadership performance. Exploring these mental biases is key to overcoming obstacles to flawed leadership decisions.

Overconfidence. Overconfidence is a tendency to overestimate our knowledge, opinions, and skills. Nobel Prize-winning psychologist and economist Daniel Kahneman called overconfidence "the most significant of the cognitive biases,"[2] in part because it makes us more vulnerable to all the other mental biases that affect decision-making. Numerous studies show that most people are overconfident. For instance, a recent survey found that 93 percent of Americans consider themselves to be better than average drivers, a statistical impossibility. It's not much of a stretch to imagine that most leaders think of themselves as better-than-average leaders. But that's a dangerous belief, because when we're overconfident, we miss things, stop paying attention to the details, and undervalue others' input. Not only does overconfidence often alienate followers, it leads inevitably to mistakes and poor decision-making.

CHUCK: OVERCONFIDENCE

Growing up in Colorado, I had been skiing since I was nine. When I was 48 years old, I had been skiing for almost 40 years without suffering a serious skiing accident. Then, one bright sunny day in March 2008, I was racing feverishly down the mountain with a former Olympic downhill racer, A.J. Kitt, when I hit a deep patch of spring snow and double-ejected out of my skis. I cartwheeled several hundred feet down the mountain until I finally came to a stop. I was unconscious, cracked two vertebrae in my neck, and had a brain bleed. I was taken off the mountain for the first time in my life by highly trained ski patrol personnel and rushed to the hospital.

Four months later, I was still in the care of a team of healthcare professionals from several different disciplines in an effort to fully recover from my accident. While sitting with my neurologist, he told me, "The only patients I see with injuries like yours are expert skiers skiing on bright sunny days on intermediate runs."

[2]Daniel Kahneman, *Thinking, Fast and Slow* (New York: Farrar, Straus and Giroux, 2011).

Stunned, I responded, "That's exactly what happened to me! Why is that?"

"It's because you're just not paying attention," my doctor replied.

That's when I learned that overconfidence almost killed me.

Our successes often reinforce overconfidence in our leadership judgment. When things go well for us for a long time, we begin to think we'll always be successful. We forget that success is fragile and usually requires significant effort. Overconfidence affects not just our own decision-making quality but can have a profound impact on our organization's culture, fostering a climate of overconfidence that permeates the entire organization. When you are successful, other team or organization members are more likely to emulate your behavior, either because they admire you or because your overconfidence sends the message that being overconfident is "the way we do things around here." If overconfidence is so potentially damaging, why is it so persistent in individuals and organizations? Our work at think2perform, along with recent research, suggests that overconfidence is an asset—at least for a time. Self-confidence breeds success. The more consistently a leader is successful, the more they risk becoming overconfident. Success causes overconfidence, which generates more success. Until it doesn't. That's because overconfidence interferes with the openness to learning required for long-term growth. Overconfident leaders, and the overconfident organizations they create, risk becoming complacent, even arrogant. In such a climate, growth stalls, and early successes are unsustainable.

TIPS FOR AVOIDING OVERCONFIDENCE

- Practice humility. Recognize that most of us overestimate our abilities and accept that we are more fallible than we might like to think.
- As Stephen Covey famously said, "Seek first to understand, then to be understood." When others offer ideas, tap into your curiosity rather than rushing to judgment.
- Proactively seek out feedback. Ask your boss, coworkers, and family members to share their views about your performance. That can help you identify blind spots and develop a more accurate picture of your capabilities.

Confirmation Bias. Confirmation bias is a tendency to selectively pay attention to information that reinforces our beliefs, ignore information that conflicts with what we think, and interpret ambiguous information as supporting our views. Confirmation bias is most likely to affect us when dealing with highly charged emotional issues or deeply held beliefs. Though we can never eliminate confirmation bias, we can minimize its negative impact on our decision-making. For instance, influential leaders deliberately seek out varied points of view before making a decision. Take Chris Klinke's predicament during the Cho Oyu ascent when faced with the biases of his Sherpas, Dawa and Temba. Chris wanted to reach the mountain's summit as much as his Sherpas did, so it might have been tempting to pay more attention to their arguments for continuing their climb. Had Chris not analyzed the situation from all angles, he and his team might not have lived to tell their story.

TIPS FOR AVOIDING CONFIRMATION BIAS

- Adopt a learning mindset. Assume you don't know anything about the challenge you face. Read relevant articles, ask for input about your situation on a LinkedIn group, or sign up for a webinar on the subject.
- Become your own "devil's advocate." Write down the assumptions you are making about your decision options and challenge each assumption with a counterargument.
- Discuss your ideas with others, especially those who tend to see things differently from you. Concentrate on trying to understand their points of view, not poke holes in their ideas.

Overoptimism. Overoptimism is the bias that can cause us to overestimate how frequently we will experience favorable outcomes and underestimate how often we will experience less desirable results. Roughly 80 percent of all people demonstrate overoptimism bias. Overoptimism is not the same thing as having hope. Being hopeful is about envisioning a positive future. Overoptimism involves taking a positive future for granted. It's when our emotions lead us to distort data to the point at which our desire to make something happen far outweighs a realistic possibility of success. According to research, over-optimism is a common trait in entrepreneurs, and it's likely why many of them ultimately fail. It's especially hazardous for leaders. Overly optimistic leaders can damage a team's morale and sense of engagement. When you are excessively optimistic, others may see you as insensitive to their struggles or challenges. Liz Wiseman, a leadership researcher and executive advisor, explains why:

> *The good thing about optimists is that they're positive and hopeful, and you tend to need heavy doses of that in senior leadership because sometimes it can be difficult to even get out of bed in the morning and say, 'I believe we can make this work,' says Wiseman. "But what happens with optimists is they're often so focused on what's possible, and so convinced that the team is going to be able to make something work, that they don't see the messy process of getting there.*[3]

Another drawback of being an excessively optimistic leader is that you may influence those around you to buy into unrealistic expectations about the progress and outcome of a project or change initiative. Then, when things don't go as advertised, your followers feel frustrated or misled, undermining trust in your leadership going forward.

DOUG: OVEROPTIMISM

I was born with the optimism gene. That sometimes leads me to be excessively optimistic. I tend to think that things will work out for me and those around me. So, when it comes to decisions, I may not spend as much time as I should fact-checking the data.

A while ago, I served for about a year as a temporary senior executive for a large financial services organization. I was optimistic that I could make some key strategic changes that would improve their

---

[3]Leah Fessler, "The Best Leaders Aren't Optimists," *Quartz*, April 30, 2018, https://qz.com/work/1263261/the-best-leaders-and-bosses-arent-optimists.

financial results. But to achieve that, people on the frontlines would have to buy into some new ways of doing business. Though I tried to be realistic about my ability to pull off a major culture change, I realized in retrospect that I had been overly optimistic about my chances. Though I got a lot of positive feedback from people about the new systems, ultimately, they didn't take hold the way I'd hoped. It was painful to watch gravity sucking things back to where they had been. The people resisting change knew that they could wait me out since I was a temporary exec.

Though this experience was disappointing, I'm still glad I made the effort. The organization may not have changed in the big way I'd hoped. But I know there are people in the company who got to experience new possibilities for making a difference in clients' lives, and I think they'll carry what they learned into their work as leaders going forward.

When you're a senior leader responsible for setting the strategy and allocating resources to support significant changes, it's even more crucial that you guard against excessive optimism in yourself and at all levels of the organization. When things don't go exactly as planned, excessive optimism can leave your organization under-resourced and woefully unprepared to change course. For example, consider how the United States "managed" COVID-19 in the early days of the pandemic. Believing the virus would naturally dissipate by early summer 2020, the federal government and many states failed to do enough to slow the spread of the virus. Therefore, they were not prepared to deal with the spike in infections that soon overwhelmed many health-care systems.

Excessive optimism is challenging to manage because some measure of optimism is important if we hope to inspire others. Very few people are motivated to rally around a negative or consistently pessimistic leader. So as leaders, we need to be measured optimists. It's a little like eating. Eating the right amount is essential for health. But overeating is bad for health. It's easy for optimism to morph into over-optimism, and when that happens, it is tough for us to see the actual facts of a situation.

TIPS FOR AVOIDING EXCESSIVE OPTIMISM

- Use quantitative data when planning and predicting the outcome of a decision. Benchmark your plan based on statistics such as average costs, time, or staffing required to implement decisions comparable to the ones you are considering.
- Refine your plan by factoring in any specifics about your situation that would affect the timing or cost to achieve a particular outcome. For instance, be conservative in your estimates if the anticipated decision outcome has never been attempted before. Allow room in your plan for mistakes in estimating needed resources.
- Practice Daniel Kahneman's "premortem approach":[4] Imagine it's a year after you've made a decision and that the outcome has been negative. Create a scenario about what went wrong and why. Then consider likely threats and steps you can take to prevent them.

HOW TO DECIDE

In many ways, decision-making is the quintessential job of a leader. Therefore, one of the critical actions you can take as a leader is to use a decision-making process that reliably results in wise decisions. Consider the typical decision-making processes people learn in Management 101. Most models tend to oversimplify the decision process, reducing it to a linear progression of logical steps:

1. Gather data about a problem that requires a decision.
2. Identify options for deciding how to address the problem.
3. Decide on the best option.
4. Implement the decision.

While there is no doubt that logic plays a role in making good decisions, optimal decision-making goes beyond logic. It requires moral and emotional intelligence. Years ago, Doug saw that in the absence of moral and emotional competence, he and others would make leadership decisions that didn't turn out so well. Doug determined that he

---

[4]Gary Klein, "The Pre-Mortem Method" (January 14, 2021) *Psychology Today*, https://www.psychologytoday.com/us/blog/seeing-what-others-dont/202101/the-pre-mortem-method.

and others could consistently make better decisions when they used their moral and emotional competence to do the following:

- Increase self-awareness of what they were experiencing (thoughts, feelings, and actions) when faced with a challenging situation.
- Shift decision-making drivers from outside stimuli, such as fear-producing circumstances, to internal stimuli, such as principles and values.
- Adopt the most realistically positive and productive perspective about the situation at hand.

These principles formed the basis of the 4Rs, a model for decision-making that helps people reliably activate their moral and emotional competencies to make effective, values-based decisions.

WHEN IT COMES TO DECISIONS, 4Rs MAKE ALL THE DIFFERENCE

Every positive decision a leader makes includes four steps:

THE 4Rs

1. **Recognize** what you and others are experiencing.
2. **Reflect** on the big picture, principles, and values.
3. **Reframe** your thinking as needed.
4. **Respond** by deciding to do something—or not.

One of the most powerful features of the 4Rs process is that *it interrupts your brain's default responses to external situations.* Think of this effect as hitting the "pause" button on your brain's automatic program for decision-making. You may not always be able to prevent your brain from kicking up an emotional storm in the face of a significant leadership challenge, but you can, by practicing the 4Rs, keep your emotions from "hijacking" your rational thinking. And thanks to the brain's plasticity, when you hit the "play" button again, whatever you did during the pause begins to develop new mental pathways that improve your response the next time you make a decision.

The 4Rs Improve the Way We Process Information

Often when we need to make a significant leadership decision, we react emotionally to stimulation, "from the outside in." The 4Rs give us the tools to respond to leadership challenges "from the inside out." They change the power balance between the reflexive emotional center of our brain (which, as we've noted before, sacrifices accuracy for speed) and the reflective, rational center of our brain (which is more accurate but not as fast). The 4Rs give us better access to our logical, thinking brain. But they do more than that: The 4Rs significantly improve the quality of the data upon which we make those thoughtful decisions.

RECOGNIZING

The first of the 4Rs, *recognizing*, depends mainly on self-awareness, the emotional competence that research shows has the largest positive impact on leadership performance. Recognizing includes the following:

- Recognizing what's happening to me
- Recognizing what's happening to those around me
- Recognizing what is stimulating me and those around me

Recognizing is the critical first step in which we survey our own experiential triangle of thoughts, feelings, and actions, and as needed, when we gather information about the experiential triangles of those we want to influence, such as our teams or families. In Chapter 4, we introduced you to the freeze game, one of the easiest and most effective ways to recognize what's happening with you. The more you play the freeze game, the more self-aware you'll become about your thoughts, feelings, and actions. In addition to playing the freeze game yourself, you can learn about others' experiential triangles by asking them to play the freeze game with you. If that's not feasible, imagine what those significant others might be experiencing in response to a situation that affects them.

By consistently practicing recognition, you will transform yourself from a *reflexive responder* to a *reflective recognizer*.

REFLECTING

The second R, *reflecting*, is the process of focusing on what matters most to you. The primary purpose of reflecting is to shift the things that influence your decisions and actions from external to internal stimuli. *External stimuli* might include a wide range of frightening or upsetting situations, for example, needing to lay off a group of employees, discovering that your teenager is a drug abuser, or being reprimanded for a personal ethical lapse. *Internal stimuli* come from within you. Internal stimuli have three primary sources:

- The big picture of your life
- Principles
- Values

When you reflect on the big picture, you ask yourself:

> *In the big picture, what do I want this decision to mean, not just in this instance but over the course of my life?*
> *What do I want the impact of my leadership to be in the long term?*
> *How do I want to present myself in life and as a leader?*

When you reflect on principles, you ask yourself:

> *What principles, e.g., integrity, responsibility, compassion, or forgiveness, do I most need to demonstrate when I respond to this situation?*

When you reflect on values, you remind yourself of your top five values, then ask yourself:

> *What values are most important to me when deciding how to respond to this situation?*

Other questions to consider during the reflection phase include the following:

> *How is this situation affecting my ability to achieve my most important leadership goals?*
> *What mental biases might be coloring my understanding of the situation, and how might they influence a potential decision?*

DOUG: MAKING REFLECTION A HABIT

For me, reflection is most effective when it's part of my daily routine. For years I tied reflecting on my values to activities related to water. For instance, when I brushed my teeth, drank a glass of water, or washed my hands, I would say my values to myself, turning them into action statements using verbs: Love your family. Be happy. Seek wisdom. Behave with integrity. Do something of service for someone today. Make healthy choices. Then I would spend a few moments thinking about everything and each person I was grateful for.

I never stopped my reflection rituals, even during some very dark times. But for a few years, I was on autopilot—repeating my values without really thinking. I now realize that reflection only works when done mindfully. I can't just go through the motions. So, these days I'm careful to pay attention to what I'm saying to myself when reflecting on my values and what I'm grateful for.

On the surface, the 4Rs may look like an orderly, step-by-step process. In reality, the 4Rs weave in and out throughout the decision process. Recognition and reflection often seem to happen simultaneously. Once you make a conscious choice to pause to recognize your experiential triangle, things move very quickly. As soon as you recognize thoughts, feelings, and actions, you'll probably find you're also beginning to reflect on what matters most to you. That's a good thing because the sooner you can get into a calm, reflective state, the less likely you are to make a premature, ill-considered decision.

REFRAMING

The third R, reframing, begins by taking the results of your reflections and considering whether or not you need to change how you interpret the factors affecting a required decision. More often than not, reflecting flows into a realization that you need to change how you think about the situation. For example, Erin Livermore, a finance manager for a global media company and mom of two special needs children, has a lifelong mantra: "I can do it myself." She stakes a lot of her self-esteem on her ability to keep all the balls in the air at work and home.

She hates asking for help almost as much as she hates people asking if she'd like some help. At work, the more her boss delegates to her, the happier she is, interpreting that as a vote of confidence. But a year into her current job, the downsides of her Lone Ranger work style began to catch up with her. For months she had been doing two jobs, her own and that of a fellow manager who had resigned on short notice. Pride in her ability to do it all eventually was overshadowed by the profound exhaustion she felt at the end of every day. She developed headaches, felt irritable, and her kids missed her ordinarily cheerful demeanor.

Erin's "frame" of basing her self-image on her solo achievements also limited her development as a leader. When Erin first took over responsibility for her team, her impulse was to do as much as possible herself. Reflecting on why she operated that way, Erin realized that she thought she could do many team tasks faster or better than her employees or that she shouldn't burden them. Her boss saw what was happening and began coaching Erin on delegation skills, helping her reframe the very meaning of delegation. Today, Erin understands that delegation is a gift she gives to her employees, one that accelerates their development and demonstrates her trust in them. It allows her employees to feel the same sense of accomplishment she feels when her boss delegates to her. Erin appreciates the help her boss gave her in cultivating her delegation skills. She's proud of how her team members have stepped up to the plate, and her employees feel valued and trusted. Reframing from "I'll do it myself" to "It takes a village" has made Erin far more effective as a leader. (Just don't ask if you can help her make dinner.)

Reframing contributes to effective decisions even if you discover you don't need to change your perspective about the situation at hand. That's because this third R acts like a spotlight on the most effective option or options for action, inspired by the previous two Rs. Whether you literally reframe a situation (as in most instances) or validate your existing frame (occasionally), the thoughtful process of the third R helps ensure that the decision you ultimately make is wise.

Consider the following questions while reframing:

How has reflection changed the way I think about this situation?
Do I need to change my thinking about this situation or not?
What different choices are available to me if I think about this situation in a new way?

Just as recognizing flows into reflecting, reflecting seems to flow naturally into reframing. And just as the first two Rs may have danced together in your mind, reflecting and reframing may move back and forth in tandem. In Erin Livermore's case, the 4Rs process began by reframing her assumptions about the best way to lead her team, a reframing offered as part of the feedback from her boss. That led Erin to reflect on how her value of independence, taken to an extreme, could get in the way of her career growth and her team's productivity.

As you move through the reframing phase, you may notice a feeling of relief, as though you can breathe more easily. That's because reframing, though a cognitive process, is also emotionally freeing. When we reframe, we can see more possible choices. We feel lighter. Whether or not we change our frame in some fundamental way, we can be confident that the decision we are about to make is measured and values based. Armed with a realistically positive frame, we can now make a wise decision.

RESPONDING

The fourth R, responding, might appear to be the easiest of the 4Rs to master. At its simplest, responding is about making a decision. It's about doing something or choosing not to do something. Questions you may want to ask before making a final decision include the following:

What should I do?
Should I take a particular action or not?
For each action I could take, what could be the unintended consequences of those decisions?

It's tempting to jump to a decision as soon as we've cycled through the first three Rs. Sometimes, as soon as we have reframed our situation, we're off and running with a smart decision. At other times, we may feel unsure about our decision, and perhaps we need to revisit some earlier phase of the 4Rs process. For instance, we may need to reflect further about whether we've fully taken our values into account. Or we may need to be more creative in reframing our situation to open up the most productive choices about how to proceed.

Finally, having moved through the first three Rs, we can now take advantage of those conventional decision-making models, applying quantitative methods to identify and evaluate options when the leadership or organizational challenges are complex and would benefit from data science applications. However, returning to those 35,000 decisions that fill each day, it's a safe bet that most of your choices as a leader and human being don't require sophisticated analytical tools. The decision-making differentiators that genuinely make a difference are the moral and emotional competencies at the heart of the 4Rs decision-making model.

...

U.S. snowboarding coach Rick Bower's transformation in the years between the Sochi and Pyeongchang Olympics is a powerful example of the 4Rs decision-making model in action. Rick left Sochi feeling upset about the team's performance and disappointed with himself. He spent the next few years reflecting on what had happened and why it happened. That reflection allowed Rick to explore other ways of leading the team as they approached the 2018 Games in Pyeongchang. Rick reframed what successful coaching meant and ultimately chose a different way of leading his team. His shift to a more collaborative coaching model that better addressed athletes' emotional needs contributed greatly to the team's tremendous success in both the men's and women's events.

The most obvious advantage of the 4Rs decision-making model is its ability to get us unstuck from impulsive, emotionally driven decisions and focus on the values that ideally should drive our actions as leaders. As necessary as values and consideration of the big picture are to wise decision-making, they are not sufficient. The quality of our reframing, the third R, is equally important. Productive reframing depends on our ability to be expansive and creative when reimagining our approach to a leadership challenge. To discover new ways of framing a challenging situation, we need to let go of many things we're comfortable with—our expertise, points of view, education or training, or conventional wisdom. That may sound radical. But being open to innovative solutions to challenges is essential to exceptional leadership.

In the next chapter, "Let Go of What You Know," you'll discover the vital role of learning agility in making high-quality leadership decisions. As you'll see, being willing to jump off the cliff of the known and comfortable to explore unfamiliar territory will exponentially enhance your leadership impact.

CHAPTER EIGHT

Let Go of What You Know

Darby Coleman began her career as an executive assistant to the CEO of a start-up leadership development consulting firm that worked primarily with U.S. government agencies. By the time she left the company 10 years later, she was director of operations. Darby didn't just climb the ladder—she built it. Darby created every role she assumed as the firm grew. Darby successively developed the human resources, finance, operations, technology, and marketing functions for the company. Darby managed to accomplish all that without any formal training in those fields. In fact, Darby doesn't have a college degree in anything. What she did have was a thirst for learning and an openness to apply what she already knew to new and challenging situations.

Darby had dropped out of college when she found out she was expecting a child and became a mom at 20. When asked how she managed to accomplish so much so quickly in her professional life, Darby explains:

> I was scrappy. I had to learn on my own. I remember the time my boss said, "I need someone to manage this $800K project" and even though I didn't have experience in project management, I jumped at the opportunity. The business didn't have a training budget, so whatever I needed

to know, I would just figure it out. There was a lot of Googling and a lot of YouTubing involved in advancing my career. One way or another, I'd find the resources I needed to solve problems and expand my skills. I read a lot, I listened a lot, and figured out how to translate what I learned to our context and needs.

Darby's leadership growth would not have been possible without a high degree of learning agility. As Monique Valcour, internationally recognized management professor and executive coach defines it, *learning agility* is "the capacity for rapid continuous learning from experience. It means giving up what may have worked in the past."[1] When it comes to learning agility, Darby had an advantage: She knew what she didn't know. She didn't start her career as an expert in anything. So, she had nowhere to go on the learning curve but up.

Contrast Darby's career trajectory with yours. Suppose you are a high performer who wants to take your leadership to the next level. You may already be very knowledgeable in your chosen field. In that case, your challenge is to figure out when you need to let go of your expertise and open yourself to new ways of thinking and behaving. It's a paradox that the more intelligent you are, the more challenging it may be to learn and grow. As learning organization pioneer Chris Argyris explained in his seminal *Harvard Business Review* article, "Teaching Smart People How to Learn," ". . .because many professionals are almost always successful at what they do, they rarely experience failure. And because they have rarely failed, they have never learned how to learn from failure."[2]

Argyris's research also found that generally successful leaders often find it challenging to take responsibility for their occasional failings and may instead blame their bosses, clients, or other team members. But scapegoating others is ultimately career-limiting. As discussed in Chapter 3 "Aim to Be Your Ideal Self," unwillingness to admit mistakes or failures is a moral lapse that erodes your credibility in the eyes of those you hope to influence. Beyond that, it stunts your professional growth. You can't learn from a mistake you aren't willing to own.

[1] Monique Valcour, "4 Ways to Become a Better Learner," *Harvard Business Review* (December 2015), https://hbr.org/2015/12/4-ways-to-become-a-better-learner.
[2] Chris Argyris, "Teaching Smart People How to Learn," *Harvard Business Review* (May–June 1991).

That's why "Let go of what you know" also means letting go of the need to be right. There is little to be learned from doing everything right day after day, especially when many of the "right things to do" lose their effectiveness as times and circumstances change. Learning agility involves being able to flex as the environment in which you operate becomes more complex. For example, Darby parlayed her talent for learning to become an expert in many business areas. But despite her well-deserved leadership titles, she did practically everything herself. She had to, because in such a small firm there was no one else to help. Now that she's working at a much larger company, Darby has a new learning challenge. As Darby tells us,

> The skill I am most working on right now is delegation. I'm not used to having other people I can rely on to do the work and have their own dedicated roles. It's helping me stretch because the skill of delegating and my identity as a curious learner who wants to take on the challenge myself can conflict with each other.

THE BUSINESS CASE FOR LEARNING AGILITY

In the last 10 years, learning agility has become a critical skill for leaders at all levels. As the global organizational consulting firm Korn Ferry points out, "Learning agility, sometimes described as 'knowing what to do when you don't know what to do,' requires an open and receptive mindset. Those who demonstrate strong 'learning agility' often excel at being able to study, analyze, and understand new situations and new business problems."[3]

Whether you're a community leader or a CEO, you live in an uncertain world. Conditions change rapidly, issues are complex, and there's no hope that life will settle down anytime soon. Because the world is so volatile, the skills we have and the expertise we've always relied on can quickly become outmoded. Korn Ferry has done significant research on the impact of learning agility for leaders. Their work found strong links between high learning agility and the success of individual executives. Korn Ferry's research has shown learning agility to be a significant predictor of long-term success, with high learning-agile

[3]"The Organisational X-Factor: Learning Agility," *Focus*, Korn Ferry, https://focus.kornferry .com/leadership-and-talent/the-organisational-x-factor-learning-agility/

individuals 18 times more likely to be identified as high-potential employees than their low learning-agile colleagues. They are also twice as likely to be promoted. Another Korn Ferry study found that companies with highly learning-agile executives had 25 percent greater profit margins than their peer group. In light of these benefits, it is disconcerting that only 15 percent of the global workforce is considered to have high learning agility.

The lack of learning agility among most people has contributed to an ever-widening global skills gap. In Gartner, Inc.'s 2018 *Shifting Skills Survey*, more than 7,000 employees were asked to assess their level of proficiency in in-demand skills. Eighty percent of those surveyed said they lack the skills needed for their current roles and future careers.[4] According to *The State of Skills 2021: Endangered*, a survey of more than 5,000 global workers, managers, and leaders, the ongoing coronavirus pandemic has only sped up "skill extinction."[5]

By the way, this second survey polled participants about the skills they wanted to develop for themselves—not skills that their employers wanted them to have. It's hard to imagine being able to close the rapidly growing global skills gap without a significant improvement in the learning agility needed to accelerate the acquisition of new skills.

EXERCISE: ENHANCING YOUR LEARNING AGILITY

1. What new skill could help you the most in addressing emerging challenges of your leadership role or roles?
2. On a scale of 1–10, how curious are you about learning the new skill you identified? Is there a gap between your need to develop that new skill and your interest in developing that skill? If so, how could you increase your interest in developing that skill?
3. What would be the best way for you to learn that skill?
4. What skills or expertise might you need to let go of or rely on less to be a more effective leader?

---

[4]Gartner, Inc., "Motivate Employees to Reskill for the Digital Age," 2018, https://www.gartner.com/smarterwithgartner/motivate-employees-to-reskill-for-the-digital-age
[5]Degreed, Inc. "The State of Skills 2021: Endangered," 2021, https://stateofskills.degreed.com.

CULTIVATING A LEARNING MINDSET

In our work with leaders, we have found that willingness to "let go of what you know" is the overarching component of learning agility. It's one thing to be curious about the latest and greatest trends. It's another thing to accept that, in Albert Einstein's words, "We cannot solve our problems with the same level of thinking that created them." That means removing the filter of "the way we always do things," allowing what you read or hear to soak in, and exploring how to use new information to strengthen your effectiveness as a leader. For instance, many think2perform leadership clients have read all the best-selling leadership and performance enhancement books. Many also spend time and money attending workshops or signing up for webinars that experts promise will offer tools for upping their leadership game. But exposure to information about new approaches to leadership does not necessarily translate into meaningful improvement in concrete leadership behavior. For example, every year, our company sponsors Evolution, a future-focused leadership conference. We're always gratified that enrollment is high, and we're proud to connect participants with groundbreaking thought leaders in leadership and performance effectiveness. Almost 100 percent of our participants review our conference as highly positively. However, we've discovered over the years that, despite our conference's popularity, not all participants make use of what they have experienced during the conference to become better leaders, improve employee engagement, or increase financial results. When it comes to the learning value of our conference, our data indicate it has a meaningful impact on the leadership performance of 60 percent of participants. We're gratified but not satisfied. We're relentless. We want to make a meaningful difference in the lives of everyone we touch, not just 60 percent. That is why, before we begin to work with leaders in an organization or with participants in one of our programs, we now ask for their commitment to actively use what they learn from us to enhance their skills. By "prequalifying" clients based on their motivation to learn, we increase the odds that we'll have the impact on performance we aim for and that clients will get the return on investment they expect in our services.

Another way of framing "motivation to learn" is to think of it as having a "learning mindset." What does a learning mindset look like in practice? One of the best examples we know is Joanie Goulart, a prominent leader in the field of solutions to end homelessness. When we first spoke to Joanie, she was executive director of a large residential community for low-income senior citizens in Minneapolis. Joanie considers lifelong learning to be at the heart of her leadership approach. As Joanie says,

> *For me, being an effective leader means not getting in your own way and assuming you know everything. I never felt that I did and that's been helpful. My ego doesn't play a role. I'm quick to ask for help and collaboration. I'm always learning from the people around me. I try to keep my eyes open to things other leaders are doing. The way I learn is hands-on connecting with people. My preferred learning style is pulling people in so we can learn together.*

Joanie has discovered that her learning-centered leadership approach is effective and personally rewarding. As she told us:

> *Every day I learn something different. I really try to surround myself with people who are different. I just love going into someone's office and saying to a colleague "Let's talk it through." We all need to do that since we all come with our different perspectives. I work to lean into the discomfort of those differences. I remind myself that I only know what I know. I want to soak up other people's experiences.*

After many years dedicated to supporting the needs of vulnerable senior citizens, Joanie wanted to apply her leadership skills in a new context. She expanded her impact by joining a nonprofit dedicated to ending homelessness in people facing various barriers, including mental health challenges and chemical dependency. Joanie's decision to transition to a new organization was itself a measure of her learning mindset. Everything about her new role was a learning challenge. It meant leaving the comfort of a familiar organization, a staff who felt like family, and a client demographic that she had come to feel she deeply understood. It meant establishing credibility as a senior leader with followers who didn't know anything about her. It meant figuring out how to be a good leader of people who worked in a role she had never done herself. It meant working with a smaller group of direct reports who themselves had very large teams. It meant for her less "boots on the ground" direct work with clients and upping her game as a strategic thinker and coach to the front-line managers who reported to her. In Joanie's new job, almost every part of the organizational context was different. The only thing that didn't change was Joanie's strong learning agility, a skill that is paying off as she rises to the challenges of her new position. Without a learning mindset, Joanie might never have left the emotional security of her former job. Without learning agility, Joanie might not be achieving her purpose of making a difference in the lives of society's most vulnerable citizens.

EMPATHY-FUELED LEARNING

As you've probably noticed, the eight essentials of leadership intelligence don't operate independently. They are all interconnected. For example, when we spoke to Joanie Goulart, she reminded us of a critical connection between learning agility and empathy, two leadership essentials we explore in this book. In Joanie's former role heading up a low-income senior housing community, she discovered that learning came not just from colleagues, but from the residents of the senior community she led. As Joanie wisely discovered, to learn from others, especially those most different from you, you must approach them with an attitude of empathy. In Joanie's words:

> If I'm able to go and talk to someone who is different, I think of it as a huge gift. I try to avoid applying my own lens to someone else's experience. For instance, I work constantly to think of how we can help people who come with different backgrounds, such as someone who is of lower literacy.

> A lot of that is about empathy. To learn and educate yourself you need to be empathetic. You can't lead effectively if you're busy judging others. I don't believe we can meet the diverse needs of people if we don't understand them.

> Using empathy, I've learned that a person's worth is not defined by the life they've had, or their educational level. Two hundred residents live in the senior community where I formerly served as executive director. They are some of the most wonderful people I've ever known. Maybe they've been to prison, or were homeless for 15 years, or grew up in abusive homes, or have had periods when they don't know where their next meal is coming from. Because of those experiences, they have so much wisdom to offer. You need to treat everyone with kindness and respect in order to learn from them.

Nothing Joanie has done throughout her career in the nonprofit sector has been motivated by fame or fortune. Despite that, Joanie's empathetic, learning-centered leadership has not gone unnoticed. For example, in 2017, Joanie received the prestigious Caregiver of the Year award presented annually by LeadingAge Minnesota, an aging services advocacy organization.

STRENGTHENING YOUR INDIVIDUAL LEARNING AGILITY

As with most skills, learning agility comes more easily to some of us than others. Some of us are more naturally curious and more open to new experiences. Others of us may hang on too tightly to our expertise, habits, and usual ways of learning. Katie Morgan Glass discovered that she had to "let go of what she knew" when she said goodbye to her job at Gartner, a global research and advisory firm, to become an independent learning solutions consultant. At Gartner, Katie had access to the organization's highly regarded Leadership Academy and the good fortune to work for a manager who was a great coach. When she became a freelancer, she suddenly lost those resources. As Katie tells it:

I had to reimagine what my learning environment was going to be. One of the first things I did was hire a business coach. My biggest mindset change was the realization that I don't have to have all the answers. I can figure things out. I'm never going to have the full picture, so I can just try things and see how they work. I had to be agile. I put myself through my own training.

I also learned to separate my performance from my identity. My skills are a tool set. They are not who I am. I view mistakes as experiments, and if something doesn't work out, I don't take it as a personal failure. I've made a lot of progress in letting go of the perfectionistic tendencies that the culture encourages.

Like Katie, we all need to figure out how to deal with the challenges our environment creates for us. Given your unique leadership circumstances, what can you do to strengthen and deepen your learning agility? We believe that four key practices make all the difference when it comes to learning agility:

- Be curious.
- Choose growth over comfort.
- Resist defensiveness.
- Experiment.

BE CURIOUS

It may be hard to admit, but many of us lack curiosity. Even when it comes to something as simple as listening to a friend talk about a problem, we may barely listen before making assumptions about their situation, then interrupting prematurely to present what we think is a clever solution. But when we don't listen, we don't learn. We don't realize that our thoughts about a situation might lead to a more effective solution if we stayed in curious mode for a while longer. That would give us time to ask questions about our friend's circumstance, giving us a fuller picture of the problem our friend is facing. In addition to learning more about our friend's circumstances, curiosity would help us communicate that we actually care about them and want to learn together to help them deal with a difficult time. As the late, legendary Stephen Covey said in his mega-bestselling book, *7 Habits of Highly Effective People*: "Seek first to understand, then to be understood."

Curiosity is a learning practice that goes far beyond listening to other people's stories, as crucial as that is both to being a helpful leader and creating a bond between you and those you hope to influence. Imagine going through a day in which your default attitude was one of curiosity. Consider these scenarios:

> *You see a member of your team approach a task in a completely different way from how you did when you were in her position. Instead of judging her approach as wrong or inefficient, you call on curiosity. You ask her about her approach, and how it benefits her and the team's overall results. As a result of your dialogue, you realize that your team member has developed a best practice you and she can share with others.*

You notice in the news that there is a lot of talk about AI (artificial intelligence), a topic you know nothing about. You work in a traditional organization that doesn't use AI in its systems. But you imagine that in the future, AI will become part of every organization's business processes. So, you sign up for an introductory webinar about AI, start reading about it, and ask colleagues what they think about it.

You're doing well as a first-line production supervisor and hope to advance. You've heard that strategic thinking is an important skill for a more senior manager. So, in your weekly one-on-ones with your manager, you start asking him how the tasks your team is working on contribute to the company's strategy. You also begin to read articles on strategy and strategic thinking. What you learn convinces you that you could apply strategic thinking principles to your team's work, even though your team is low in the company hierarchy.

Caroline Soares parlayed her gift for curiosity into an exciting new job. Caroline is both a lifelong learner and a thought leader in the corporate learning space. Caroline was a pioneer in the digital learning arena. Today, she is the associate vice president of client services and delivery for Emeritus, a global provider of world-class higher education programs. Several years ago, Caroline's previous employer underwent a major corporate restructuring, eliminating the organization that she directed. Caroline was understandably disappointed. She had been highly regarded by her company's clients and beloved by her team. It would have been tempting for Caroline to feel bitter, but she isn't the type to waste time hanging on to the past. Caroline immediately defined her reality as one of exploration. She set a short-term goal to help her team members land new roles successfully. She used her sense of curiosity to get as much information as possible about her outgoing team's career aspirations so that she could be an effective advocate for them. At the same time, Caroline networked extensively to identify new opportunities for herself.

In conducting her job search, Caroline could have sought a position that looked a lot like her previous role. Instead, Caroline took a broader approach. She was curious. Caroline took time to explore what was new and changing in the world of organizational learning.

She looked at opportunities anywhere in the rapidly expanding arena of online learning, whether or not they mapped perfectly to her existing skill set. Caroline's curiosity led her to discover Emeritus, a learning experience platform committed to providing affordable and accessible learning programs to individuals, companies, and governments around the world. Emeritus' focus on higher education was a departure from the last three corporate learning jobs in which Caroline had excelled. Emeritus was growing and wanted to hire someone who would help clients develop high-quality offerings. But they didn't know the exact skill set they needed for this new role. So as part of considering Caroline for the job, they asked Caroline to tell them what she thought they needed. So, she tapped into her curiosity once again. She asked a lot of questions, digging deep and really trying to understand what Emeritus hoped to accomplish. As Caroline said, "Talk about learning on the job! This was learning while applying for the job!" By capitalizing on her curiosity and growth mindset, Caroline was able to craft a compelling job description that ultimately landed her a role on Emeritus' senior leadership team.

CHOOSE GROWTH OVER COMFORT

Learning-agile people are willing to be uncomfortable in pursuit of growth. They are pioneers who venture into unknown territory and put themselves "out there" to try new things. They take "progressive risk." Learning-agile leaders don't pursue risk because it's thrilling, but because they can learn from the risks they take to identify new opportunities. Learning-agile people volunteer for jobs and roles where success is not guaranteed and failure is a real possibility. They stretch themselves beyond their comfort zones in a continuous cycle of learning and confidence-building that ultimately leads to success.

Choosing growth entails taking on unfamiliar challenges that allow you to develop new skills and perspectives. To develop your capacity to choose growth over comfort, do something that seems worth doing but scares you.

THE PARADOX OF GROWTH VERSUS COMFORT

Our colleague Ray Kelly poses these two questions to his clients to demonstrate the choice we need to make if we want to learn and grow:

1. What do you prefer, comfort or discomfort? Nearly all say "Comfort".
2. Would you rather be comfortable or grow? Most people say "Grow".

People want to grow but stay comfortable. But growth and comfort are incompatible. You can grow. Or you can be comfortable. You can't do both.

The behavioral choice many people make is to choose comfort over growth. That's partly why learning agility is in short supply worldwide.

Don't wait to feel comfortable before deciding to act in a way that helps you grow. To practice choosing growth over comfort, find something to do that is meaningful and makes you uncomfortable but is not so important that failure will have serious personal consequences. Accept the discomfort you feel as an inevitable part of doing something new. Let others know what you are doing to help you deal with the usual pain of behaving differently and ask for their help and support.

Also, when choosing an action you hope will help you grow, take advantage of self-talk. There are lots of ways you can speak to yourself internally. University of Michigan professor Ethan Kross suggests that the best way to engage in self-talk is to talk to yourself in the second or third person. If you speak to yourself in the first person, for instance, saying something like, "I'm going to feel uncomfortable," is likely to intensify your discomfort. Instead, talk to yourself as if you are your coach. For example, you might say, "Doug, to succeed in this new way of behaving, you will have to face some discomfort. I know you can do this. You've done a lot of new things in the past. Doing this new thing will help you deal successfully with all the changes in your life right now."[6]

[6]Ethan Kross and Oslum Ayduk, "Self-Distancing: Theory, Research, and Current Directions," *Advances in Experimental Social Psychology*, Volume 55, 2017, Pages 81–136

RESIST DEFENSIVENESS

Being defensive is the opposite of "letting go of what you know." It can be hard to avoid feeling defensive when someone criticizes or challenges you. Self-preservation has deep roots in the human brain. But as Katie Morgan Glass learned, there is a difference between your performance and your identity. You may make mistakes, but you are not your mistakes. You may feel negative emotions about making a mistake, but you are not your emotions. Learn from those emotions, but don't let them drive you. As Susan David encourages us in her best-selling book, *Emotional Agility*,

> *One of the greatest human triumphs is to choose to make room in our hearts for both the joy and the pain, and to get comfortable with being uncomfortable. This means seeing feelings not as "good" or "bad" but as just "being." Yes, there is this relentless assumption in our culture that we need to do something when we have inner turmoil. . .. What we really need to do, though, is also what is most simple and obvious: nothing. That is, to just welcome those inner experiences, breathe into them, and learn their contours without racing for the exits.*[7]

To practice nondefensiveness, view feedback as a gift. Regardless of someone's motivations for giving you feedback, their input always provides an opportunity to learn more about yourself. We all have blind spots, and others' feedback usually has at least a grain of truth in it. So, when someone offers feedback, take a breath. Resist the temptation to defend your behavior to them or preserve your self-esteem by making excuses in your head. When you hear feedback, ask yourself, "What can I learn from what I am hearing?"

Finally, make it a habit to thank those who offer you feedback. Expressing appreciation for their input doesn't mean that you agree with everything they say. But it will protect a valuable source of data about your "real self." And by modeling openness to feedback, you will encourage a culture of learning among those you influence.

---

[7]Susan David, *Emotional Agility: Get Unstuck, Embrace Change, and Thrive in Work and Life* (New York: Avery, 2016).

EXPERIMENT

The fourth learning agility practice is to experiment. Many of us, especially high achievers, tend to be impatient. When dealing with a problem, we often choose the first or most obvious solution rather than considering whether it is indeed the optimal course. So, for each problem you face, make time to try out various new approaches. Also, encourage yourself and others to experiment with "wild and crazy" ideas. Experimenting with several options may seem inefficient or time-consuming, but it allows you to discover new ways of doing things that can produce better results in the long term.

WHEN FACING A CHALLENGE, ASK YOURSELF

- How would I usually deal with a situation like this? What are the drawbacks to adopting the usual approach?
- What could be keeping me from trying a new approach to this situation?
- How could I overcome the constraints holding me back from experimenting with some new approaches?
- What two or three new ideas could I try out to deal with this situation?

CULTIVATE LEARNING AGILITY IN THOSE YOU LEAD

Strengthening your own learning agility is no doubt important. But as with all leadership essentials, you are also responsible for encouraging learning agility in those around you. Fostering a culture of learning in the team or organization you lead amplifies the positive impact of learning under challenging circumstances. No one demonstrates the performance value of encouraging a learning culture better than Richard Sheridan. Richard is a co-founder of software development company Menlo Innovations and best-selling author of *Joy, Inc: How We Built a Workplace People Love*. Richard's company is uniquely organized to promote learning agility. One example of a learning-centered approach to managing the company is Menlo Innovation's use of "pairing," in which two people sit together at a single computer all day working on the same task. Many of us might think that's a highly inefficient approach to work. But as Richard explains in *Joy, Inc.*:

Pairing fosters a learning system, builds relationships, eliminates towers of knowledge, simplifies onboarding of new people, and flushes out performance issues.

In the paired environment of Menlo, we are continuously building our skills. Each pair partner brings his or her own unique experience and knowledge to the conversation. When pairs work together, they often learn something new about their pair partner's unique breadth of experience.

. . .Learning happens every minute of every day while actual work is being done. One person in the pair teaches her new partner what she learned the previous week.[8]

Menlo's approach to learning does much more than develop skills and accelerate business performance. It fosters a culture of engagement precisely because the work environment is learning-centered. In a 2019 PwC survey, 78% of global business and human resources leaders identified learning and development opportunities as important to the future of their organizations. Still, only half of those organizations were taking action to create those opportunities. That gap reflects how vulnerable many organizations, and their leaders, are when it comes to attracting and retaining the people they most need to fuel performance. In commenting on the importance of lifelong learning in today's constantly evolving world, the survey researchers note:

Organisations can help employees make successful transitions by emphasizing the importance of diversity of experiences and lifelong learning. Employees themselves are pushing for continuous learning and development opportunities. For companies hiring younger employees, the ability to learn and progress is now a key employment criterion and a factor in their own brand building.

[8]Richard Sheridan, *Joy, Inc.: How We Built a Workplace People Love* (New York: Portfolio/Penguin, 2013).

This calls for corporations to deliver learning tailored to individual needs. Organisations cannot merely rely on education institutions in a landscape of changing jobs and skills requirements.[9]

REFLECTION

What kind of learning opportunities do you currently offer to members of your team or organization?

What opportunities could you provide to encourage others to strengthen their learning agility?

...

Many leaders hang their hats on being experts when it comes to effective leadership. In most organizational settings, people who know a lot are rewarded for their expertise through promotions, bonuses, or the satisfaction of knowing that they have superstar reputations. But in today's VUCA world (volatile, uncertain, complex, and ambiguous), expertise has an alarmingly short half-life. In the face of unprecedented challenges—whether organizational or societal—leadership will increasingly depend not on what leaders know but on *what leaders do when they don't know what to do.* As you'll see in the next chapter, the most influential leaders tackle the challenges of uncertainty by setting purposeful goals. As you'll also discover, achieving goals requires a learning mindset. Your success in achieving goals that matter depends on your willingness to experiment with fresh approaches to goal achievement. As Albert Einstein famously said,

The world we have created is a product of our thinking; it cannot be changed without changing our thinking. If we want to change the world, we have to change our thinking. . .no problem can be solved from the same consciousness that created it. We must learn to see the world anew.

---

[9]PwC, "Preparing for Tomorrow's Workforce, Today: Insights from a Global Survey of Business and HR Leaders," 2018.

Before Doug's father died, he told his family that he wanted this epitaph on his gravestone: "And Yet I Am Still Learning." Whenever Doug thinks about his dad, he sees that epitaph in his mind's eye. Coincidentally, the brilliant seventeenth-century Spanish artist, Francisco de Goya, titled one of his last works, "I Am Still Learning," a haunting self-portrait that showed the artist facing old age yet still committed to growth and learning. Like Goya, Doug's father recognized that learning is a never-ending journey. Ultimately, your leadership effectiveness rests on a life-long commitment to learning.

CHAPTER NINE

Achieve Purposeful Goals

For the last 40 days, polar explorer Eric Larsen and his partner Ryan Waters had been battling the most severe weather conditions they'd ever experienced. After two trips to the South Pole, a previous trip to the North Pole, and once to the summit of Mount Everest, Eric was one of the most accomplished explorers on the planet. Only 50 people in history had ever attempted what he and Ryan were determined to achieve: skiing unassisted 480 miles across the Arctic Ocean to the North Pole. Now their goal was in jeopardy. With 10 days left before they were scheduled to be airlifted from the North Pole, they still had 200 miles left to cover. The air temperature was a brutal minus 40 degrees Fahrenheit. Eric stared across the lunar-like landscape, exhausted and trying to catch his breath after 8 hours of struggle, pulling his 300-pound sled across the unforgiving ice. They were low on food and fuel. Ryan was battling worsening frostbite on his legs. In Eric's book about the expedition, *On Thin Ice*, he recalls that day: "The prevailing thought going over and over in my head was, why continue? Why go on? We are just going to die out here, and my son will never know who I was." Thirteen unimaginable days later, moving across 200 miles of thin or floating ice and swimming through open water, Eric and Ryan miraculously reached the North Pole. That they succeeded against overwhelming odds is a tribute to Eric's approach to goal achievement.

SELF-AWARENESS AND GOAL ACHIEVEMENT

One of Eric's tenets for a successful expedition is selfishness. Contrary to popular beliefs about teamwork, in the extreme conditions that Eric and his teammates operate, taking care of oneself is vital to personal survival and critical to being a good teammate. Working in unmerciful weather conditions requires constant self-awareness. Knowing how you're doing, what you need, and when you need it requires an ongoing cycle of checking in with oneself to ensure those needs are met. Ignoring your needs could result in loss of limb or life—yours or your teammates'. If you fail to take care of yourself, you could become a dangerous burden for those around you. If you aren't vigilant about self-care, you won't be strong enough to care for others.

Eric's emphasis on self-awareness echoes what we tell leaders: You can't succeed in reaching your goals if you focus solely on the goal itself. As Eric tells it,

> There are two successes in goal achievement; one is achieving the goal. The second is how we achieve it. If we are all skiing to the South Pole, the goal is to reach it as a team. Someone may not be as strong; someone else may have equipment failure or suffer an accident, but we all need to be caring for ourselves, so we have the potential to help one another.

To ensure we are always in shape to take care of others, Eric advises, "As you're pursuing your goals, check in with yourself. Ask yourself, 'How am I doing at this moment?'"

In light of Eric's polar explorations, Eric's question brings new meaning to the concept of the freeze game.

It's clear from Eric's story that self-awareness is essential whenever reaching our goal requires significant personal sacrifice and long-term effort. Our journeys may be less daunting than Eric's adventures. But achieving any meaningful goal involves taking care of ourselves so we can reach the finish line.

SECRETS OF SUCCESSFUL GOAL ACHIEVEMENT

Eric and his expedition partner Ryan accomplished their goal of skiing to the North Pole because they did a lot of things right. First, they set a goal worth achieving and one they had committed to wholly. Once they set their goal, they identified everything they needed to do to reach their goal. They made a plan that detailed needed equipment, supplies, and timing. They lined up the air transportation they would need to get them to their starting point and, later, return from their destination. Once en route, they followed their plan, adapting it as necessary to deal with unwanted events, such as equipment failures, harsh weather, or extreme physical fatigue. Finally, they found ways to fight the discouragement they often felt when circumstances jeopardized the success of their mission. Though Eric and Ryan had never heard of the WDYWFY Goal Achievement Process that we introduce in this chapter, everything they did to accomplish their goal was consistent with the WDYWFY model.

WDYWFY Goal Achievement Model

WDYWFY (pronounced "Widdy Wiffy") is a unique goal achievement model. WDYWFY stands for "What Do You Want for Yourself?" It differs from most goal achievement models in four ways.

First, the process begins with self-awareness about what you deeply want for yourself, informed by your values. Out of that awareness, you can make the best decisions about doing new things or doing things differently. As important as it is for you as an individual to pay attention to what you want for yourself, as a leader, it's even more important to know what those you hope to influence want for themselves. When you communicate to followers that you care about their goals for themselves and want to help them achieve those goals, you foster a powerful bond with them. You solidify that bond by supporting followers in accomplishing goals that are personally meaningful to them. That increases their engagement in working with you to achieve goals important to your mission as their leader.

Second, the WDYWFY goal achievement model sets a high bar for choosing goals. Conventional wisdom suggests that setting goals is easy while achieving goals is hard. Anyone who's made a New Year's resolution that soon fell by the wayside might agree. But in the WDYWFY model, a *want* doesn't necessarily qualify as a *goal*. There are lots of things we want. But wants only become goals when we're able and willing to do what it takes to achieve them. In the WDYWFY model, *goals are wants that have passed the "acid test."*

The Acid Test

> Am I able to do what's needed to get what I want?

> Am I willing to do what it takes to get what I want?

The acid test consists of two questions: First, am I able to do what's needed to get what I want? Second, am I willing to do what it takes to get what I want? Only when you can answer "yes" to both questions does something you'd like to have or do qualify as a goal. When you set a goal that passes the acid test, you're already far more likely to achieve that goal than if you stayed in the realm of wishful thinking—wanting things that you weren't able or committed to working toward.

The third distinction between WDYWFY and other goal achievement models is that, unlike many goal achievement models, WDYWFY is not a linear stepwise process. Though the WDYWFY model defines a series of steps, the steps intertwine. In the case of the first step related to setting a goal, for instance, you immediately need some sense of what actions would be needed to reach that goal. Only when you look ahead to potential future steps to see what your desired goal would entail in terms of effort and commitment can you determine whether something you want rises to the level of an authentic goal. That's why the notion that setting goals is easy doesn't ring true. Setting goals—goals that are really goals—is hard.

Fourth, WDYWFY, unlike most other goal achievement models, explicitly recognizes that course corrections are part of the process. Typical goal achievement models assume that once you make a plan to achieve a goal, it's simply a matter of following the plan to a successful conclusion. WDYWFY, on the other hand, factors in the logistical and emotional landmines that frequently affect the implementation of a plan to accomplish a goal. WDYWFY's goal achievement process explicitly includes strategies for overcoming the inevitable obstacles that threaten your ability to achieve goals.

The WDYWFY Goal Achievement Process is not an easy path. That's not just because setting worthwhile goals is hard. It's also because reaching purposeful goals is hard. It's far easier to keep doing what we've been doing, even if what we're doing is not helping us or those we lead. Fortunately, goal achievement, though not easy, is also not complicated. It's simple, as long as we genuinely care about improving our lives and the lives of those around us. With all that in mind, let's turn to the steps in the WDYWFY Goal Achievement Process.

WDYWFY:
The Five Profoundly Simple Steps for Goal Achievement

---

1. Have a Goal

2. Have a Plan

3. Implement the Plan

4. Control Direction

5. Throw off Discouragement

DOUG: ROY GEER AND WDYWFY

My friend and mentor Roy Geer originated the WDYWFY model in the 1960s. Over the last 60 years, thousands of people have used the WDYWFY model to help them define and achieve their most meaningful personal and professional goals.

I had the good fortune of meeting Roy in 1974 when Roy was 47 and I was only 22. That's when Roy shared with me a life-changing insight: Goal achievement is as straightforward as implementing five profoundly simple steps. I soon realized that goal achievement is indeed simple, but definitely not easy.

Roy left this earth in 2017 after a long and well-lived life. His legacy lives on in many ways, including one of his greatest gifts, the WDYWFY model of goal achievement. What better gift to all of us than his insights about using our skills and determination to make the world a better place? Thanks, Roy! Your work lives on in the hearts and achievements of those you taught and who, in turn, share your wisdom with others.

Step 1: Have a Goal

As the alignment model tells us, our goals, whether for personal or professional purposes, come out of the vision we have as moral and values-driven leaders, or in other words, our ideal selves. Goals are mileposts that measure our progress toward that ideal self. As the alignment model also suggests, our vision of our ideal self is aspirational and clear, but not specific. Goals make that vision clearer and connect us to our purpose, that direction we want to chart for our lives. For instance, Eric Larsen and Ryan Waters didn't decide to go to the North Pole for bragging rights; they envisioned helping to change the catastrophic trajectory of global warming. Their vision to do that translated into a specific goal of making an improbable 480-mile trek to the North Pole and filming a documentary to show people the damage caused by climate change. Eric says this about the value of setting goals:

> We set a goal to get to the North Pole. Both of us were focused on that goal. It was the main reason why we were on the Arctic Ocean. Anytime things got rough (which was constantly), we reminded ourselves of the overall goal of our journey. However, we also used a lot of short-term goals to serve as benchmarks of our progress as well as helping to keep us motivated.

QUANTIFIABLE VERSUS STATE OF BEING GOALS

Quantifiable goals are those we generally envision when we think about setting a goal. Eric's goal to ski to the North Pole is an example of a quantifiable goal. Eric would know when he reached his goal because he'd arrive at a location where GPS coordinates would confirm that he was standing on the North Pole. Quantifiable goals answer two questions: *How much?* and *By when?* They are also the most comfortable goals because they allow us to easily track whether or not we are achieving what we hope to accomplish.

State of being goals are qualitative goals that represent our high-level sense of who we would like to be. State of being goals are just what they sound like. They represent a desired state of being. Examples of state of being goals might include "Being a good leader" (now, not sometime in the future) or "Being a great spouse/partner/parent/grandparent/son/daughter" (now, not sometime in the future). State of being goals are worthwhile goals, for obvious reasons, even though we can't quantify them. Fortunately, the key activities we need to perform to achieve a certain state of being *can* be quantified. For instance, sometime after Doug's mom passed away early in 1996 at age 63, Doug realized that he needed to explicitly state that he wanted to be a great son for his dad, who was then 70 years old. Doug decided to define at least two key activities to achieve his goal: (1) Talking with his dad by phone for one hour every Sunday afternoon; (2) Visiting his dad, who lived two and a half hours away at least one weekend per month. In addition, Doug established other key activities related to spending time with his dad, such as on holidays. We quantify key activities for state of being goals just like any other type of goal by answering questions: *What is the activity? When will I do it? How frequently will I do it?* You'll find a more complete list of questions for defining key activities when we discuss step 2 of the WDYWFY Goal Achievement Process, "Have a Plan."

DOUG: STATE OF BEING GOALS

There is a catch when it comes to figuring out whether you've truly accomplished a state of being goal. For instance, even if I quantified the key activities associated with being a great son, I might not know for certain if those activities actually made me a great son. The best resource for confirming that would be my dad. Dad could maybe even tell me what he would suggest my key activities should be. I was fortunate that my dad thought the key activities I did choose were right on target. And over the years, he let me know that he thought I became pretty good at being his son.

REFLECTION: CHOOSING PURPOSEFUL GOALS

Take a few minutes to think about and answer these questions:
Where do you want to take your life or your organization (your goal or goals)?
What would getting there look like?
What would it feel like to achieve those goals?

> As you reflect on these questions, notice what comes up in your mind and heart without judgment. Don't censor yourself by worrying about whether your ideas are realistic. Reflecting on possible goals is only a first step toward creating a more fulfilling life for yourself or improving the lives of others in your family, community, or workplace. You can always fine-tune your ideas as you move through the WDYWFY Goal Achievement Process.

Setting and achieving qualitative goals are essential because they help satisfy a need for meaning and significance in our lives. And because qualitative goals are grounded in our need for a meaningful life, they help us keep working to achieve goals when things don't go well or as planned. That said, even when we believe we want to achieve a goal, the process of getting there is hard. Why? Motivation is a fleeting thing. On a good day, motivation may disappear, and on a bad day, it may never bother to show up. When it comes to goal achievement, it's human nature that most of us don't have an abundance of motivation or self-discipline. In *The Power of Full Engagement,* authors Jim Loehr and Tony Schwartz cite research indicating that the average person spends only about 5 percent of their energy as a result of self-discipline. Even outstanding performers spend only about 15 percent of their energy as a result of self-discipline. Most of what we do is based on habit or routine.[1] Brain science helps explain why. We have neural pathways in our brain that reinforce current or habitual behavior. Pursuing goals requires changing our behavior and establishing new habits, and our brains don't initially have neural pathways to reinforce that new behavior. To reach our goals, we need some powerful reasons to change our behavior, and that's where motivation and self-discipline come into play. We need to use our limited motivation and self-discipline to create goal-achieving habits.

[1] Jim Loehr and Tony Schwartz, *The Power of Full Engagement: Managing Energy, Not Time, Is the Key to High Performance and Personal Renewal* (New York: Free Press, 2003).

MOTIVATION AND GOAL ACHIEVEMENT

We can leverage two types of motivation in changing behavior and achieving goals: intrinsic and extrinsic. When we engage in behavior based on extrinsic motivation, we act in a certain way to earn a reward or avoid punishment. Examples of positive extrinsic motivation in organizational settings include bonuses, awards, and promotions. Most organizations spend a lot of effort trying to create the perfect reward and recognition system. However, there is evidence that such motivational systems work only for a short period. So, when positive rewards fail, organizations may use negative extrinsic motivators such as performance plans, demotions, or the ultimate, being fired (the result of losing the "keep your job contest"). Extrinsic motivators are also common in families, as in the case of parents who "pay" their children for each "A" on their school report cards.

In their article "The Neuroscience of Leadership," David Rock and Jeffrey Schwartz argue that this "carrot-and-stick" approach to motivation has some merit:

> *Many existing models for changing people's behavior are drawn from a field called behaviorism. The field emerged in the 1930s and was led by psychologist B.F. Skinner and advertising executive John B. Watson, building on Ivan Pavlov's famous concept of the conditioned response: Associate the ringing of a bell with food, and a dog can be made to salivate at the sound. The behaviorists generalized this observation to people and established an approach to change that has sometimes been caricatured as: "Lay out the M&Ms." For each person, there is one set of incentives— one combination of candy colors—that makes the best motivator. Present the right incentives, and the desired change will naturally occur. If change doesn't occur, then the mix of M&M colors must be adjusted.[2]*

Though extrinsic motivation can be compelling initially, they tend to lose effectiveness over time.

---

[2]David Rock and Jeffrey Schwartz, "The Neuroscience of Leadership," *Strategy+Business* (May 2006).

CHUCK: EXTRINSIC MOTIVATION FATIGUE

When each of my kids turned 6, they started getting an allowance for doing some weekly chores. They liked it initially. At first, each Saturday morning, they quickly finished their tasks, then ran to me or their mom with their hands out for their allowance. But by the time they got to be 13 or so, they were bored. They stopped caring about their allowance—and they also stopped doing their chores consistently.

Intrinsic motivation, on the other hand, has a lot more staying power when fostering successful goal achievement. Intrinsic motivation is the motivation responsible for fueling behavior driven by internal rewards. In other words, the motivation to engage in certain behavior arises from within the individual because it is naturally satisfying to them. For example, when you consistently engage in activities aligned with your purpose, values, or sense of self, you are tapping into intrinsic motivation. That is why self-reflection and self-discovery are so crucial to the process of setting and pursuing goals. To make progress in achieving goals, or in other words, to develop a new behavior, you need to be aware of what motivates you at the deepest level. Simon Sinek's bestselling book, *Start with Why: How Great Leaders Inspire Others to Take Action*, emphasizes the power of internal motivation. Knowing our "Why"—our purpose or reason for being—clarifies the meaning that inspires our goals and objectives. Because internal motivators such as our purpose spring from our ideal selves, they are far more compelling and sustainable over time than extrinsic motivators.

Although intrinsic motivators are more reliable spurs to goal achievement than extrinsic motivators, not all intrinsic motivators are created equal. Psychologist Jennifer Crocker and colleagues identified the interpersonal and emotional impact of two types of intrinsically motivated goals: self-image goals and compassionate goals. Self-image goals are those we set to boost our status relative to others or to acquire desirable things for ourselves. During a job interview, for example, we may have a goal of being seen as qualified and successful. Activities we engage in during a job selection process might include dressing, speaking, and acting the part of someone we imagine our prospective employer would want to see in a candidate for the job. As necessary and functional as a self-image goal may be in this situation, achieving self-image goals may have a disturbing result. Landing that plum job may expose us to an "arrival fantasy": we thought that getting our dream job would result in our having a wonderful life going forward. When our fantasy job turns out to be not so perfect because no job, in fact, no achieved goal, results in our living happily ever after, we may crash emotionally. As a result, we may feel disconnected from others, perhaps even depressed, because success in achieving a self-image goal is, at its core, a lonely, self-centered accomplishment.

Compassionate goals, on the other hand, help us feel connected to others. That's because compassionate goals, by their very nature, are those we set to serve others. In working toward compassionate goals, we inevitably demonstrate caring behavior. Those we hope to serve can sense that we care about them. In turn, they grace us with appreciation and camaraderie that enhances our feelings of connection to them.

At the risk of being judgmental, it's not a big stretch to assume that compassionate goals are more personally satisfying and have a more significant impact on others' well-being, primarily because they align us with universal principles of responsibility and compassion. That said, self-image goals are not wrong. We need to achieve self-image goals if we want others to be confident in us. The key is to diversify our goals, that is, to create a balance between self-image goals and compassionate goals. Self-image and compassionate goals both have a place in our lives. However, research suggests that weighting the pendulum in the direction of compassionate, other-focused goals will have the most positive impact on our leadership effectiveness and on those we hope to influence. At the same time, focusing primarily on compassionate goals rather than self-image goals will energize us by instilling a greater sense of meaning and purpose in our lives.

EXERCISE: DISCOVER YOUR INTRINSIC MOTIVATORS

To capitalize on the power of intrinsic motivators in your life, take a few minutes to list the reasons why accomplishing the goals you identified during the *reflection* in step 1 (Have a Goal) would contribute to your sense of purpose.

This doesn't mean you can't ever set goals that may seem "selfish." Goal achievement is a rightfully selfish process, provided your goals are aligned with universal principles (integrity, responsibility, compassion, forgiveness) and personal values, (for example, family, happiness, wisdom, service, and health).

SMART Goals

SMART goals describe and quantify goals, so you clearly know when you have accomplished a goal. SMART is an acronym for goals that are **S**pecific, **M**easurable, **A**ttainable, **R**esults-based, and **T**ime-bound.

- *Specific* means that the goal is clearly identified or defined.
- *Measurable* means we can measure the goals to see if we've achieved our objective.
- *Attainable* means we have the ability to achieve our desired goal.
- *Results-based* means the goal has a clearly defined outcome that makes a practical difference to a situation.
- *Time-bound* means we can identify a specific date by which we will achieve the goal.

Let's compare a goal that's not SMART with one that is. "Being a better leader" wouldn't qualify as a SMART goal because it's specific, measurable, result-based or time-bound. It might be attainable, but we can't know for certain because the end state of the goal isn't clear. In contrast, consider this goal: "Increasing my score for the Leading Employees competency on a 360-degree feedback instrument from mid-range to high by the end of 12 months." This goal would meet most SMART criteria, since it is specific, measurable, results-oriented, and time-bound. Determining whether this goal is *attainable*, however, depends on the acid test. As you'll recall, the acid test is the answer to two questions: Can I do what's needed to achieve this result? Am I willing to do what it takes to achieve this result? Before you can answer either question, you need to jump to step 2 in the WYWFY process, "Have a Plan," which focuses on developing a plan to achieve your goal. You need to know what key activities would be required to improve your score for Leading Employees by the end of the next 12 months. For instance, you might need to increase the frequency of delegating essential tasks, empower team members to make more decisions, be more prompt about offering feedback, provide challenging developmental opportunities to employees, and so on. You may be capable of doing all that, but you need to be honest about whether you are willing to make the changes that would lead others to rate you higher in the competency of Leading Employees. Only after you've previewed the plan to improve your ratings, and said yes to the two acid test questions, does your desire to improve your ratings in the area of Leading Employees qualify as a goal. That iterative process of determining whether something you want is really a goal is what makes setting goals harder than you might think. But all that effort pays off: by the time you complete the first step of the WDYWFY process, you are well on your way to successfully reaching your goal.

Step 2: Have a Plan

Now that you have a goal, it's time to focus on the specific actions you need to take to achieve your goal. Self-awareness tools such as reflection, the freeze game, and soliciting feedback can give you a baseline for understanding how you currently behave and how others view you relative to the changes you will likely need to make to achieve your goal. Once you're clear about your current behavior relative to how you'd like to act, you're ready to make a plan to close that gap.

Knowing what behavior needs to be eliminated, reduced, increased, or added is the essence of having a plan. Behaviors that have the greatest impact on successful goal achievement are called *key activities*. In its strictest definition, a key activity is something *I must do*. "I" means that I and no one else is responsible for performing a key activity. "Must" means a key activity is nonoptional, and "Do" means that the key activity is action oriented. If you've done a good job with step 1, deciding on a goal, you already have a preview of key activities. Key activities answer as many of the following questions as possible:

- What is the activity?
- When will I do it?
- How long will I do it when I do it?
- How often will I do it, if more than once?
- With whom will I do it, if with someone other than just myself?

CHUCK: DON'T IGNORE A KEY ACTIVITY

Being healthy has always been important to me, but years ago, I used to think there was only one key activity needed for a healthy life— exercise. But I was deluding myself about everything involved in living a healthy life. I was ignoring the key activity of healthy eating because I didn't particularly like paying attention to what I ate. The importance of a healthy diet finally sank in when my doctor told me that it was the fifth year in a row that my cholesterol level was over 200. I realized then that no matter how many miles I ran or how many weights I lifted, my health markers would not improve unless I started improving my eating habits.

Here is an example of key activities that could be part of a plan to improve your competency in Leading Employees, as measured on a 360-degree feedback instrument.

- Delegate one important task each week to capable team members.
- Conduct monthly one-on-one feedback and coaching sessions with each team member.
- Develop and implement a system for involving team members in decision-making by the end of next month.
- Institute weekly half-hour Zoom "Open Door" sessions to listen to concerns and answer questions.

EXAMPLE: GOAL ACHIEVEMENT PLAN		
My Goal: Ensure that my team meets all performance goals while I am on 12-week maternity leave		
Key Activities "I Must Do":	• Hold a two-hour meeting on Monday at 9:00 a.m. with the team to discuss work plans during my absence. • Have team members rotate responsibility for facilitating weekly team meetings, beginning four months before planned leave. • Copy all team members on routine email from my supervisor (except confidential information). • Delegate all possible activities to appropriate team members beginning two months before planned leave. • Coach team members as needed and at least weekly on new assignments. • Appoint and coach an acting team leader beginning two months before planned leave. Make additional leadership training available every Wednesday and Thursday from 9–10 a.m. beginning immediately. • Communicate team strategy and performance objectives at each team meeting from now until planned leave. • Participate remotely in team meetings every other week while on leave.	
Resources I Need to Perform My Key Activities:	• Find budget to send acting team leader to a leadership development program. • Training by IT in product development performance tracking system for acting team leader. • Upgraded technology devices for periodic work from home.	
People I Need to Support Me and How:	Name	Support I'll request
	Jan, my department head	• Coaching on how to delegate work for an extended absence. • Support to acting team leader.
	Acting team leader	• Call on me when needed, but don't be afraid to make decisions without my input.
Control Direction (Track Progress and Correct Course as Needed):	• Review performance metrics every Friday. • Ask Jan to provide **bi-weekly** assessment on team performance and engagement. • Solicit feedback from acting team leader on performance, successes, and challenges. • Suggest changes to plan based on feedback from Jan, acting team leader, and team members.	
Throw Off Discouragement (How I'll Manage Emotions):	• Meditate twice a day. • Get one more hour of sleep per night. • Recognize that having a new baby is an emotional time, and it's okay to feel the way I feel. • Trust that my team will do a good job when I'm not there. • Take a 15- to 30-minute walk every day.	

Also, think about specific resources—people, equipment, and so on, needed to achieve your key activities. Ask a coach, mentor, or other support person for their help as part of your plan. If they agree, solicit their feedback on your goal's value and ask for suggestions about any changes or additions to your key activities. Entering key activities and any related tasks in your calendar will increase the odds of staying on track with your plan. Also, schedule regular check-ins with your coach, mentor, or other support people to promote accountability and commitment and to help you adapt your plan as needed.

CHUCK: KEY ACTIVITIES

I can't stress enough the importance of knowing your key activities. One of my senior executive clients, Peter, told me how pleased he was that everyone in his organization knew the firm's goals for the year. "For the first time I remember, everyone is clear on our year-end objectives," Peter remarked confidently.

Since it was only June, Peter and his organization still had six months to reach their goals. After a few seconds, I responded. "That's terrific, Peter! Now, how confident are you that each person knows their key activities?"

"I'm not sure." Peter thoughtfully reflected. That prompted him to start reviewing key activities with his direct reports. Later, Peter thanked me for asking that question, adding that they might have missed their year-end targets had he not focused on key activities when he did.

In addition to documenting your goals, tell others about your goal and plan for achieving it. Gail Matthews, a psychologist at Dominican University, conducted a study in which participants were asked to engage in different tasks related to goal achievement. Her research found that the people most successful in reaching their goals were those who wrote down their goals and activity commitments and sent weekly progress reports to a friend.

Our work with thousands of clients confirms Matthews' work. Documenting goals and key activities in writing and enlisting support from others, for instance, a coach, partner, or spouse, dramatically increases the likelihood that you will reach your goals.

Step 3: Implement the Plan

So far, all the work you've done to create purposeful goals and develop a plan to achieve them hasn't changed your life, others' lives, or your organization at all. With step 3, Implement the Plan, the heavy lifting is about to begin.

Trish Moll sat in a cold, overly air-conditioned training room early on a Saturday morning in Chicago. Trish was determined to achieve the success she expected since she began her career as a financial advisor a few years earlier. Barely able to cover her monthly expenses, Trish had signed up for the "Sweat Hogs" training program with the last $600 she had. Trish, now a senior executive with Ameriprise Financial, reflected on this experience:

> *Every Saturday morning, we met, and it was about 15 of us all focusing on what we had to do to bring on one new client each week. Our leader had us start each session by singing a song about our weekly goal. At first, it felt silly, and I was skeptical about the approach. But I had tried everything else and was failing. Once I narrowed my goal and committed to what I had to do each week, things started moving in a positive direction. Within the year, I doubled my production and income, all because the group focused on the micro-goal of acquiring one new client each week.*

Trish's approach of working on "micro-goals" mirrors the process James Clear recommends in his best-selling book, *Atomic Habits*. Clear suggests that instead of trying to work twice as hard in any given time frame, we focus on improving by 1 percent each day. Most of us can't work twice as hard, so we give up. Clear advocates making good habits easier. In this case, good habits are those key activities that will help us achieve our goals. As Clear says, "Ultimately, your habits matter because they help you become the type of person you wish to be. They are the channel through which you develop your deepest beliefs about yourself. Quite literally, you become your habits."[3]

[3]James Clear, *Atomic Habits: An Easy & Proven Way to Build Good Habits & Break Bad Ones* (New York: Avery, 2018).

Step 4: Controlling Direction

Controlling direction is about tracking progress and redirecting as needed. We rarely implement a goal achievement plan that doesn't require change. "Control direction" is a critical WDYWFY step because it allows us to keep score and adjust as needed. Consider this example: if an airplane takes off from New York for Los Angeles, it is off course 97 percent of the time. Air traffic controllers track where the plane is and provide input that calls for frequent directional and altitude changes, often to provide minimum separation from other aircraft or to accommodate weather systems. The plane takes off and lands in the right places, but without keeping score and redirecting, it might end up in Alaska instead of Los Angeles.

Andy Wallace, CEO of OneWall Communities, understands the importance of controlling direction. On a cold, snowy afternoon in early 2012, Andy and his two business partners were holed up in a one-bedroom flat on the upper east side of New York City, faced with a serious threat to their business. For the past four years, they had been focusing on building a real estate firm that managed a portfolio of properties serving the senior and student housing markets in the Northeastern United States. Along with other real estate firms, they had anticipated opportunities that the Silver Wave (retiring baby boomers) and increasing college enrollments would be creating in assisted senior and student living. They had been successful at raising money to acquire smaller multi-unit housing properties on the East Coast, but market conditions were changing. Larger, well-capitalized real estate firms were starting to compete in senior and student housing spaces, driving up prices and borrowing costs, squeezing OneWall's ability to be profitable. Andy and his partners came to a harsh realization that snowy day: They couldn't compete with the big guys. They had to shift their business's direction to survive.

Andy's partner Nate had begun to formulate a change in strategy. Rental housing in or adjacent to major cities on the Eastern Seaboard had become unaffordable for many workers, resulting in painfully long commutes from outlying areas. Nate proposed that they focus on offering affordable workforce housing in apartment communities farther from city centers but close to mass transit lines providing access to those metropolitan areas. The properties they targeted to purchase were less expensive, financing was cheaper, and competition to acquire them was not as great.

By shifting direction to serve a previously overlooked market, OneWall stayed true to its ultimate goal—establishing a successful regional real estate firm. Ten years later, the company has more than 100 employees and owns properties with 3,500 units in New Jersey, Maryland, and Pennsylvania. Beyond their financial success, Andy and his partners are proud that their strategic redirection has allowed them to create great, affordable apartment homes with attractive lifestyle amenities for thousands of working families.

As Andy's experience illustrates, the purpose of planning is not to come up with the perfect plan but to chart a course so that as events unfold, you can make needed adjustments while staying clear about the overall direction of your goal.

Step 5: Throw Off Discouragement

Achieving new goals is often painful. Why? Because when you set out to achieve goals, you often need to do things you haven't done before. That involves doing more, doing it more effectively, or doing something altogether new. Such changes can create physical or emotional pain because you're stretching yourself. When you do new things, you're likely to make more mistakes than in the past, which never feels good. To stay the course and realize the impact of your efforts, you need to "throw off" the inevitable discouragement that comes with chasing a new goal. Take Eric Larsen's reflection on his expedition to the North Pole.

> *Finally, about the 40th day, we realized we were never going to catch a break, and if we didn't change our pace, we wouldn't meet our pickup date at the North Pole on time.*
>
> *Once we adjusted our mindset and reset our pace, our confidence and motivation improved. We started dealing realistically with the situation at hand. Instead of wishing it was different, we accepted reality and made the necessary changes.*

Throwing off discouragement requires tapping into our resilience and getting support from others. We call people who have a vested interest in helping you achieve your goals "enablers." In the world of addiction, an "enabler" is a term used to describe someone who helps feed our addiction and is therefore considered a negative influence. When it comes to achieving purposeful goals, we use the term "enabler" in the positive sense as someone who not only cares about whether or not we reach a particular goal, but also is someone who wants to see us live our best selves. You need those positive enablers to help you bounce back when you get off track, when your resilience is low or when you don't feel motivated to perform key activities. Enablers can be family members, close friends, or business colleagues. To help you, enablers need to know your goal and be familiar with its key activities. In Eric Larsen's 480-mile journey to the North Pole he and his expedition partner, Ryan, were enablers for each other, as were their family members and support teams back home.

LEADING OTHERS TO ACHIEVE PURPOSEFUL GOALS

WDYWFY helps you achieve your own goals. But it can do so much more. One of the greatest gifts a leader can give to a follower—employee, child, athlete, junior colleague—is to teach WDWFY to them and offer coaching and support as they work on achieving their most-valued goals. The WDYWFY Goal Achievement Model assumes that a leader working with followers, clients, or colleagues prioritizes what others—*not* the leader—want for themselves. In many organizations, goal achievement is all about getting members to adopt goals you and your fellow leaders care about, then executing on your preapproved plan to accomplish those goals. That approach is a recipe for underperformance. Your followers don't necessarily care about the same goals that you do. They may "go along" with goals you encourage them to adopt. But to influence followers, you need a good match between what your followers want for themselves and what you, as their leader, want them to want.

When leaders "weaponize" WDYWFY, it becomes a stumbling block to successful goal achievement by followers. WDYWFY is meant to help you and your followers pursue their passions and give their best efforts to animate your shared purpose and goals. However, some leaders misuse WDYWFY to punish people for failing to accomplish goals that the organization cares about, even if there is no connection between a follower's goals and what the organization wants to achieve. One way of weaponizing WDYWFY is to include the process in an organization's performance management system. Performance management in organizations is explicitly designed to set and track goal achievement in areas that support an organization's strategy or key performance indicators. WDYWFY, on the other hand, includes goals that spring from an individual's hopes and dreams. Integrating WDYWFY into a performance management system virtually guarantees that individual wants are ignored and pursuit of them may even be used as an excuse for dismissal.

Helping followers set appropriately challenging goals is not always easy. Coaching colleagues, employees, team members, family members, and anyone you seek to influence begins with your genuine belief that most people want to be better at doing whatever they do than their current performance indicates. Most of us want to be the best we can be, whether in our careers, family life, friendships, or community contributions. If you've hired the right people, they will want more success than the organization needs them to want. So, as a leader, you need to discern whether the goals that followers share with you rise to the level of performance that you believe they can achieve and that they, in their heart of hearts, want to achieve. When authors Doug and Chuck were senior managers in the financial services industry, they often ran into direct reports who pulled their punches when it came to the goal-setting part of the WDYWFY process. Despite Doug's and Chuck's best efforts to communicate the spirit of WDYWFY, which is all about leveraging people's deepest desires, some employees proposed goals that fell far short of what Doug and Chuck knew they could and ideally would want to accomplish. When Doug had a conversation with someone who was, in his view, lowballing a sales performance goal, Doug would typically comment, "If you achieve your goal, we fail." Such feedback was not meant to be coercive. It was intended both as a wake-up call and a vote of confidence in that employee's ability to perform at a level that would be in the business's best interests and at the same time, personally gratifying to that employee.

COACHING OTHERS ON SETTING GOALS

Start by asking people questions along these lines:

- *How good do you want to be here [in your organization or team]?*
- *Where would you like to take your expertise, career, or positive impact in this context?*
- *Why are those goals important to you?*

Many people are not used to answering questions like those just listed and, at first, may give vague, fuzzy answers, not because they're not important to them but because they've never been asked before.

Continue asking these questions, even if you don't at first get satisfying answers. Over time, people's answers and their commitment to those aspirations will become clearer and more compelling to them.

Instead of holding people accountable to *your goals*, focus on becoming a resource to help others accomplish *their goals*.

The sweet spot for empowerment happens when the goals your people want for themselves are aligned with your team's mission.

As regional vice president, Chuck had regularly spent time having WDYWFY conversations with each of his direct reports and expected them to do the same with those they led. He always wanted to know what his team wanted for themselves because he understood it was part of his responsibility as their leader to help them get what they wanted, both in their careers and their lives outside of work. Because of this practice, when Chuck was preparing to leave his job temporarily to attend an executive management program, he already had a head start in using his own development opportunity to help create meaningful development opportunities for others on his team.

Let's assume that you've helped someone move through the early steps in setting a goal and developing a plan to achieve that goal. Your role as a coach continues as that person embarks on implementing a goal. If you're lucky, the person you're leading through the goal achievement process is determined to succeed and won't let any obstacles get in their way. Frequently, though, those you coach, despite their good intentions, may have trouble when it comes to following through on implementing their goal. To help those you lead to move forward on their goals, you may have to apply some "tough love," as illustrated in Doug's first-person advice in the following box.

DOUG: COACHING OTHERS TO ACHIEVE THEIR GOALS

When doing a check-in with someone on goal achievement, whether with a team member or a coaching client, the process is straightforward. Imagine that you are working on a goal, and I am the leader supporting you in accomplishing your goal. I begin by asking one or two questions.

Question 1: *Are you on target to achieve your goal?*

There are only two possible answers to this question, *yes* or *no*.
If you say yes, I congratulate you and encourage you to keep doing what you're doing.
If you say no, I will ask you another question:

Question 2: *Are you not on target because you are executing the plan and it's not working, or are you not on target because you are not executing the plan?*

If you admit *I am not executing the plan*, I say (humorously but not jokingly) *Do you need more data?* Most likely, you are confused by my question, furrow your brow, and say *What?*
I then respond: *You have demonstrated so far that not working the plan doesn't work. Not working the plan isn't helping you achieve your goal. Do you want to try not working the plan a little bit longer to see if it starts to work, or would you rather try executing the plan?*
If, on the other hand, you say *I am executing the plan, and it's not working,* then we jump to step 4 of WDYWFY, which is "Control Direction." That's because the plan we thought would work is not working. If executing the plan isn't working, we have to change the plan or change the goal.
I'll also encourage you to avoid becoming frustrated because most goal-achievement plans are not perfect. Perfect execution of an imperfect plan won't work because the plan wasn't perfect. The execution of an imperfect plan will not allow us to reach the goal. Almost every plan requires frequent course correction.

•••

Setting and achieving purposeful goals is undoubtedly one of the keys to leadership intelligence. Like all eight leadership essentials, goal achievement is a team sport. Just as Eric Larsen and Ryan Waters needed each other to reach the North Pole, we need others, both those we lead and those we follow, to help us reach our goals. Andy Wallace needed his business partners to open the door to significant business success. Trish Moll needed the Sweat Hogs group to help her gain new clients. We're confident you'll achieve success in reaching your goals if you follow the WDYWFY Goal Achievement process in your leadership roles and overall life. Finally, as a leader, don't forget to "pay it forward" by finding ways to help others you care about achieve their goals.

CHAPTER TEN

Empower Others

By January 1997, coauthor Chuck was a successful regional vice president for American Express Financial Advisors (now Ameriprise Financial). Because of his stellar performance, consistently in the top 5 percent of his peers, Chuck's leaders decided to accelerate his development by enrolling him in an intensive four-month program at Harvard Business School's prestigious Advanced Management Program, held on the school's campus in Cambridge, Massachusetts. There was a catch. To attend, Chuck had to give up his leadership of the region while attending the program. However, the company didn't have the bandwidth to name an interim regional vice president in his absence. So, Chuck needed to figure out how to keep the region humming while he was away. It didn't take long for Chuck to figure out that his absence was both a challenge for him to manage and an opportunity to support the growth of the regional team he led. Later, Chuck would realize that some of his most important leadership lessons began well before he set foot on the Harvard Business School (HBS) campus.

Chuck had nine months until D-day, the start of his HBS program. He pulled the team together to announce he would be attending the HBS program. Chuck painted an optimistic and realistic picture for his team: this, he emphasized, was a golden opportunity for them to develop and grow since he would need them to take on additional responsibility while he was gone. Since Chuck had routinely made time to understand each high-potential team member's goals, he had a pretty good idea about which areas they wanted to strengthen. Chuck also paid attention to team members already demonstrating highly successful results in their current positions. From this analysis, Chuck focused on a small group of people he could empower to act with autonomy and effectiveness in his absence.

For the next nine months, Chuck worked closely with his group of high potentials. During this time, Chuck prioritized mentoring, giving feedback, clarifying expectations, and answering questions so that each person would feel confident performing their portion of the regional vice president position successfully while Chuck was at Harvard.

As Chuck boarded his plane to Boston in early September, he felt relieved, confident that the region was in good hands and his team was fully prepared to lead effectively in his place. While Chuck was attending the Harvard program, his team performed so well that when he returned, Chuck had a dilemma: How could he now assume his former role without rolling back the opportunities he had created for the team only four months earlier? The answer was deceptively simple: Chuck decided not to reassume his former role. Fortunately, soon after Chuck returned, an opportunity opened up for him to head up a larger region. And the people he had groomed so carefully to lead while he was at Harvard were all promoted.

WHAT IS EMPOWERMENT?

Chuck's story is a case study about empowerment and its wide-ranging benefits. Empowerment means sharing power with others as much as possible, while considering where they are in their development. The essence of empowerment is that when team members are empowered, they are encouraged to act with authority, make decisions, and perform various acts consistent with their competence and motivation.

In their seminal work on situational leadership, noted leadership experts and authors Ken Blanchard and Paul Hersey emphasize the importance of tailoring one's leadership approach both to the ability level and motivation level of individual followers. On any given team, people vary in the strength of their skills and their desire to perform at a high level. Some people are highly skilled but lack the motivation to do their work. Others may be eager to serve but lack the skills to succeed. If people lack the skills or motivation to succeed, your well-meaning efforts to be an empowering leader will backfire. That's why it is essential, as Chuck did in the months before his departure for the Harvard program, to assess each follower's skills and interests in the context of the leadership needs of your team and to provide any coaching needed to ensure that the people you empower are up to the challenge.

EMPOWERMENT AND DELEGATION ARE DIFFERENT

Safra slowly closed her office door, fearing that she'd made one of the biggest mistakes of her young leadership career. After five years of continued success in an administrative position, Safra, now in her early 30s, was tapped to open a new location of her company in a major U.S. city. Safra was a "go-getter," a "figure it out on the fly" type who got results. She was resourceful, creative, and not afraid to push the limits. Now she was being evaluated in a position where she had to work through others and be more deliberate in getting results. A few months ago, Safra had received feedback that she was too much of a "micromanager" and didn't give people the latitude they sought to make day-to-day decisions about some of the tasks for which they were ultimately held accountable. To respond to that feedback, Safra handed off one of the most important projects for her growing business to several key people, unfortunately without considering their readiness. After four months of waiting patiently, Safra finally called a meeting with the team to get a status update. In total disarray and with little to show for their efforts, the team had tried desperately to pull itself together and present its progress. However, it was clear that Safra's team had failed to rise to the occasion. Safra was in shock as she sat in her office after the meeting. "What do we do now?" Safra asked herself.

Finishing this project on time was critical to the success of her office and her leadership reputation. As she sat staring at the ceiling, Safra wondered what it would take to dig herself and her team out of this hole.

How did Safra come to mismanage her team? As a new leader, Safra read about "empowerment" in the latest management journals. She was intrigued by the idea of empowerment since research showed it was often associated with stronger job performance, greater job satisfaction, and higher employee engagement. Sadly, though Safra had good intentions, she confused "empowerment" with "delegation."

What is the difference between "empowerment" and "delegation?" Usually, there is an overlap between the two, and that overlap can be confusing. When you delegate, you assign a particular task or tasks, usually routine responsibilities, to someone you expect will be able to complete them without further direction. Empowerment is both more and less than delegation. When you empower someone, you may or may not delegate full authority to someone to complete a task. But in every case, empowering someone means you give that person overall autonomy to make decisions relevant to their role. Empowerment differs from delegation in that empowered team members understand the vision and mission of the team or organization and make autonomous decisions aligned with the team's vision and mission. When you empower someone, you don't assume that the empowered person can operate completely on their own. As an empowering leader, you provide coaching and resources that enable empowered team members to perform at their best.

THE COST OF EMPOWERMENT MISSTEPS

Years ago, we worked with a very successful bank in the United States that routinely recruited top executives from its competitors. Our client mistakenly believed such talented hires would be able to hit the ground running without much, if any, direction. So, they left newly hired executives to their own devices, trusting they'd "figure it out." Our clients didn't understand that much of their new executives' previous success had been organization specific. Their star hires' accomplishments had been achieved in the context of their prior organization and with the help of their former team members. The bank's new executives didn't have any magical skills to help them get things done in their new organizational context. Nine to twelve months after they were hired, many of these executives would be struggling and not meeting expectations. At that point, senior leadership would step in and have a performance management conversation with the floundering executive, putting them on notice that "this has got to get better or else." Another six to nine months would pass, usually with little or no improvement in results, leaving human resources no choice but to put the new leader into the final phase of the performance planning process. To save their supposedly brilliant hire, their leader would finally step in and "micromanage" the floundering executive, but it was often too late. Many of these new hires had dug themselves into holes so deep that they ultimately were let go. Given the time and expense of hiring executives at that level, this was a tremendous cost to the organization and a hit to morale when someone at that level left.

As performance consultants, we helped the bank's senior leaders see that, while a newly hired executive was talented and had tremendous industry experience, they lacked institutional knowledge about how to be effective in their new organization. Too often, organizations confuse talent and experience with skills and knowledge. Skills and knowledge need to be developed in a certain context in order to achieve success in a particular organizational context. For example, take National Basketball Association (NBA) Hall of Famer Michael Jordan's mid-career decision to move from the NBA to Major League Baseball. Clearly, Jordan was talented and had tremendous success in the NBA. But in the wildly different context of professional baseball, he lacked the skills and knowledge to perform at the level he needed to succeed in the new sport.

To prevent our bank client from continuing its expensive and unproductive hiring practices, we recommended that they provide extensive support, structure, and direction during each new executive's first 12 months. This support included regular one-on-ones with their leaders, joint calls with peers or leaders to observe how experienced executives handled specific interactions, and mentoring from veteran colleagues. Within a year of investing in developing newly hired executives, the bank saw dramatic improvements in new executive performance and retention.

EMPOWERING OTHERS IS MOTIVATING

Empowerment is a powerful leadership tool because it taps into the internal motivators of the people you want to influence. In the *Harvard Business Review* classic, "One More Time: How Do You Motivate Employees?"[1] distinguished professor of management Frederick Herzberg points out that challenging, interesting work and

---

[1] Frederick Herzberg, "One More Time: How Do You Motivate Employees?" *Harvard Business Review* (September–October 1987).

opportunities to achieve and take on more responsibility motivate employees to give their best efforts and improve their performance. Empowerment works precisely because it activates people's desire to do challenging work and excel at what they do.

Our work with hundreds of firms, large and small, confirms what we've already shared in the context of goal achievement: most people want to be better at their job than their organization needs them to be. Most want to excel and be above average. They may not all want to be a CEO someday, but most people want to contribute and know that what they do is making a difference. Our human desire to perform at our best applies far beyond the office walls. Most of us want to be better family members, community members, team members, and overall human beings. Empowering others is the most effective way to optimize others' ability to excel in whatever they do or hope to be.

CLARIFY EXPECTATIONS

While empowerment involves giving others as much autonomy as possible, successful empowerment happens within a framework. Empowered people need to understand expectations. They need to understand and buy into the overarching goals of your organization or team. They need to know how far they can go. Over the last two decades, Southwest Airlines has racked up countless awards for customer satisfaction. Employees routinely give the company high marks for being a good place to work. The airline's stellar reputation is in large measure a result of its culture of empowerment. Ginger Hardage, former senior vice president of culture and communications for Southwest Airlines, describes its culture as "freedom within a framework." Hardage expanded on this idea in an episode of the podcast *The 80 Percent.*

> You have this basic framework: they [Southwest frontline employees] need to get your flight out on time; they need to check you all in. They have certain things that are part of the framework, but what they can do outside of that framework that gives them total freedom to use their personality. So, I'd encourage listeners to think about that in their own organizations. You've got certain jobs that have a framework, but don't create such a strict framework. . . . And that's what leads to great employee

engagement and also longevity with the company. If people are feeling like they're able to be themselves and bring their total selves to work every day, that makes such a difference.[2]

Another example of freedom within a framework comes from Kim Sharan's experience during the spinoff of Ameriprise Financial from American Express in 2005. Kim, at the time chief marketing officer, was the lead executive driving the transition to a new brand. As she recalls:

Once we defined the end state—ensuring that the market acknowledged the company as a completely new entity—all the other pieces fell into place. CEO Jim [Cracchiolo's] leadership team took on their roles in a remarkable way. Everyone knew what they needed to do and that it was important to rely on one another. We had to adapt quickly. There would be no turning back or recycling questions about our why. Now we had to solve the problems involved in defining the what and the how. Empowering our teams to do that in a bold way was something that worked very well. Empowering them meant not giving them the answer, but instead, the permission to think big and broadly. We had set the vision of where we wanted to go, much like giving them the big broad-brush strokes of a painting. But then we challenged the team to fill in the canvas with possibilities.

Before Chuck left for the Harvard program, he also established freedom within a framework for the leaders who would support the region's advisors in his absence. He identified goals for each area of responsibility. When it came to recruiting, for example, Chuck defined a hiring goal and what basic activities were needed to hit that goal. Apart from the high-level expectations Chuck set, he encouraged his team to use their individual skills and strengths to deal with the challenges of their new roles.

REFLECTION: FREEDOM WITHIN A FRAMEWORK

What would "freedom within a framework" look like within your organization or team?
What performance expectations and boundaries are non-negotiable?
In what ways can you encourage individuality and independent decision-making?

---

[2]"Employee Communication Solution to Engage the Frontline," n.d., Axonify, Accessed December 13, 2022, https://axonify.com/podcast/building-a-culture-of-frontline-empowerment-at-southwest-airlines/.

PROVIDE RESOURCES

Effective empowerment isn't just about freedom within boundaries. It's also important to consider tools and resources that people need to be truly empowered. For instance, Southwest Airlines gate attendants can decide to provide snacks and drinks for passengers awaiting delayed flights, with no higher-level approval needed. When Chuck was preparing to be away from his job, he spent time thinking about additional resources that might be necessary for his leaders to achieve success when adding new responsibilities to their existing roles. In some cases, that led to hiring additional administrative support or increasing some leaders' travel budgets.

EMPOWERMENT DONE RIGHT

As Chuck's story and our bank client's hiring issues demonstrate, empowerment must be done carefully. Done poorly, empowerment can be traumatizing, erode trust, and set the organization back, not just in terms of results but, most importantly, by discouraging others from stepping forward to take on future opportunities. Sloppy empowerment, such as leaving decision-making to followers without the proper guidance and support, is likely to demoralize followers and impair their performance.

However, when you provide the right amount of coaching and resources, followers become highly effective ambassadors and enablers of your mission. That's because they see that you care about giving them the tools to be effective and that, in turn, leads them to trust that you care about them and their professional development. Empowerment done well can be a huge step forward in an organization's growth, strengthening its people's skills and motivation and contributing to outstanding results. Empowerment is as much an opportunity for the leader to grow by letting go as it is for individuals and teams to grow by taking on new challenges.

REFLECTION: EMPOWERMENT

Where do you spot opportunities to empower others to stretch themselves and grow in your organization?

What resources do team members need from you to feel empowered in their roles?

THE GIFT THAT KEEPS ON GIVING

As we've seen, empowerment has many benefits. When you empower your team members, they are happier, perform at higher levels, and are more likely to remain with you and your team. When team members are empowered, customers, clients, and other stakeholders are more satisfied and loyal, leading to stronger results in the ways that matter most to your organization.

There's yet another benefit to empowerment. When you empower your immediate followers, you encourage them to empower their own followers. In Chuck's case, the opportunity he offered his team to step up while he was away also created development opportunities for more junior team members. Chuck met with each of his leaders to identify high-potential leaders on their own teams and help them map out a game plan for "second-level" development. What began as Chuck's individual opportunity to attend Harvard cascaded into opportunities for leadership development across his organization.

As a leader, one of your most vital points of influence is your willingness to share power with others. That means trusting those you lead to make decisions aligned with your organization's mission and values. Empowering others is essential because as a leader, you can't go it alone. The only way to get the best results for your organization is to help everyone operate at their full power. Ultimately, that's what empowerment is all about.

PART THREE

CLIMBING LEADERSHIP MOUNTAINS

CHAPTER ELEVEN

Confront Crises

On the morning of September 11, 2001, Ken Chenault, CEO of American Express, faced the shocking destruction of the World Trade Center and the damage to American Express's corporate headquarters in New York City, chronicled in Chapter 1. Meanwhile, Chuck was beginning a typical workday 1,000 miles to the west. He had stopped by a local Detroit bakery to pick up breakfast before heading to the airport on his way to an American Express leadership conference in Florida. As Chuck got to the bakery door, a customer tightly gripping his coffee cup held the door open for Chuck.

"Have you seen what just happened?" the man asked, shock on his face and agitation in his voice.

"No," Chuck responded, taken aback by how emotional the man seemed. Chuck also momentarily wondered, "Why is this stranger talking to me?"

"An airplane just hit the World Trade Center," the distraught fellow customer said.

Stunned and trying to process the meaning of what he had just heard, Chuck looked up at the TV on the shop wall to see the replay of a full-sized jetliner flying into a massive high-rise building. Then Chuck understood the magnitude of what his fellow customer had just described. As Chuck would soon discover, in addition to the complete devastation of the World Trade Center's North and South Towers, his company's headquarters, adjacent to the World Trade Center, was severely damaged by the most destructive terrorist attack in U.S. history. Soon, Chuck would also learn that 11 of his American Express colleagues lost their lives in the attack on the World Trade Center.

There would be no trip to Florida that day since all domestic flights were canceled, quickly and indefinitely. The world had changed instantly, not just for Chuck, but also for the 500 financial advisors and staff he led as group vice president of sales for one of the American Express Financial Advisors' most successful regions.

Chuck's organization managed over $5 billion in assets for more than 100,000 clients in Southeast Michigan. With most of the world turned upside down and the stock markets closed for the next four days, Chuck knew that his people and their clients would be paralyzed with fear and hungry for direction. Chuck immediately set up daily meetings with his 30-person management team and conference calls for all his advisors and staff. His plan was simple: tell people what he knew and when he knew it and give them a chance to share their concerns and ask questions. Each day at 7:45 a.m. eastern standard time, Chuck would open the phone lines. He'd spend about 15 minutes giving a status update and then take questions and comments until everyone on the call had a chance to be heard. Depending on the day's events, some calls would last just 20 minutes, while others could take over an hour. Chuck and his managers would follow up on any open items from those calls immediately so that they could provide direction and resolve issues for their people. Chuck and his team knew that how they responded and provided leadership during this crisis could be a differentiator affecting their investors' decision-making and their employees' willingness to stay. Jumping ship financially in the middle of a crisis with the stock market in free fall could lock in horrific losses for their clients. Chuck and his team also realized they needed to model the robust communication they wanted their 300 financial advisors to provide to their clients. Those calls and meetings continued five days a week for over a month until everyone agreed the post-9/11 situation had become more stable. That intense communication positioned the region's advisors to be a calming influence on their clients and appropriately guide their financial decision-making.

It's no coincidence that so many of the leadership stories in this book happen in the context of crises. Take Ken Chenault's masterful leadership as CEO of American Express in the aftermath of the 9/11 terrorist attack on the World Trade Center, which clearly influenced Chuck's response to the financial crisis that followed. Or Ameriprise CEO Jim Cracchiolo's decision to decline government funding during the 2007–2009 "Great Recession." How about mountaineer Chris Klinke, who saved lives on one of his Everest teams' ascents by holding firm to the leadership essentials he had learned and practiced countless times? Recall other inspiring organizational leaders, such as Terry Rasmussen, president and CEO of Thrivent, and a Fortune 100 Company senior leader. Tami Pinchiaroli, a Fortune 100 Company senior leader. Each made quick, life-preserving decisions to protect their employees, preserve morale, and support productivity in early 2020 when the coronavirus pandemic abruptly transformed their workplaces into potential deathtraps.

All leaders at some point face crises that call them to perform at their best under the worst of circumstances. As crises escalate on the world stage—terrorism, climate change, economic disruptions, pandemics—crisis leadership has emerged as a critical knowledge area for leaders everywhere. But, really, how specialized are crisis leadership competencies? We believe that the most critical skills a crisis leader needs are not much different from the skills a leader needs to excel every day. In fact, the very idea of a normal, steady-state leadership environment may be a myth. Organizational life and leadership are full of crises. Crisis itself has become routine. How many days does a leader get when things are calm and trouble-free? Instead, situations like these are commonplace:

An important customer is dissatisfied.

A key team member decides to work elsewhere.

An unexpected revenue shortfall occurs.

A supply chain is disrupted.

A project falls seriously behind schedule.

A global crisis threatens your operations.

Noted leadership theorist Peter B. Vaill coined the metaphor "permanent white water" to describe the environment in which situations such as these arise. As Vaill explains, ". . .these whitewater events are novel, they're surprising, they don't fit into neat categories, they force themselves on your attention, and they will always arrive in some form or another."[1]

Vaill's description of whitewater events neatly captures the nature and pervasiveness of crises. Whatever you call them, these days, crises are hard-wired into your life as a leader. The recent explosion of literature and educational programs about crisis management might lead you to believe that effective crisis management requires specialized skills. We think that's largely a myth. Do an online search of crisis leadership, and you're likely to find that the skills cited most often as crucial are oddly familiar. Take, for instance, leadership expert Daniel Goleman's short list of crisis leadership skills: self-awareness, self-control, social awareness, and relationship management.[2] While successful crisis leadership may sometimes require unique capabilities, such capabilities are outweighed by the importance of mastering the eight leadership essentials at the heart of this book. If you practice the eight essentials daily, you'll be ready to lead effectively when the next crisis inevitably arises. How then, can you use the leadership essentials to lead effectively during crises? Here are a few examples:

SELF-AWARENESS

As the leadership logic chain demonstrates, self-awareness is the foundation of wise decision-making. In the case of crisis leadership, self-awareness is the first crucial step in responding to a crisis. During a crisis, everyone, including you as a leader, is under stress. You need self-awareness to recognize exactly what you are feeling and take steps to manage your own inevitable stress. Managing your stress is crucial, and not just because it will improve the quality of your individual decisions under duress. Self-management and self-control will free you to support others around you who are also experiencing stress because of the crisis situation.

During crises, it's common for you and your team to experience highly charged emotional responses, such as self-pity, guilt, or blaming

[1] Peter B. Vaill, *Learning as a Way of Being: Strategies for Survival in a World of Permanent White Water* (San Francisco, CA: Jossey-Bass, 1996), p. 14.
[2] Korn Ferry, "4 Leadership Skills for Crisis Management: Daniel Goleman Shows How Having a Strong Emotional Intelligence Can Help Navigate Difficult Situations," https://www.kornferry.com/insights/this-week-in-leadership/leadership-skills-for-crisis-management.

others. To avoid getting stuck in unproductive emotions, remind your-self and those around you that many of the most devastating crises you'll face are not of your making. Even if you or your team might be partly responsible, the autopsy can wait.

To access self-awareness during a crisis, however, you need to "get ahead of the crisis" by regularly practicing self-awareness tools. As our colleague, sports psychologist Rick Aberman says, "If the first time a pitcher uses the freeze game to calm down is during the bottom of the ninth inning, it's too late." Similarly, it would help if you practiced self-awareness thousands of times so when a crisis erupts, self-awareness comes more easily.

INTEGRITY AND RESPONSIBILITY

When it comes to crisis leadership, the principles of integrity and responsibility loom large. A crisis leader needs to keep two aspects of integrity top of mind. First is the need to tell the truth. As you've seen earlier, one way of framing telling the truth is to think of it as *accurately defining reality*. For example, when Hurricane Katrina approached the Louisiana coastline in September 2005, government leaders' denial of the danger of the Level 5 storm left the region unprepared for its impact, resulting in catastrophic loss of life and property.

Failure to accurately define reality can arise for many reasons: a sense that it's too much work, a desire to avoid conflict, a preference for cutting corners, and perceptions of insufficient resources or time con-straints. In contrast to such excuses, influential leaders value and expect an undying commitment to reality in their organizations. This com-mitment to integrity and defining reality, no matter the situation, out-come, or consequence, begins with a search for the unvarnished facts of each case. Effective crisis leaders collect data and insist on assessing reality accurately. Defining reality accurately includes establishing a culture of organizational transparency in which people feel encouraged and supported to bring up issues, challenges, or mistakes. Promoting a culture of transparency in an organization begins with building high levels of trust where people feel comfortable speaking the truth. As Stephen M.R. Covey emphasizes in *The Speed of Trust*,[3] "Trust always

---

[3] Stephen M.R. Covey, *The Speed of Trust: The One Thing that Changes Everything* (New York: Simon & Schuster, 2006).

affects two outcomes—speed and cost. When trust goes down, speed will go down and costs will go up. When trust goes up, speed will also go up and costs will go down."

While that's true every day, trust is even more crucial during crises. It needs to move freely everywhere in an organization, so people feel they have the support and information they need to deal with extremely difficult circumstances.

During a crisis, it's critical to avoid either excessive optimism or catastrophic thinking—both of which are unproductive extremes. As a leader, you need to call on self-awareness to prevent denial. You can't afford to pretend that things are not as bad as they seem or that if you ignore the situation, it will go away on its own. Never encourage your followers or other stakeholders to minimize the seriousness of the crisis you are all facing. On the other hand, make sure you aren't exaggerating the severity of the crisis. Don't be an organizational hypochondriac. Occasionally, insecure leaders characterize a problem as a major crisis, hoping that when they solve the hyped-up problem, they'll get extra credit for their intervention. That rarely works, but it does add to stress in those with whom they work. In short, be honest with yourself and others affected by the crisis. Communicate so everyone knows the answers to these questions:

- What is really going on? What are the consequences of a failure to resolve the crisis in a given time frame?
- What needs to be done to minimize the negative impact of the crisis situation?
- What opportunities might be hidden in this difficult situation?

A second major aspect of the integrity principle as it applies to crises is the need to maintain your alignment with the integrity principle (and, therefore, all the principles) throughout a crisis. A crisis is not an excuse to take moral shortcuts. Whether you're having one of those rare easy days as a leader or facing a potentially catastrophic situation, acting in concert with principles and values is equally important. When protecting employees during the coronavirus pandemic, companies differed significantly in their actions. An analysis of corporate decisions about sizing their workforces in the face of business declines during 2020 revealed that a company's bottom line was not the deciding factor regarding layoffs. Many companies with the deepest pockets slashed their workforces to maximize profitability. In contrast, other companies with far less in the bank did all they could to keep their employees on the payroll. In the view of researchers, these choices were a function of values such as integrity and responsibility. One of the most disturbing examples of prioritizing corporate finances above all else was when mortgage company Better.com CEO, Vishal Garg, abruptly fired 900 employees (via Zoom) a scant two weeks after the company received an early $750 million cash infusion from venture capital partners.

Fortunately, there are also many positive role models for staying true to integrity and responsibility during crises. As we noted in Chapter 5, one of the best examples of holding to the principles of integrity and responsibility was Ameriprise Financial's actions during the global financial crisis. Though it might not have been unethical to accept U.S. government TARP funds then, the company's senior leaders set a higher bar for integrity. Ameriprise had a strong balance sheet and didn't need the money, so they decided not to take it. They also stayed true to the principle of responsibility when they continued their commitment to ensure that each share of their money market funds would continue to be equal to one dollar, although not legally required. That was when some other financial institutions allowed their money market shares to drop below one dollar per share, resulting in losses for their clients.

EMPATHY AND COMPASSION

A leader's empathy and compassion are never needed more than during a crisis. Both are key to dealing with crises because they are the "software" for taking care of the people affected and those you will rely on to be part of the solution. During a crisis, everything changes. In addition to a heightened stress level, a crisis breeds a high degree of uncertainty. There is no smooth sailing. The ride is bumpy, and there's no warning of the rocks underneath the whitewater, threatening to tear the raft apart. As a leader, you need to appreciate that those you are trying to influence during a crisis may be emotionally hijacked and unable to think clearly. When you show empathy and compassion, you help people get unstuck. By responding empathetically and being compassionate, you create a climate of safety that helps those around you release enough of their fear to access the logical and creative parts of their brains, where the best crisis solutions can be found. When it comes to crisis leadership, some leaders believe they don't have time to be compassionate. They may view empathy as "coddling" employees at a time when their team needs to move instantaneously to solve the technical problem at the root of the crisis. But the logic of that approach won't work when people are emotionally overwhelmed. That's why empathy and compassion are "must haves," not "nice to haves," in the arsenal of effective crisis leadership. For example, Ken Chenault's empathy and compassion following the horror of 9/11 helped people feel like they still belonged to an important cause. In the throes of a destabilizing crisis, Ken related to American Express employees in a way that strengthened their psychological connection to the company. His empathy and compassion helped people get unstuck. Because Ken gave them permission to fully feel their emotions, they were more quickly able to move beyond the nightmare of the terrorist attack and refocus on their work.

Finally, use your empathetic skills to recognize that one of the most compassionate steps you can take is to turbocharge your communication efforts, as Chuck did in response to the post-9/11 crisis. Chuck knew that there was no such thing as "too much communication." The daily meetings he held lasted as long as needed to ensure that the region's employees had accurate information and knew that their concerns were understood and addressed.

WISE DECISION-MAKING

During a crisis, the decisions that get the most attention are generally those intended to solve the core technical problems that define the crisis. In the aftermath of Hurricane Katrina in 2005, those goals included adequate medical care for the injured, housing for the displaced, rebuilding critical infrastructure, and financial support for those who lost work. In the 2010 BP Deepwater Horizon explosion and oil spill in the Gulf of Mexico, the goal focused on stopping the leak, which despite all efforts, lasted a horrifying 87 days until the well was finally capped. The Deepwater disaster illustrates the devastation

that can happen when leaders fail to decide how to anticipate and plan
for crisis scenarios.

> *Over the course of months following the blowout, it became painfully*
> *clear the company never bothered to develop response plans specific to this*
> *drilling site. . .and the government never forced them to do so. Instead*
> *the government accepted lacking, inaccurate and out-of-date response.*[4]

BP's failure to make wise crisis-prevention decisions resulted in the
deaths of 11 Deepwater rig workers. It also caused incalculable damage
to the Gulf ecosystem, killing and injuring marine wildlife representing
more than 8,000 species, shuttering area marine-based food industries,
and harming countless coastal community residents' physical and mental health. Given such disturbing impacts, it's undeniable that leaders
need to practice wise decision-making as it applies to daily operations,
long-term strategies, crisis prevention, and actual worst-case crisis events.

Other crisis decision areas are those that surround the core technical problems themselves. Usually, such decision areas involve addressing the emotional needs of crisis stakeholders, most notably by deciding
how best to communicate information about the crisis to various stakeholders. Each stakeholder group has its own information needs. The
first step in deciding how to address stakeholders is to identify the
distinct needs of each audience. For instance, when Chuck led a
regional group of American Express financial advisors based in Detroit
through a highly publicized transition following a mass resignation of
managers, he identified key audiences for his messaging: advisors, clients, leaders, and media. According to Chuck,

> *We needed to keep all four audiences informed and continuously un-*
> *derstand their needs. Advisors wanted to know what the company was*
> *doing. Clients wanted to know what the advisors were doing. Our com-*
> *pany's senior leaders wanted to know what was happening on the ground.*
> *And the media wanted to know "who was winning," because our crisis*
> *was something of a sport to them.*

[4] Oona Watkins, "A Look Back to 2010: 87 Days Too Late, BP Finally Stops Deepwater
Horizon Blowout," *Oceana* (July 14, 2020), https://usa.oceana.org/blog/look-back-2010-87-
days-too-late-bp-finally-stops-deepwater-horizon-blowout/.

LEARNING AGILITY

On April 11, 1970, 56 hours into the U.S. Apollo 13 mission to the moon, a routine maintenance task caused the spacecraft's oxygen tanks to explode. Nothing had prepared the three astronauts onboard or the staff at NASA Mission Control in Houston, Texas, to deal with this catastrophic event. Against all odds, NASA flight controllers and engineers called on their learning agility to improvise a succession of novel procedures that brought the astronauts home safely five days later. The Apollo 13 saga has been extensively chronicled in the media and was the subject of the 1996 Academy Award-winning film *Apollo 13*, starring the legendary actor Tom Hanks.

The Apollo 13 mission was famously dubbed a "successful failure" because of the inventiveness of experts who orchestrated the miraculous return of the astronauts. Less well documented, however, were the prelaunch technical issues that NASA experts ignored in their haste to launch the third human-crewed moon mission. In other words, the explosion might never have happened had the development team been more willing to learn from the problems they encountered before the launch. So, the Apollo 13 space mission is a unique example both of the dangers of low learning agility and the incredible importance of high learning agility.

What is so important about learning agility for a leader facing a significant crisis? As we saw in Chapter 8, "Let Go of What You Know," learning agility is not just about learning. It's about being comfortable with not knowing everything we need to know. It's about the ease with which we can shift from relying on established routines to experimenting with new approaches. It's about applying what we *do* know to new situations. It's about responding with curiosity rather than distress to new challenges. Learning agility is a "soft skill" that includes our ability to develop new "hard skills" in record time.

With the Apollo 13 emergency in mind, it doesn't take much imagination to recognize that learning agility is a leadership essential with an outsized impact on our ability to deal with the core technical problems contributing to a particular crisis. Peter B. Vail, who originated the "permanent whitewater" concept, points out these two defining components of crisis events:

- They frequently have novel components and character.
- They don't fit neatly into any capability the organization already possesses.[5]

These two characteristics of a crisis event cry out for learning agility. Since crises by nature are novel, one-off events, there is no way to anticipate all the skills leaders, or followers for that matter, need to possess in advance of an unknown future event. Because of this, learning agility is our insurance policy against the downsides of crises. We are not psychics who can predict the future capabilities we need to deal with impending crises. But we can be prepared for future crises if we and our teams cultivate learning agility. Learning agility will equip us with the capacity to explore and quickly develop the new skills we need to deal with the challenges of future crises.

PwC's 2021 Global Crisis Survey underscores the importance of learning to successful crisis leadership. While most global leaders surveyed reported that the coronavirus pandemic had negatively affected their organization's performance, a surprising 20 percent of respondents said that overall, the crisis had a positive impact on their organization. For those organizations reporting positive results, a key differentiator was their learning mindset. In particular, the organizations that emerged stronger were those that systematically worked to capture what they learned from every project and program. They regularly conducted "after-action reviews" (AARs) and incorporated learnings from AARs into their long-term strategy.[6]

ACHIEVING PURPOSEFUL GOALS

When it comes to a crisis, defining relevant "purposeful goals" may not be as straightforward as it first appears. For example, an obvious goal may be to return conditions to a state preceding the crisis. As the coronavirus pandemic that erupted in 2020 has made painfully obvious, there is no such thing as going back to the way things were. When a crisis ends, the landscape is permanently altered. The ocean is never as

[5] Peter B. Vaill, *Learning as a Way of Being: Strategies for Survival in a World of Permanent White Water* (San Francisco, CA: Jossey-Bass, 1996).
[6] PwC, "Global Crisis Survey 2021: Building Resilience for the Future, 2021," https://www .pwc.com/gx/en/issues/crisis-solutions/global-crisis-survey.html.

clean as it was before an oil spill. Marriage partners are never as innocently trusting as they were before an episode of infidelity. An organization that successfully navigates a crisis can become too risk averse for fear of the next crisis just around the corner. During a crisis, it's unrealistic to set a goal of wiping the slate clean. On the plus side, setting crisis resolution goals doesn't necessarily include accepting certain permanent post-crisis losses. Crises can give leaders a chance to achieve goals that might not have been possible otherwise. President John F. Kennedy is widely quoted as pointing out that the Chinese word for crisis is composed of two characters: one represents danger; the other, opportunity. It's important to recognize both. Our conversations with leaders revealed that they saw opportunities in crises to achieve purposeful goals that might not have been possible or implemented as quickly in the absence of a crisis.

In early March 2020, Thrivent CEO Terry Rasmussen decided not to waste any time closing their Minneapolis corporate offices in the face of the coronavirus pandemic. Within three weeks, the entire headquarters staff of 7,000 professionals had transitioned to at-home work. This change accelerated the rollout of Thrivent's strategic plan by 18 months. As Terry explained, "Our strategic goals had included becoming more digital and doing far less face-to-face work. We had planned to ease into this gradually. Instead, we had to do it in weeks, sometimes within days."

EMPOWERING OTHERS

Empowering others is always a vital tactic and key to your effectiveness. It's a win-win: for leaders because they can't accomplish team goals independently. Empowering others encourages followers to trust their leaders and give their best efforts to achieve shared goals. For followers, it's also a win because empowered followers feel respected and trusted. They have higher self-esteem and feel safe to make on-the-spot decisions that keep customers happy or address urgent problems.

During times of crisis, empowering others is even more essential. In a crisis, there is even more to do than usual. There are many more moving parts. Problems are new, so you and your team need to develop solutions on the fly. You simply don't have time to train people in skills to address each critical challenge. That means you need to trust people to be self-sufficient and to make wise, independent decisions in the moment. As McKinsey senior partners Gemma D'Auria and Aaron De Smet emphasize:

> *During a crisis, leaders must relinquish the belief that a top-down response will engender stability. In routine emergencies, the typical company can rely on its command-and-control structure to manage operations well by carrying out a scripted response. But in crises characterized by uncertainty, leaders face problems that are unfamiliar and poorly understood. A small group of executives at an organization's highest level cannot collect information or make decisions quickly enough to respond effectively. Leaders can better mobilize their organizations by setting clear priorities for the response and empowering others to discover and implement solutions that serve those priorities.*[7]

Suppose you haven't been empowering your followers all along. In that case, you can't expect them to have the resilience and motivation to tackle the unfamiliar issues that crop up continuously throughout a crisis. That's why practicing empowerment every day, in good times and bad, is your best insurance for successfully managing the human and organizational challenges of significant crises.

···

Crises are, by their nature, full of uncertainty and ambiguity. In difficult times, the eight leadership essentials are even more essential, though that may seem illogical. Consistently practicing the eight essentials will elevate your daily leadership performance and prepare you to overcome the inevitable disruptions that ever-looming crises cause. Practicing the eight leadership essentials will also influence those you lead to develop *their* crisis leadership capabilities. And when you join forces with your crisis-prepared followers to tackle the worst of days, you can't help but turn today's crises into tomorrow's successes.

---

[7] Gemma D'Auria and Aaron De Smet, "Leadership in a Crisis: Responding to the Coronavirus Outbreak and Future Challenges," *McKinsey & Company* (March 16, 2020), https://www .mckinsey.com/business-functions/people-and-organizational-performance/our-insights/ leadership-in-a-crisis-responding-to-the-coronavirus-outbreak-and-future-challenges.

CHAPTER TWELVE

Recovering from Leadership Setbacks

Trish Moll's leadership career began at a very early age. A good student well-liked by her classmates, Trish founded her elementary school's first girls' basketball team. In high school, Trish was elected to student government, ultimately becoming student council president. In Trish's view, leadership was always a collaborative venture.

"It was never just about me," Trish insisted. "It was always important to me to be with people who had similar goals and objectives, people like me who wanted to accomplish something."

Along the way, Trish had mentors who helped crystallize her view of the future. Probably her most influential mentor was her dad, himself a leader as a Deputy District Chief in the Chicago Fire Department and a small business owner. "My dad and I would sit at the kitchen table for hours, talking about what was going on in my life and what I wanted for my future. He never told me what to do. He asked questions because he wanted me to think through how to make my own decisions."

Though Trish's dad believed in a good education, her working-class family didn't assume she would choose to attend college. So, when

Trish told her parents she wanted to further her education after high school, they were supportive. When deciding on a college major, once again, Trish's dad was influential. He told Trish, "If you want to have money, you need to make money."

Trish took her dad's insight to heart and decided to study finance and marketing. When Trish graduated, she had her pick of entry-level jobs at various financial services companies. Ultimately, Trish accepted an offer to become a financial advisor for IDS (now Ameriprise Financial).

Trish did so well during her first year on the job, that by her second year, her company promoted her to training manager. That's when her first professional setback struck. "My production suffered," Trish explains candidly. "I couldn't be both a successful financial advisor and an effective training manager, which was what the company expected. I almost lost my job, and they definitely didn't want me to be a training manager anymore."

Trish didn't let that bump in the road stop her. She enrolled in a group training program focused on acquiring new clients. Being around like-minded people who all wanted to be successful was hugely motivating. Before long, Trish had doubled her production and was invited to attend the company's prestigious annual national conference.

Trish was then tapped to be a training manager for the second time and, not long after, was promoted to district manager. Trish relished the challenges of being a leader. Her record as a producer and manager in the franchise track of the company eventually got the attention of higher-ups. They wanted her to become a full-time corporate leader. Trish wondered, "Can I successfully climb the corporate ladder?"

She wasn't entirely confident about that, but she had a vision of herself at future national conferences, standing at the front of the room with other senior leaders, and inspiring her colleagues to do well while doing good. So, she took a considerable risk and sold her successful independent financial practice to become a full-time corporate leader. Trish flourished as a senior leader in Ameriprise, eventually being asked to serve as a franchise field vice president. When a regional vice president position opened up, Trish applied for the job. Trish was one of three finalists for the position and hoped she would get the nod. Her optimism was dashed when the external candidate, a friend, told Trish that he had been offered the job. It was a shocking way to get the news that she wasn't going to move ahead.

Trish wondered why she hadn't been chosen. After all, she had a strong track record of outstanding results and had developed and promoted other women leaders in the firm. As Trish reflected on her experience:

> *After receiving the news that I hadn't gotten the position, I was so down and wondered, "Do I still have a place at this firm? But in the days that followed, I got calls from almost every member of the senior executive team telling me to hang in there and that there was still a future for me here.*

Trish trusted what she heard, worked through her hurt feelings, and doubled down on her efforts to achieve her ultimate goal, which was to lead at an even more meaningful level. Thanks to Trish's self-management skills, she was ultimately able to put her disappointment into perspective:

> *The worst leadership experience of my life became my best. I got some direct and concrete feedback from my leader, who let me know what I needed to do to be the number one candidate next time. I trusted the feedback and my leaders, applied what I learned, and feel like I've achieved even more success. I saw the bigger picture and in the process, I got the opportunity to demonstrate that I could be resilient.*

Over the next several years, Trish excelled in her leadership roles, gaining an enviable reputation for developing next-generation leaders. Trish's resilience and commitment to continuous learning paid off. In 2021, Trish was promoted to a position as an Ameriprise franchise regional vice president.

EXPECT BUMPS IN THE ROAD

As Trish Moll's story demonstrates, even successful leaders encounter adversity periodically during their careers. Personal setbacks, like the organizational crises discussed in the previous chapter, are inevitable parts of being a leader. Your leadership journey, like life itself, will not be an easy hike. It will be more like climbing a mountain. As we learned from adventurer Chris Klinke, climbing to the top is danger-ous. No matter how well you prepare, unpredictable conditions can assault you. Storms can leave you stranded; wind can steal your tent; high altitude can leave you without enough oxygen to sustain good judgment—or escape death. Chris's challenges on Cho Oyu Mountain mirror the unforgiving environments leaders encounter wherever they lead.

Influential leaders aren't those who never suffer a setback. They are the ones who do what it takes to get themselves and others safely down a treacherous mountain. They learn from whatever kept them from reaching the summit. Then they climb again.

HOW DID THIS HAPPEN?

Recovering from a leadership setback begins with understanding its source. Some setbacks are beyond your control. For example, many competent leaders were among the estimated 20 million U.S. workers who lost their jobs in 2020 because of the coronavirus pandemic and related shutdowns. Other setbacks may be those you help create. Nine years after the legendary Steve Jobs co-founded Apple, he was forced out by its board partly because of employee complaints that he drove them too hard.

Leadership setbacks sometimes happen when, despite your best efforts, you lack the skills or competence to fulfill your role at the level your superiors expect. This type of leadership setback can be difficult to accept because when you're working hard to do a good job, you expect to be rewarded for your efforts. But working hard isn't the same as producing excellent results.

Without self-awareness, you might believe you did a great job but were sidelined through no fault of your own. Such a misperception can blind you to the reality of your situation and thus recognition of the changes you need to make to get back on track. In contrast to well-meaning but ineffective leaders, effective leaders are brutally honest about their performance.

When trying to understand the causes of your situation, consider the possibility that you might have unconsciously contributed to this setback because you aren't emotionally invested in your role. If you're not passionate about your leadership position, your superiors, peers, and followers will notice your lack of spark, making you more likely to lose a promotion, your current role, or your job itself. You might feel frustrated about that type of setback without realizing that you are at least partly responsible. That was the case with Nadia, who loved her job as a manager with a humanitarian nonprofit organization. Her team was responsible for soliciting corporate donors to support their work helping refugees from the Middle East seeking asylum in Western countries. Nadia was highly regarded by her team for her warm and collaborative style. The team worked well together and excelled at bringing new corporate donors on board.

But as the coronavirus pandemic intensified in 2020, donations to Nadia's organization dropped dramatically. Their donors were cash-strapped because of the economic impact of the pandemic on their operations. Executives at Nadia's nonprofit seemed to blame Nadia for their financial woes. Nadia's manager scheduled endless Zoom meetings with her, focused on finding ways to boost her team's sagging results. At first, Nadia worked hard to coach her team members about how to be more persuasive with current and prospective corporate donors, but to no avail. By the fall of 2021, Nadia had burnt out. Despite her team's best efforts, corporate funding had virtually dried up. The social environment of the office she and her team had previously enjoyed was a distant memory. These days her job was all drudgery, no joy. She lost her enthusiasm for her job and gave up trying to motivate her team. Finally, the organization decided to let Nadia go and replace her with someone they believed would be more successful in raising funds. When Nadia's boss gave her the bad news, she was shocked. Nadia had been a great performer until the past year and never thought her job was at risk. It would take Nadia many months of reflection to recognize that she was in many ways responsible for getting fired.

Finally, a leadership setback can strike because your behavior has fallen out of alignment with your values or purpose. For example, leadership misconduct is an increasingly common cause of senior executive derailments. As Dr. Jim Loehr notes in his book *Leading with Character*, "In 2018, CEO dismissals for ethical lapses exceeded dismissals for financial performance or board struggles for the first time in history."[1] Ensuring that your actions are consistent with your values is the most potent way to prevent leadership setbacks of your own making.

As painful as setbacks can be, they are often powerful tools for learning and growth. Paraphrasing Winston Churchill's maxim, "Never let a good crisis go to waste," we would add, "Never let a good setback go to waste." With the help of the 4Rs—*recognize, reflect, reframe,* and *respond*—you can recover stronger, wiser, and more purposeful than before.

RECOGNIZE YOUR RESPONSE

Jeffrey Sonnenfeld and Andrew Ward's research analyzing more than 450 CEO successions between 1988 and 1992 at large, publicly traded companies found that most fallen leaders—almost two-thirds, don't recover. They explain why:

> *What prevents a deposed leader from coming back? Leaders who cannot recover tend to blame themselves and are often tempted to dwell on the past rather than look to the future. They secretly hold themselves responsible for their career setback, whether they were or not, and get caught in a psychological web of their own making, unable to move beyond the position they no longer hold. This dynamic is usually reinforced by well-meaning colleagues, and even by family and friends, who may try to lay blame in an attempt to make sense of the chaos surrounding the disaster. Sadly, their advice can often be more damaging than helpful.[2]*

Rick Aberman, a psychologist who specializes in executive and sports performance, sees a related reason why some leaders don't recover:

> *What gets in the way of a comeback is their anger. A lot of that anger results from being separated from all they were used to, from the pain of being rejected. The setback triggers a sense of being abandoned. Their anger toward others is their own inner conflict about what happened*

[1] Jim Loehr, *Leading with Character: 10 Minutes a Day to a Brilliant Legacy* (Hoboken, New Jersey: John Wiley & Sons, Inc., 2021).
[2] Jeffrey A. Sonnenfeld, and Andrew J. Ward, "Firing Back: How Great Leaders Rebound After Career Disasters," *Harvard Business Review* (January 2007).

being projected onto others. Anger directed outward keeps them in denial about their own contribution to what's happened. It protects them but keeps them stuck.

As Sonnenfeld, Ward, and Aberman suggest, emotions play a huge part in your response to a leadership setback. Whether or not you are responsible for the setback you face, it's a traumatic experience. It's normal to have strong feelings. When Steve Jobs lost his job at Apple, he was devastated. In the commencement address he gave at Stanford University in 2005, Jobs described his initial reactions:

I really didn't know what to do for a few months. I felt that I had let the previous generation of entrepreneurs down—that I had dropped the baton as it was being passed to me. I met with David Packard and Bob Noyce and tried to apologize for screwing up so badly. I was a very public failure, and I even thought about running away from the [Silicon] valley.

Not everybody responds to a setback in the same way. Like Steve Jobs, you may struggle with feelings of failure. Or you may be angry about the perceived injustice of being "punished" for a situation you couldn't control. You might blame others for the setback. No matter what you feel initially, recognize that your initial feelings are standard parts of a grieving process. But it's not these feelings themselves that are problematic. It's hanging on to them, being unable or unwilling to let those feelings go, that keeps you from recovering after a setback. If you stay stuck in highly charged emotions for too long, you're no longer in a grieving process; you're in a stall. Getting emotionally unstuck is essential for overcoming a setback. So, the first step in recovering from a setback is to call on self-awareness to keep track of where you are in the grieving process. Paying attention to your experiential triangle— your thoughts, feelings, and behavior—is never more critical than when you're in the throes of a personal crisis. It's ironic that by becoming more aware of your reactions to a setback, you're better able to release them. Using the tools of recognition, such as the freeze game, will set the stage for you to reflect on more positive approaches to life after your setback. So, make it a point to play the freeze game described in Chapter 4 several times daily.

EXERCISE: PLAYING THE FREEZE GAME AFTER A LEADERSHIP SETBACK

Call a timeout from whatever you're doing. Ask yourself the following questions:

- How do I feel about the situation I'm in (e.g., fearful, angry, sad, accepting, hopeful)?
- What are my attitudes and beliefs about the situation I'm in (e.g., it's all my fault; it's not my fault; it's a disaster; when a window closes, a door opens)?
- How am I reacting physically, and how am I behaving in response to this situation (e.g., my blood pressure is high; I'm not sleeping; I'm being irritable with others; I'm kinder to others in difficult circumstances)?

REFLECT ON YOUR SETBACK

Once you've acknowledged and accepted your experience, the best way to move forward after a setback is to be reflective. Although reflection includes figuring out what caused your setback, reflection does not mean brooding about the past. You want to understand how you may have contributed to your setback to avoid making similar mistakes in the future. But it's the future that your reflection should focus on the most.

In Steve Jobs' case, after he'd wrestled with feelings of guilt and failure, he began to reflect on his circumstances. As Jobs explains, ". . . something slowly began to dawn on me—I still loved what I did. The turn of events at Apple had not changed that one bit. I had been rejected, but I was still in love. And so, I decided to start over."

When you reflect following a setback, a fundamental question to ponder is, "Who am I?" Both Jim Loehr and Rick Aberman point out that leaders often fail to recover from setbacks because their sense of self is overly dependent on their professional role. When such leaders make mistakes that jeopardize their position, they risk losing their sense of self. To counter this obstacle to recovering from adversity, Jim and Rick remind everyone they coach after a setback that "you are not your job."

Reflecting on your state of alignment with principles and values is also essential. In Chapter 3, coauthor Doug told a story about falling out of alignment in a significant way. Ironically, during one of the most challenging times in Doug's life, when he was clearly out of alignment, he never stopped practicing his reflection rituals, such as repeating his values while washing his face, brushing his teeth, or drinking water. But in contrast to previous years, Doug had stopped being mindful about his practice. He repeated his values by rote, without paying attention to what he was saying to himself. It was only when he re-established his commitment to mindfully reflecting on his values that his recovery began.

Another crucial area for reflection is to contemplate your "big picture." What is your reason for being? What is your purpose? According to Jim Loehr, leaders whose purpose emphasizes personal gain rather than serving others are at high risk of failure and have a low probability of recovering from their failures. Jim told us this story to illustrate his point:

> There was a guy I got to know whose whole entire being was to become a billionaire before the age of 50. He started out on a very fast track, but as he got closer to 50 it was all about him; it was all about his wanting to be in that special billionaire class. The closer he got to 50, the riskier his decision making was. Eventually the risks he took were so great that the whole thing imploded. He lost absolutely everything. Because his purpose was so self-serving, he's never resurrected from his failure. I believe that so much of what drives people and sustains them is trying to do something good in the world and realizing that life isn't about you.

In contrast to the 50-something billionaire wannabe, Trish Moll's purpose included helping others develop. In reflecting on her setback, she realized there were good reasons why she didn't get the nod the first time she put her hat in the ring for a regional vice president position. Accurate self-awareness and staying focused on a service-related purpose helped Trish move past her setback and into a more successful career.

When reflecting on a setback, consider these questions:

- How have my attitudes or behavior contributed to my setback?
- Given what I now know, how might I have responded differently in this situation?
- Have I stayed true to universal principles and my values? If not, what can I do today to act in alignment with principles and values?
- What is my life purpose, and how can I stay true to my purpose despite this setback?
- What are my goals for moving beyond this setback? Do I want to resume my previous role, or should I aim for a new position that better fulfills my purpose?
- Who can give me additional insight into the situation and feedback about how I might reframe and respond to it (e.g., my boss, a mentor, or in some cases, a person or team that has been affected by my behavior)?
- What are the opportunities for learning that this setback has opened up for me (e.g., this experience could help me become a better people manager)?

REFRAMING FOR THE FUTURE

A successful leadership comeback does not necessarily mean landing the same role you had before. For instance, losing one CEO job, then getting another is hardly the only definition of success. Your most successful comeback could very well be an entirely different leadership role. U.S. President Jimmy Carter lost reelection in 1980, partly because of his failure to secure the release of long-held American hostages in Iran. As he later told researchers Jeffrey A. Sonnenfeld and Andrew J. Ward, "I returned to Plains, Georgia, completely exhausted, slept for almost 24 hours, and then awoke to an altogether new, unwanted, and potentially empty life."[3]

Despite the pain of his loss, Carter refused to wallow in anger or self-pity. Instead, he used his credentials to carve out a new career

[3]Jeffrey A. Sonnenfeld, and Andrew J. Ward, "Firing Back: How Great Leaders Rebound After Career Disasters," *Harvard Business Review* (January 2007).

devoted to promoting peace, advancing human rights, and alleviating human suffering. In 2002, Carter was awarded the Nobel Peace Prize "for his decades of untiring effort to find peaceful solutions to international conflicts, to advance democracy and human rights, and to promote economic and social development."[4]

If you make a career-limiting mistake, use it as an opportunity to examine your deepest life interests. You may discover that such a setback is a gift, which gives you an opening to pursue a dramatically different leadership role—one that offers you far more enjoyment and meaning than before. When Nadia, the development manager for the nonprofit devoted to helping refugees, was fired, she realized that she was still deeply committed to helping refugees. But she didn't want to be part of a fund-raising machine. Instead, she wanted to work more directly with refugees, helping them deal with the daily challenges of adapting to a new country. Within a few months, she landed a job enrolling individuals, charitable organizations, and churches in programs to welcome Middle Eastern refugees to U.S. Midwestern communities. In her new role, she helped provide funding for refugee families to secure housing, learn English, and train host families to support refugee families resettling into nearby communities.

Reframing harvests the fruit of your reflections. Reflecting either reinforces your commitment to a worthwhile purpose or leads you to formulate a new, less self-centered, and more service-oriented purpose. Reframing allows you to let go of attitudes that could keep you stuck in an unproductive past. Then reframing creates a space where you can move confidently into a new future.

When it comes to leaders in high places, Jim Loehr is eloquent about the reframing needed for a leader to make a comeback. Here is an example of reframing that Jim offers to the leaders with whom he works:

> *My passion is to be a great success because I want to help. I want to make the world better. I want to make others better in whatever type or organization I lead. My identity is about much more than my job. My identity is my mission; that is, what I want to accomplish for my organization and others. When I make mistakes, I will learn from them. I will get back up and pursue whatever I'm chasing because I'm chasing it for the right reason.*

[4]"The Nobel Peace Prize 2002," *NobelPrize.org*, September 16, 2002, Nobel Prize Outreach AB, https://www.nobelprize.org/prizes/peace/2002/summary/.

An overarching theme regarding leadership setbacks is to reframe them as growth opportunities rather than disasters. When reframing, ask yourself these questions:

- What is the story about this setback that I can legitimately tell myself and others that provides the best path to a different and better future?
- How can I change my interpretation of this situation and similar situations to enhance my leadership effectiveness in my current organization or elsewhere? (For instance, avoid making negative assumptions about an employee's request based on previous experiences with them or other employees. Instead, give employees the benefit of the doubt and, whenever possible, be kind.)
- What ideas and attitudes could I adopt to create options for dealing more effectively with this and similar situations in the future?

RESPOND WITH COURAGE

Responding may seem to be the simplest part of rebounding from a leadership setback. However, as we've often said, simple doesn't mean easy. Simple *does* mean that once we've reframed our situation, the actions we need to take to recover from adversity are straightforward.

Research tells us that the more serious the setback, the less likely a leader will recover and resume a leadership position of equal stature. But statistics can be misleading. For example, just over a third of fired CEOs land in another CEO position. Such was the case with Jamie Dimon. Fired from his position as chief financial officer of Citigroup in 1998, he was hired in 2000 as CEO of Bank One. When JPMorgan Chase bought Bank One in 2004, Dimon became the merged company's president and chief operating officer. A year later, he became CEO of JPMorgan Chase.

As heartening as Dimon's career trajectory may be to leaders under fire, we do not define recovery from leadership setbacks as success in landing an equivalent position. The most satisfying recoveries may happen when a setback prompts a purpose-driven change of career direction.

Sometimes, career setbacks that seem devastating from the outside may be easier to weather when your sense of purpose isn't exclusively tied up in your career. Such was the case for tennis great Andre Agassi, who managed one of the most incredible comebacks in tennis history. Once ranked the number 1 tennis player in the world, in 1997 he dropped to 141st place, before battling his way back in 1998 to being a top player and regaining his number 1 spot in 1999. When his rankings, reputation, and winnings tanked, Agassi focused on boosting his performance, but not because he loved tennis, which he famously did not. In his 2009 memoir *Open*, Agassi wrote, "I play tennis for a living even though I hate tennis, hate it with a dark and secret passion and always have."[5] Instead, Agassi saw the sport as a way to serve his purpose of helping children. As Agassi told *Time Magazine*, "I knew at 18 years old that I can't be inspired just for the sake of winning a tennis match. Giving opportunity to children through education became my passion for staying on a court."[6]

In fact, in 2004, when Agassi was just 23 years old, he established the Andre Agassi Foundation, dedicated to helping underserved children access high-quality education. Since the foundation began, more than $180 million have been raised to benefit the foundation's mission. The foundation have also funded a charter school in Agassi's hometown of Las Vegas, giving young children in underserved communities the opportunity to have a good childhood and follow their hopes and dreams.

Most of you will hopefully never experience setbacks as dramatic as those of Andre Agassi or Jamie Dimon. But in your leadership world, your mistakes and failures will still significantly impact your followers. So do your best to respond effectively. Share your reflections and reframing with your stakeholders, such as leaders, mentors, and followers affected. For instance, ask your leaders and mentors for advice before taking action. Initiate a meeting with your manager to share what you have learned from the mistake or failure, and review what you plan to do to repair any damage you've done and prevent similar problems in the future. Also, meet with anyone affected by your mistake or failure. Accept responsibility for any adverse effects you've caused.

[5]Andre Agassi, *Open: An Autobiography* (New York: Knopf, 2009).
[6]Ibid.

SELF-CARE DURING A SETBACK

A leadership setback is not just an emotional blow—it's a physical assault that triggers stress responses throughout your whole body. When experiencing a setback, it's easy to abandon the healthy habits you usually practice, such as adequate sleep, healthy eating, and other rituals that are even more crucial during times of personal crisis. It's also common for leaders facing adversity to retreat like a wounded animal to a dark cave. That may mean isolating yourself, abandoning your networking activities, or becoming more irritable with family members and friends. Though such actions are tempting default mechanisms in times of crisis, none of these behaviors helps you regain equilibrium following a significant setback.

To combat any such unproductive responses, you need to practice self-compassion. Rebounding from a setback requires paying even more attention than usual to self-care routines, such as eating well, exercising, and getting adequate sleep. As discussed earlier in the book, self-empathy and self-compassion are essential leadership tools in good times and bad. They are never more needed than during times of personal adversity. One of the most important benefits of self-care during setbacks is that such practices shorten your emotional recovery time, giving you the focus and stamina to return to a meaningful leadership role more quickly.

MINIMIZING SETBACKS WITH THE EIGHT ESSENTIALS

Though the 4Rs are highly useful in guiding your recovery from a leadership setback, leveraging all eight essentials expands a leader's ability to recover from leadership setbacks. We already know we can't eliminate setbacks, no matter how much we try to be perfect leaders. As we've emphasized repeatedly, setbacks are an inescapable and valuable part of your leadership journey. As the famous anthropologist Joseph Campbell pointed out in his book, *The Hero with a Thousand Faces,* in every culture, the stories of great leaders follow a common trajectory that includes early successes, profound challenges, setbacks, and eventually a triumphant return to greatness.

In our coaching and consulting work with thousands of leaders, we have found that the more grounded leaders are in the eight essentials, the less likely they are to fall prey to leadership failures for which they are responsible. Even if these leaders experience setbacks, their command of the eight essentials reduces the most personally disabling effects of a setback and helps them regain their footing as influential leaders. Trish Moll, whom you met at the start of this chapter, is an excellent example of someone who relied on the eight essentials to accelerate her path to executive leadership after being passed over for a highly desirable promotion. For example, Trish Moll stayed true to her ideal self by continuing her work of helping upcoming leaders grow and develop. She was self-aware, unhesitatingly accepting feedback from superiors that gave her a more complete picture of her real self.

MAKE MISTAKES MATTER

Most leadership setbacks happen, at least partly because we make mistakes. High-achieving leaders are often intolerant of their own mistakes. The perfectionists among us have a lot of trouble dealing with losing a coveted role or getting fired. That's because we are congenitally disposed to being hard on ourselves. If you have a track record as a high-performing perfectionist leader, the only way to let go of unforgiving self-expectations is to reframe your perception of mistakes from seeing them as unacceptable failures to opportunities for learning and growth.

As a high performer, another advantage of facing a setback is that when you acknowledge it, you become humbler and, therefore, more open to other potential solutions and more responsive to others' points of view.

As leaders, the choices we make about dealing with our mistakes and others' missteps set the table for how we lead in good times and bad. Dealing honestly with our own mistakes engenders a sense of humility that makes us more tolerant of the mistakes of those around us, even more when followers see we are working to address our own mistakes. When we show compassion in helping followers recover from their mistakes, we are investing in the future of our organizations and teams.

The best leaders normalize mistakes as part of the team experience, let team members know that we recognize the learning value of failures, and challenge them to reflect and respond to the challenges their setbacks pose for them. When we tell those around us that we expect them to make mistakes, we reduce their anxiety about taking risks. That doesn't mean we're prepared to give people who make mistakes a free pass. For instance, high-performing leaders don't want to see their people make the same mistakes repeatedly. They hope to see that, as their followers develop, they will make new mistakes.

REDISCOVER YOUR REAL SELF-IDENTITY

As Rick Aberman points out, part of what makes a leadership setback so tricky is that such a setback threatens our identity as a leader or as having a particular role as a leader. To rebound after a leadership failure, you must realize that "you are not your job." Your true identity is simply "you as you." Aim to base your sense of self on principles and values—who you are, not what you do.

According to Jim Loehr, leaders who successfully recover from setbacks have a keen sense of purpose. So, recommit to living in alignment with your purpose and values instead of clinging to externals such as job titles.

ASK FOR SUPPORT

A leadership setback is a significant personal crisis. Don't try to navigate it alone. Many of us wrongly think that asking for help is a sign of weakness. It may be hard to overcome feelings of inadequacy or shame in the wake of a significant mistake or setback. However, hiding such feelings from others will only prolong the time it takes for you to rebound. When you admit you've taken a fall, others will empathize. Your family, friends, and networks can be excellent sources of emotional support, professional advice, and career contacts. As Jim Loehr points out, it helps if you're the kind of person others want to help. Jim told us about Michael, a great husband and father, someone of deep faith and with a purpose of helping others. His business was very successful. Then the pandemic hit. He shut his business down because it was the right thing to do for his staff. His income dropped from six figures to nothing. At the same time, he and his wife had a new baby with a severe health condition. Then his father, who had always been his best friend, died from COVID-19. Amid all these difficulties,

Michael tapped into his resilience. He was determined to figure out how to rebuild. So, Michael asked his friends for help. He went to the banks for loans. Everyone he contacted wanted to help him because of the way he had always treated them. Michael is back on his feet. His business is flourishing once again, primarily aided by his friends' love and the respect of others in the business community.

HELP FOLLOWERS MANAGE THEIR OWN SETBACKS

As important as it is to understand and move beyond your own setbacks, it is also vital to be a role model for others who will experience them. Being open with others about your missteps and setbacks is a gift to those you lead. As we saw in Chapter 3, "Aim to Be Your Ideal Self," admitting mistakes and failures is part of being a good leader. Your honesty about setbacks permits others to be less than perfect. Admitting mistakes and failures also communicates a favorable vulnerability that strengthens your bond with those you seek to influence. By sharing your setbacks and strategies for dealing with them, you are more accessible. People connect with you because they've made their own mistakes. That leads followers and associates to think, "This person is real." When you step off the leadership pedestal, followers step up to offer you more loyalty and commitment to your shared purpose. Finally, your actions provide a roadmap for others about how to emerge stronger from any setbacks they experience.

•••

In *A Farewell to Arms*, Ernest Hemingway wrote, "The world breaks everyone and afterward many are strong at the broken places." Just as life's wounds leave scars, you may never be the same following a leadership setback. And that may be the best thing that could have happened to you. As Steve Jobs discovered, a setback can make you a better leader—*if* you practice the skills we've discussed in this chapter and throughout the book. Success teaches us little. Setbacks and failures teach us a great deal, but only if we are open to learning their lessons.

AFTERWORD

For decades, we have dedicated ourselves to helping others develop practical skills to fulfill their purpose and inspire those around them to succeed. This book boils down the fundamental leadership skill set to "eight essentials." Though we've worked mostly with business clients in our professional lives, we have come to realize that these eight essentials are important in all areas of our lives. We have come to understand that everyone is a leader. We now realize that leadership is not about the nameplate on your office door. It is about how you inspire others to do good, whether on the job, at home, or in your community. Everyone has an opportunity to influence others to make a positive difference. The eight essentials are tools you can use, not just in your professional life but anywhere people need you.

Examining our personal and professional lives, we are convinced that the eight essentials are fundamental skills for everyone who wants to make the world a better place, not just traditional business leaders.

As we complete this book, among the most disturbing global challenges we face include a war on the European continent and a deadly pandemic. The COVID-19 virus has already killed more than six million people worldwide. Even more widespread are viruses of another kind, such as intolerance of those who hold views that differ from ours. Many of us feel angry at those who don't accept what our respective tribe believes is right for everyone else. We are under threat by the pervasive belief that people of our color, gender, religious faith, ethnicity,

219

sexual orientation, etc., are superior to others who aren't like us. These beliefs underlie disturbing moral viruses, flawed beliefs that distort our moral compass and threaten our world every bit as much as the more prominent global crises that dominate the daily news.

The implications of choosing to sit by and wait for someone else to deal with the world's problems are potentially catastrophic for ourselves, our families, our communities, and our way of life. If we ignore these threats, worldwide peace and security will fade. Global and domestic health issues will worsen. Global financial issues will worsen. Globally, the sick will get sicker, and the poor will get poorer. As our book title suggests, we can't afford to wait for someone else to fix the global problems that threaten human civilization. The last decades have demonstrated that we can't afford to sit by and wait for elected officials and other members of world governments to fix things. The risks are too high if we do. There aren't enough formal leaders around to tackle all the crises emerging and escalating every day. We simply can't wait for others to "fix it." It's up to us to do our part. Fortunately, as Chapter 1 emphasizes, "We are the leaders we have been waiting for."

As the first-century Jewish scholar Hillel said, "If not you, then who? If not now, then when?" To Rabbi Hillel's famous call to arms, we would add, "And if you, then how?" How do you help fix our world? We hope we have helped you answer that question—by enlisting the eight essentials that support your growing leadership intelligence.

LEADERSHIP INTELLIGENCE IS AN ACTION SPORT

As we hope you've noticed throughout this book, leadership intelligence and its eight related essentials are not some fuzzy, high-level concepts. Leadership intelligence is about taking deliberate, concrete action steps. That is why we call leadership intelligence an "action sport." Making the world a better place begins with owning that you are a leader and deciding to act like one. Manny Padro is a successful business owner, an active church and community leader, and a great husband, father, and grandfather. Manny's family moved from Puerto Rico to North Philadelphia when he was five years old. His family was poor and lived in a dangerous and racially divided neighborhood. As Manny recalls, "When I was in the fifth grade, my only goal was to make it home from school without getting beaten up." Manny achieved that goal and began his entrepreneurial career delivering newspapers. He attended Pennsylvania State University and became the first college graduate in his family. Manny now lives in Salt Lake City, where he leads a private wealth management practice. But some of his most meaningful accomplishments have nothing to do with his professional career. In everything he does, Manny is purpose-driven. For instance, he feels a deep sense of responsibility to make a difference and is passionate about helping reduce poverty in the United States. Manny has stepped it up as a community leader devoted to helping kids in impoverished families access life-changing opportunities. As part of his purpose, Manny has written a game-changing book, *Get a Leg Up: The Learn-Earn-Give Toolset for Teenage Purpose and Optimism.*[1] In *Get a Leg Up*, Manny offers a how-to roadmap for teenagers and young adults to help them create happy, fulfilling, and successful lives. Manny's compassion and optimism shine throughout his book, providing invaluable insights and tools not just for disadvantaged youth but also for community leaders, counselors, and educators who aspire to end child poverty.

Another leader who decided not to wait for others to fix it is Target Corporation's Brenda Bjerke. Brenda is a senior director of information risk management and has employees in India and the United States. Brenda calls on the eight essentials to address the ongoing impact of a global health crisis. As she told us:

> *You have to double down on having effective dialogue and communication. We can't surprise each other. In a time like this one has to be relatable, do everything you need to do plus more. A lot is going on. I work in diversity, and we have real situations where members of our workforce have dealt with hate crimes. Everybody is facing hardship in their own ways, some more severe than others. You have to care about the people. You have to get to know what's important. You also have to be transparent and be able to establish trust.*

...

Most of us are very busy people. We have demanding jobs and daunting family responsibilities. Some of us feel that the most we can

---

[1] Manny Padro, *Get a Leg Up: The Learn-Earn-Give Toolset for Teenage Purpose and Optimism* (Lioncrest Publishing, 2022).

do is to put our heads down and try to get through the day. But even in the face of work and family overload, you can't wait for someone else to improve your situation. Remember that whatever you are doing or not doing at any moment influences those around you. Be mindful of the type of influence you have on others. Use the eight essentials to inspire those around you and become the best leaders you can be.

Maybe you'll use your leadership influence as corporate, nonprofit, or government leader. Maybe you'll devote yourself to leading a community organization, amateur sports program, or your family. No matter your roles and responsibilities, each is a leadership position, and each offers you the opportunity to infuse your life with greater purpose and meaning by making a positive difference. Whether you're a CEO or a community volunteer, you can be the leader we are all waiting for, the leader we desperately need to make your part of our world a better place.

Our think2perform colleague, Kris Petersen, often says, "Leadership is about being selfless and doing what is right." That is the essence of leadership intelligence. That is what the eight leadership essentials is all about. Let us all sign up for that.

ACKNOWLEDGMENTS

From Doug:

I am blessed with an incredible family whose support and example have done so much to make this book possible. My family blessings begin with my wife, Beth Ann. Living in alignment with my values is very important to me, and I know no one who more consistently aligns behavior with values than Beth Ann. In keeping with our book's title, Beth Ann never "waits for someone else to fix it." My children and their spouses inspire me daily with their leadership at work and home: Alan and Sari, Mary and LaCresia, and Joanie and Ryan. Together, these accomplished and loving couples have blessed me with my grandchildren Dylan, Conroy, and Reese.

My profound appreciation goes to Kay May, who is in a league of her own. Kay and I have been working together since 1979, which spans most of my career. As my friend and business partner, she has supported me both when things were going well and when they weren't. Kay is a central figure in any professional success I have enjoyed.

I'm very fortunate to have partnered with my coauthor, Chuck Wachendorfer. Though Chuck and I share a common vision of leadership, Chuck's experience added new perspectives to my understanding of essential leadership skills.

There is also a unique group of people I would like to acknowledge. We call ourselves the Shoemakers. The Shoemakers and "friends of Shoemakers" are committed to doing our best to align our real behaviors and selves with our values and ideal selves. Sadly, a young member of our Shoemaker group, Clayton Schnitker, passed away while we were writing this book. I will always be grateful to Clayton and the other Shoemakers who carry on his commitment to enhancing our leadership impact at work, home, or anywhere else that needs us.

From Chuck:

Where would any of us be without our parents? Mine taught me my first lessons in leadership through the various influencing roles they played in their lives and the expectations they had for me to be a positive influence in my own life. Whether in our family, at school, playing sports, or participating in Scouts, they encouraged, supported, and expected me to impact others positively. With loving gratitude, I thank you, Mom, and Dad.

In business, I am eternally grateful for what I consider my own Mt. Rushmore of leadership influences—my coauthor Doug Lennick, Brian Heath, Larry Post, and John Hantz. Each of you, over the years, generously shared and shaped how I led and developed others, as well as taught me how to expect more of myself and the teams I was fortunate to lead.

My children—Gena, Annie, and Ryan—played an invaluable role in preparing me to write this book. Being a father has been the most important leadership role in my life. Someone told me years ago that raising children was like handling a piece of glass; the longer you hold it, the more your fingerprints are all over it. Each in your unique way has helped me raise my game and learn how to be better when falling short. Every day I am grateful to be your father, and I love you all very much.

•••

Together, we want to thank our collaborating writer, Kathy Jordan, for ensuring that the book stayed true to our voice and vision. She was our best cheerleader and toughest sparring partner, constantly pushing us to sharpen our discussion of the essentials of leadership. We are also indebted to our editorial dream team at Wiley—Susan Cerra, Kevin Harreld, and Samantha Wu—for their encouragement and guidance.

Most of all, we appreciate the contributions of the extraordinary leaders we interviewed for the book. We are humbled that you took time out of your busy lives to share your stories. The impact of your leadership resonates throughout these pages. You are stellar examples of how much better the world can be when you refuse to wait for someone else to fix it.

REFERENCES

"4 Leadership Skills for Crisis Management: Daniel Goleman Shows How Having a Strong Emotional Intelligence Can Help Navigate Difficult Situations." Korn Ferry. https://www.kornferry.com/insights/this-week-in-leadership/leadership-skills-for-crisis-management.

"A Presidential Farewell: Truman's Farewell Address to the Nation." *Tru Blog*. Accessed (April 6, 2022). https://www.trumanlibraryinstitute.org/farewell-address/.

"Bloomberg—Are You a Robot?" n.d. www.bloomberg.com. https://www.bloomberg.com/news/features/2020-05-12/unilever-ceo-on-coronavirus-pandemic-purpose-led-businesses.

"Covid-19 Pandemic Will Be Over By the End of 2021, Says Bill Gates." *The Economist* (August 18, 2020). https://www.economist.com/international/2020/08/18/the-covid-19-pandemic-will-be-over-by-the-end-of-2021-says-bill-gates.

"Employee Communication Solution to Engage the Frontline." n.d. Axonify. Accessed (December 13, 2022). https://axonify.com/podcast/building-a-culture-of-frontline-empowerment-at-southwest-airlines/.

"Nobel Peace Prize 2002." *NobelPrize.org*, (September 16, 2002). Nobel Prize Outreach AB. https://www.nobelprize.org/prizes/peace/2002/summary/.

"Organisational X-Factor: Learning Agility." *Focus*. Korn Ferry. https://focus.kornferry.com/leadership-and-talent/the-organisational-x-factor-learning-agility/

2022 Edelman Trust Barometer. Edelman. https://www.edelman.com/trust/2022-trust-barometer.

227

Adams, Marilee. *Change Your Questions, Change Your Life: 12 Powerful Tools for Leadership, Coaching, and Life.* Oakland, CA: Berrett-Koehler Publishers, 2016.

Agassi, Andre. *Open: An Autobiography.* New York: Knopf, 2009.

Argyris, Chris. "Teaching Smart People How to Learn." *Harvard Business Review* (May–June 1991).

Benjamin, Ben, Amy Yeager, and Anita Simon. *Conversation Transformation: Recognize and Overcome the 6 Most Destructive Communication Patterns.* New York: McGraw Hill, 2012.

Bradt, George. "Practice What You Preach or Pay the Price." *Forbes* (April 10, 2013). https://www.forbes.com/sites/georgebradt/2013/04/10/practice-what-you-preach-or-pay-the-price/.

Businessolver. 2020 *State of Workplace Empathy: Executive Summary* (2020). https://www.businessolver.com/workplace-empathy-executive-summary.

Clarke, Paul. "'How Are You Going to Learn Properly?' JPMorgan CEO Jamie Dimon Warns of Increasing Negatives of Working from Home." *Financial News* (October 16, 2020). https://www.fnlondon.com/articles/how-are-you-going-to-learn-properly-jpmorgan-ceo-jamie-dimon-warns-over-increasing-negatives-of-working-from-home-20201016.

Clear, James. "Continuous Improvement, How It Works and How to Master It." https://jamesclear.com/continuous-improvement.

Clear, James. *Atomic Habits: An Easy & Proven Way to Build Good Habits & Break Bad Ones.* New York: Avery, 2018.

Covey, Stephen M. R. *The Speed of Trust.* New York: Free Press, 2018.

Covey, Stephen M. R. *The Speed of Trust: The One Thing that Changes Everything.* New York: Simon & Schuster, 2006.

D'Auria, Gemma, and Aaron De Smet. "Leadership in a Crisis: Responding to the Coronavirus Outbreak and Future Challenges." *McKinsey & Company* (March 16, 2020). https://www.mckinsey.com/business-functions/people-and-organizational-performance/our-insights/leadership-in-a-crisis-responding-to-the-coronavirus-outbreak-and-future-challenges.

David, Susan. *Emotional Agility: Get Unstuck, Embrace Change, and Thrive in Work and Life.* New York: Avery, 2016.

Degreed, Inc. "The State of Skills 2021: Endangered" (2021). https://stateofskills.degreed.com.

Drucker, Peter. *Managing for the Future.* London: Routledge, 1993.

Fessler, Leah. "The Best Leaders Aren't Optimists." *Quartz* (April 30, 2018). https://qz.com/work/1263261/the-best-leaders-and-bosses-arent-optimists

Gartner, Inc. "Motivate Employees to Reskill for the Digital Age" (2018). https://www.gartner.com/smarterwithgartner/motivate-employees -to-reskill-for-the-digital-age

Gates, Bill. "7 Unsung Heroes of the Pandemic." GatesNotes (September 8, 2020). https://www.gatesnotes.com/Health/7-unsung-heroes-of-the -pandemic.

Gentry, William A., Todd J. Weber, and Golnaz Sadri. "Empathy in the Workplace A Tool for Effective Leadership." *Center for Creative Leadership*. https://cclinnovation.org/wp-content/uploads/2020/03/ empathyintheworkplace.pdf?webSyncID=334b25b5-93e5-4ee4-40e3- 4e74063d531b&sessionGUID=d4b55505-37aa-cb8b-3b8b -8001e53b69cc.

Goleman, Daniel. "What Is Emotional Self Awareness." *Korn Ferry Hay Group* (2019). https://www.kornferry.com/insights/this-week-in- leadership/what-is-emotional-self-awareness-2019.

Guenot, Marianne. "World leaders had the ability to avert the COVID-19 pan- demic but failed to do it, a scathing WHO-commissioned report said." *Insider* (May 12, 2021). https://www.businessinsider.com/leaders-could-have-stopped -covid-19-pandemic-but-failed-who-says-2021-5.

Harkins, Gina "As the Navy Moved to Fire Capt. Crozier, Other Leaders Rallied Around Him," *Military.com*, (May 10, 2021), https://www.military.com/daily- news/2021/03/10/navy-moved-fire-capt-crozier-other-leaders-rallied- around-him.html.

Herzberg, Frederick. "One More Time: How Do You Motivate Employees?" *Harvard Business Review* (September–October 1987).

Hougaard, Rasmus. "The Real Crisis in Leadership." *Forbes* (September 9, 2018). https://www.forbes.com/sites/rasmushougaard/2018/09/09/the -real-crisis-in-leadership.

Kahneman, Daniel. *Thinking, Fast and Slow*. New York: Farrar, Straus and Giroux, 2011.

Kiel, Fred, *Return on Character: The Real Reason Leaders and Their Companies Win*. Boston: Harvard Business Review Press, 2015.

Kitroeff, Natalie, and David Gelles. "'It's More Than I Imagined': Boeing's New CEO Confronts Its Challenges." *New York Times,* (March 6, 2020). https://www.nytimes.com/2020/03/05/business/boeing-david- calhoun.html.

Klein, Gary "The Pre-Mortem Method", (January 14, 2021) *Psychology Today*, https://www.psychologytoday.com/us/blog/seeing-what-others- dont/202101/the-pre-mortem-method.

Kross, Ethan and Ayduk, Oslum. "Self-Distancing: Theory, Research, and Current Directions," Advances in Experimental Social Psychology, Volume 55, 2017, Pages 81–136.

Leider, Richard J. *The Power of Purpose: Find Meaning, Live Longer, Better.* Oakland, CA: Berrett-Koehler Publishers, 2015.

Lennick, Doug, and Roy Geer. *How to Get What You Want and Remain True to Yourself.* Minneapolis, MN: Lerner Publications Company, 1989.

Lennick, Doug, and Fred Kiel. *Moral Intelligence 2.0: Enhancing Business Performance and Leadership Success in Turbulent Times.* New York: Prentice Hall, 2011.

Liu, Jennifer. "88% of Executives Think They've Made Excellent Leadership Decisions During Covid—Only 53% of Workers Agree." *CNBC* (June 22, 2022). https://www.cnbc.com/2022/06/22/executives-are-overestimating -how-well-theyre-supporting-employees.html.

Loehr, Jim, and Tony Schwartz. *The Power of Full Engagement: Managing Energy, Not Time, Is the Key to High Performance and Personal Renewal.* New York: Free Press, 2003.

Loehr, Jim. *Leading with Character: 10 Minutes a Day to a Brilliant Legacy.* Hoboken, New Jersey: John Wiley & Sons, Inc., 2021.

McKeever, Vicky. "Goldman Sachs CEO Solomon Calls Working from Home an 'Aberration.'" *CNBC* (February 25, 2021). https://www.cnbc .com/2021/02/25/goldman-sachs-ceo-solomon-calls-working-from-home-an-aberration-.html.

North, Anna. "New Zealand Prime Minister Jacinda Ardern wins historic reelection." *Vox* (October 17, 2020). https://www.vox.com/2020/10/17 /21520584/jacinda-ardern-new-zealand-prime-minister-reelection -covid-19.

NPR Staff, "Shooters Quicker to Pull Trigger When Target Is Black, Study Finds." *NPR* (August 29, 2015). https://www.npr.org/2015/08/29 /435833251/shooters-quicker-to-pull-trigger-when-target-is-black -study-finds.

Parmar, Belinda "The Most (and Least) Empathetic Companies," Harvard Business Review, (November 27, 2015), https://hbr.org/2015/11/2015-empathy-index.

Parker, Kim, Juliana Menasce Horowitz, and Rachel Minkin. "COVID-19 Pandemic Continues to Reshape Work in America." Pew Research Center (February 16, 2022). https://www.pewresearch.org/social-trends/2022 /02/16/covid-19-pandemic-continues-to-reshape-work-in-america/.

PwC. "Global Crisis Survey 2021: Building Resilience for the Future, 2021." https://www.pwc.com/gx/en/issues/crisis-solutions/global-crisis-survey.html.

PwC. "Preparing for Tomorrow's Workforce, Today: Insights from a Global Survey of Business and HR Leaders." 2018.

Reiser, Andrea. "A 9/11 Story of Resilience." (September 2013). https:// andreareiser.com/a-911-story-of-resilience/.

Riess, Helen. *The Empathy Effect: Seven Neuroscience-Based Keys for Transforming the Way We Live, Love, Work, and Connect Across Differences.* Boulder, CO: Sounds True, 2018.

Riess, Helen. *The Power of Empathy: Helen Riess at TEDx Middlebury* (2013). https://youtu.be/baHrcC8B4WM.

Rock, David, and Jeffrey Schwartz. "The Neuroscience of Leadership." *Strategy+Business,* (May 2006).

Sheridan, Richard. *Joy, Inc.: How We Built a Workplace People Love.* New York: Portfolio/Penguin, 2013.

Sonnenfeld, Jeffrey A., and Andrew J. Ward. "Firing Back: How Great Leaders Rebound After Career Disasters." *Harvard Business Review* (January 2007).

Tayeb, Zahra. "The Great Divide: Business Leaders Are Split on Long-Term Remote Working. This Is What Spotify, Twitter, Goldman Sachs, and Others Have Announced." *Insider* (March 7, 2021). https://www .businessinsider.com/what-spotify-twitter-goldman-sachs-said-about-long-term-remote-working-2021-3.

Timms, Michael. "Blame Culture Is Toxic. Here's How to Stop It." *Harvard Business Review* (February 2, 2022). https://hbr.org/2022/02/blame-culture-is-toxic-heres-how-to-stop-it.

Vaill, Peter B. *Learning as a Way of Being: Strategies for Survival in a World of Permanent White Water.* San Francisco, CA: Jossey-Bass, 1996.

Valcour, Monique. "4 Ways to Become a Better Learner." *Harvard Business Review* (December 2015). https://hbr.org/2015/12/4-ways-to-become -a-better-learner.

Walter-Warner, Holden. "Jamie Dimon to Work-From-Homers: You Win." *The Real Deal* (April 4, 2022). https://therealdeal.com/2022/04/04/ jamie-dimon-to-work-from-homers-you-win/.

Watkins, Oona. "A Look Back to 2010: 87 Days Too Late, BP Finally Stops Deepwater Horizon Blowout." *Oceana* (July 14, 2020). https://usa.oceana .org/blog/look-back-2010-87-days-too-late-bp-finally-stops -deepwater-horizon-blowout/.

Winny, Annalies. "In New Zealand, A Response to be Proud of." *Global Health Now* (April 15, 2021). https://globalhealthnow.org/2021-04/ new-zealand-response-be-proud.

Wiseman, Liz. "Your Optimism Might Be Stifling Your Team." *Harvard Business Review* (May 2013). https://hbr.org/2013/05/your-optimism -might-be-stifling-your-team.

INDEX